The Gnostic Jung

The Gnostic Jung

Selected and introduced
by Robert A. Segal

Princeton University Press
Princeton, New Jersey

Published by Princeton University Press,
41 William Street, Princeton, New Jersey 08540
Copyright © 1992 by Princeton University Press
All Rights Reserved

Library of Congress Cataloging-in-Publication Data

Jung, C. G. (Carl Gustav). 1875–1961.
    [Selections. English. 1992]
    The Gnostic Jung / selected and introduced by Robert A. Segal.
        p.   cm.—(Mythos series)
    Includes bibliographical references and index.
    ISBN 0-691-09975-8 (cl.):   —ISBN 0-691-01923-1 (pbk.):
    1. Gnosticism—Psychology.   2. Psychoanalysis and religion.
    I. Segal, Robert Alan.   II. Series: Mythos (Princeton, N.J.)
    BF109.J8A25   1992
    299'.932—dc20   91-44731

Part One is composed of texts selected from the following volumes of the Collected Works of C. G. Jung: *Psychological Types*, Volume 6, © 1971 by Princeton University Press; *Two Essays on Analytical Psychology*, Volume 7, 2nd ed., © 1971 by Princeton University Press; *The Structure and Dynamics of the Psyche*, Volume 8, 2nd ed., © 1969 by Princeton University Press; *The Archetypes and the Collective Unconscious*, Volume 9i, 2nd ed., © 1959 by Bollingen Foundation, © renewed 1987 by Princeton University Press; *Aion*, Volume 9ii, 2nd ed., © 1968 by Princeton University Press; *Civilization in Transition*, Volume 10, 2nd ed., © 1970 by Princeton University Press; *Psychology and Religion: West and East*, Volume 11, 2nd ed., © 1958 by Bollingen Foundation, © renewed 1986 by Princeton University Press; *Psychology and Alchemy*, Volume 12, © 1953 by Bollingen Foundation, © renewed 1981 by Princeton University Press; *Mysterium Coniunctionis*, Volume 14, © 1970 by Princeton University Press; *The Practice of Psychotherapy*, Volume 16, 2nd ed., © 1954 by Bollingen Foundation, © renewed 1982 by Princeton University Press; *The Symbolic Life*, Volume 18, copyright 1958 by Bollingen Foundation, © renewed 1986 by Princeton University Press. Excerpts from Jung's letters are taken from *The Collected Letters of C. G. Jung*, Volume 2, © 1953, 1955, 1961, 1963, 1968, 1971, 1972, 1974, 1975 by Princeton University Press

The text of Part Two is taken from *Memories, Dreams, Reflections* by C. G. Jung, © 1961, 1962, 1963 and renewed 1989, 1990 by Random House, Inc., and is reprinted here by arrangement with Pantheon Books, a division of Random House, Inc.

The texts of Part Three are taken respectively from *Spring* (1949), © 1949 by Spring Publications (Dallas, Texas), and reprinted here by arrangement with the publisher; from *Eranos-Jährbuch*, vol. 37 (1968), © 1970 by E. J. Brill (Leiden, the Netherlands), and translated here by arrangement with the publisher; and from Bentley Layton's *The Rediscovery of Gnosticism*, vol. 1, © 1980 by E. J. Brill, and reprinted here by arrangement with the publisher.

Contents

Part 2   *Jung's Own Gnostic Myth*

Part 3   *Other Authorities on Jungian Psychology and Gnosticism*

Note on the Text

Most of the extracts from Jung's writings are mere portions of essays and chapters. In those cases the footnotes have been renumbered. All footnotes to the selected pages have been retained.

Acknowledgments

Robert Segal wants to thank Timothy Hatcher for his invaluable help with the introduction and Karen Mark-Anderson, John Pizer, Robert Edgeworth, and Adelaide Russo for their help with the translation of Gilles Quispel's "C. G. Jung und die Gnosis."

The Gnostic Jung

Introduction
The Gnostic Jung

The belief known as Gnosticism is definable in various ways. Defined most narrowly, it is an ancient Christian heresy. It arose out of Christianity in the second century and eventually died out.[1]

Defined more broadly, Gnosticism remains an entirely ancient phenomenon but is more than a Christian one.[2] It is also both pre-Christian and non-Christian. It spans the whole ancient world and encompasses Christianity rather than is encompassed by it. The Nag Hammadi discovery has established Gnosticism as at least a non-Christian, whether or not pre-Christian, phenomenon.[3]

Gnosticism here is the belief in an antithetical dualism of immateriality, which is good, and matter, which is evil. Gnosticism espouses radical dualism in human beings, the cosmos, and divinity; the primordial unity of all immateriality; the yearning to restore that unity; the present entrapment of a portion of immateriality in human bodies; the need for knowledge to reveal to humans that entrapment; and the dependence of humans on a savior to reveal that knowledge to them.

Defined most broadly, Gnosticism is a modern as well as an ancient phenomenon. It is living, not dead. Gnosticism here con-

[1] See Adolf Harnack, *History of Dogma*, trans. Neil Buchanan et al., vol. 1 (Boston: Little, Brown, 1899), chap. 4; Carsten Colpe, *Die religionsgeschichtliche Schule* (Göttingen: Vandenhoeck & Ruprecht, 1961), passim; A. D. Nock, "Gnosticism," *Harvard Theological Review* 57 (October 1964): 255–79; "Proposal for a Terminological and Conceptual Agreement with Regard to the Theme of the Colloquium," in *Le Origini dello Gnosticismo*, ed. Ugo Bianchi, Supplements to *Numen*, vol. 12 (Leiden: Brill, 1967), xxvi–xxvii.

[2] See Wilhelm Bousset, *Hauptprobleme der Gnosis* (Göttingen: Vandenhoeck & Ruprecht, 1907), passim; Richard Reitzenstein, *Poimandres* (Leipzig: Teubner, 1904), passim; Hans Jonas, *Gnosis und spätantiker Geist*, 1st ed., vol. 2, pt. 1 (Göttingen: Vandenhoeck & Ruprecht, 1954), passim; Rudolf Bultmann, *Theology of the New Testament*, trans. Kendrick Grobel, vol. 1 (New York: Scribner, 1951), chap. 15; Kurt Rudolph, *Gnosis*, trans. Robert McLachlan Wilson et al. (San Francisco: Harper & Row, 1983), 56–59.

[3] See James M. Robinson, Introduction to *The Nag Hammadi Library in English*, ed. Robinson, 3d ed. (San Francisco: Harper & Row, 1988), 6–10.

stitutes the belief in the alienation of human beings from their true selves, whether or not from any true world or divinity. Humans are not necessarily alienated from an immaterial self, world, or divinity but simply alienated from a true one of any kind.

It is far from surprising that various ancient authors and movements—for example, the apostle Paul, the John of the Fourth Gospel, and Hermeticism—have sometimes been said to be Gnostic. After all, Gnosticism flourished in the ancient world. It is, however, surprising that so many modern authors and movements have been characterized as Gnostic. Hegel, Blake, Goethe, Schelling, Schleiermacher, Emerson, Melville, Byron, Shelley, Yeats, Hesse, Schweitzer, Toynbee, Tillich, Heidegger, Conrad, Simone Weil, Wallace Stevens, Doris Lessing, I. B. Singer, Walker Percy, Jack Kerouac, and Thomas Pynchon typify the range of writers and thinkers to whom the epithet has been applied. Harold Bloom claims "that the major traditions of post-Enlightenment poetry have tended more to the Gnostic stance of misprision [i.e., misreading]."[4] Ihab Hassan calls the postmodern preoccupation with "immediate consciousness of reality" "the New Gnosticism."[5] Thomas Altizer declares that when Gnosticism is defined as "opposition to the world," "it is extremely difficult to limit the arena of modern Gnosticism."[6]

Eric Voegelin and Hans Jonas

The preeminent authorities on modern Gnosticism are Eric Voegelin, the political philosopher, and Hans Jonas, the existentialist philosopher and Gnostic scholar. For Voegelin, modern Gnosticism encompasses "such movements as progressivism, positivism, Marxism, psychoanalysis, communism, fascism, and

[4] Harold Bloom, *Poetry and Repression* (New Haven: Yale University Press, 1976), 13–14. Bloom even types himself a "Jewish Gnostic" (*Agon* [New York: Oxford University Press, 1982], 4) and has written *The Flight to Lucifer: A Gnostic Fantasy* (New York: Farrar, Strauss & Giroux, 1979).

[5] See Ihab Hassan, *Paracriticisms* (Urbana: University of Illinois Press, 1975), chap. 6.

[6] Thomas J. J. Altizer, "The Challenge of Modern Gnosticism," *Journal of Bible and Research* 30 (January 1962): 19. For an overview of the scope of what has been labeled modern Gnosticism see Altizer, 18–25; Richard Smith, "Afterword: The Modern Relevance of Gnosticism," in *The Nag Hammadi Library in English*, 532–49; above all Carl A. Raschke, *The Interruption of Eternity* (Chicago: Nelson-Hall, 1980).

national socialism."[7] Voegelin goes so far as to define modernity per se as "the growth of gnosticism."[8] Moreover, modernity for Voegelin is no recent phenomenon. It begins "perhaps as early as the ninth century."[9] Leading modern Gnostics for him include Joachim of Fiore, More, Calvin, Hobbes, Hegel, Comte, Marx, Nietzsche, Heidegger, and Hitler. Modern Gnostic individuals and movements share six characteristics that Voegelin calls "the gnostic attitude": dissatisfaction with the world, confidence that the ills of the world stem from the way it is organized, certainty that amelioration is possible, the assumption that improvement must "evolve historically," the belief that humanity can change the world, and the conviction that knowledge—gnosis—is the key to change.[10]

Where Voegelin seeks to show the Gnostic nature of modernity, Jonas seeks to show the modern nature of Gnosticism. Jonas draws parallels between ancient Gnosticism and modern, secular existentialism to prove that Gnosticism is existentialist, not that existentialism is Gnostic. For Jonas, both philosophies stress above all the radical alienation of human beings from the world.

Initially, Jonas assumed that existentialism was the key to Gnosticism because it was the key to all worldviews. Gradually, he came to see existentialism as a particular worldview and consequently to see Gnosticism not as the ancient *version* of existentialism but as its ancient *counterpart:* "There is one situation, and one only that I know of in the history of Western man, where . . . that [existentialist] condition has been realized and lived out with all the vehemence of a cataclysmic event. That is the gnostic movement."[11]

Jonas does say that Gnosticism is "a help in discerning and plac-

[7] Eric Voegelin, *Science, Politics and Gnosticism* (Chicago: Regnery Gateway Editions, 1968), 83.

[8] Eric Voegelin, *The New Science of Politics* (Chicago: University of Chicago Press, 1952), 133.

[9] Ibid.

[10] Voegelin, *Science, Politics and Gnosticism*, 86–88. On Voegelin's concept of modern Gnosticism see, for example, Ellis Sandoz, *The Voegelinian Revolution* (Baton Rouge: Louisiana State University Press, 1981), 105–15, 239–43; Eugene Webb, *Eric Voegelin* (Seattle: University of Washington Press, 1981), 197–213; Gregor Sebba, "History, Modernity and Gnosticism," in *The Philosophy of Order*, ed. Peter J. Opitz and Gregor Sebba (Stuttgart: Klett-Cotta, 1981), 190–241.

[11] Hans Jonas, "Gnosticism, Existentialism, and Nihilism," in his *The Gnostic Religion*, 2d ed. (Boston: Beacon Press, 1963), 325.

ing the meaning of modern nihilism"[12]—as if existentialism were itself Gnostic-like. He even speaks of a "gnostic" interpretation of existentialism: "the 'existentialist' reading of Gnosticism, so well vindicated by its hermeneutic success, invites as its natural complement the trial of a 'gnostic' reading of Existentialism."[13] But Jonas is really more interested in paralleling Gnosticism with existentialism than in subsuming either one under the other. Moreover, he is at least as interested in the differences between Gnosticism and existentialism as in the similarities. Where Gnosticism regards the world as demonic and hostile, existentialism considers it natural and indifferent.[14] In short, Jonas is far less intent than Voegelin in making Gnosticism modern.

The Evidence for Gnostic Influence

While in the cases of a few of the figures labeled modern Gnostics—notably, Hesse and Goethe—there is evidence of actual familiarity with Gnostic teachings, in most cases the ascription is merely thematic.[15] One critic cites scholarly works on Gnosticism that Joseph Conrad "could have read" but none that he actually did read.[16] Harold Bloom states that "Yeats's Gnosticism was in small part a consequence of his reading Gnostic texts, but primarily I think that Yeats's Gnosticism was inherent in him, temperamentally and spiritually."[17] Cleanth Brooks begins his essay on Walker Percy as a Gnostic by granting that "I am not aware that Walker Percy has ever mentioned Gnosticism in any of his writings."[18] A critic who labels Doris Lessing Gnostic blithely confesses that "I know of no

[12] Ibid., 320.

[13] Ibid., 321. See also Jonas, "A Retrospective View," in *Proceedings of the International Colloquium on Gnosticism*, ed. Geo Widengren (Stockholm: Almquist & Wiksell; Leiden: Brill, 1977), 13–14.

[14] See Jonas, *The Gnostic Religion*, 338–39. Had Jonas ever compared Gnosticism with religious rather than secular existentialism, he would have found fewer differences.

[15] On Hesse see Theodore Ziolkowski, *The Novels of Hermann Hesse* (Princeton, N.J.: Princeton University Press, 1965), 110, 126; on Goethe see Gilles Quispel, "Faust: Symbol of Western Man," in his *Gnostic Studies*, vol. 2 (Istanbul: Nederlands Historisch-Archaeologisch Instituut, 1975), 304–6.

[16] Bruce Henricksen, "*Heart of Darkness* and the Gnostic Myth," *Mosaic* 11 (Summer 1978): 35 n. 1. See also 36 n. 2.

[17] Bloom, *Poetry and Repression*, 212.

[18] Cleanth Brooks, "Walker Percy and Modern Gnosticism," *Southern Review* 13 (October 1977): 677.

evidence that Lessing is directly familiar with Gnosticism."[19] The critic who, on the basis of the work of Jonas and Voegelin, calls Thomas Pynchon Gnostic declares it "important to make clear at this early point that I am not claiming any direct influence from these writers on Pynchon. I am not claiming that he ever read them as he certainly read (and was influenced by) Henry Adams, Norbert Wiener, Max Weber, Norman O. Brown, and others."[20]

It is unlikely that many of the disparate thinkers that Voegelin categorizes as Gnostic were acquainted with their ancient forebears. Referring to one particular ancient text, Voegelin even states that "Whether Marx knew this text either directly or indirectly, we cannot say. Probably he did not. All the more, then, would the parallel in symbolic expression corroborate the essential sameness of attitudes and motives in ancient and modern gnosticism."[21]

The point is not to deny the designation "Gnostic" to any of the individuals or schools named.[22] The point is simply to contrast the basis on which most of them are called Gnostic to the basis on which Carl Jung is. Whether or not Jung finally qualifies as a Gnostic, Jung actually studied Gnostic writings and cites them throughout his corpus. Certainly Jung would not qualify as a Gnostic merely because he studied Gnosticism: to study something is not thereby to accept it. But those who label Jung a Gnostic at least link the claim to Jung's own fascination with Gnosticism. There is, then, a much sturdier basis for touting Jung as a Gnostic than for touting virtually any of the other persons named.

---

[19] Robert Galbreath, "Problematic Gnosis: Hesse, Singer, Lessing, and the Limitations of Modern Gnosticism," *Journal of Religion* 61 (January 1981): 24 n. 14.

[20] Dwight Eddins, *The Gnostic Pynchon* (Bloomington: Indiana University Press, 1990), xi.

[21] Voegelin, *Science, Politics and Gnosticism*, 40. For a damning exposé of the attribution of views to thinkers who did not know that they held them see Quentin Skinner, "Meaning and Understanding in the History of Ideas," *History and Theory* 8 (1969): 3–53.

[22] To cite the most prominent contested case, the individuals and groups that Voegelin terms "Gnostic" might be better termed "apocalyptic" or "millenarian" precisely because their goal *is* to perfect the world rather than, as in ancient Gnosticism, to escape from it. For criticisms of Voegelin's usage see, for example, Smith, "Afterword: The Modern Relevance of Gnosticism," 542–43; Carsten Colpe, "The Challenge of Gnostic Thought for Philosophy, Alchemy, and Literature," in *The Rediscovery of Gnosticism*, ed. Bentley Layton, Supplements to *Numen*, no. 41, vol. 1 (Leiden: Brill, 1980), 38–39; Stephen A. McKnight, *Sacralizing the Secular* (Baton Rouge: Louisiana State University Press, 1989), 23–24, 41–48. See Voegelin's own qualification of his usage in his *Autobiographical Reflections*, ed. Ellis Sandoz (Baton Rouge: Louisiana State University Press, 1989), 66–67.

Jung's Interest in Gnosticism

In his autobiography, *Memories, Dreams, Reflections,* Jung describes his search for objective evidence of the collective unconscious—evidence beyond his own experience of it:

> As my life entered its second half, I was already embarked on the confrontation with the contents of the unconscious. . . . First I had to find evidence for the historical prefiguration of my inner experiences. That is to say, I had to ask myself, "Where have my particular premises already occurred in history?" If I had not succeeded in finding such evidence, I would never have been able to substantiate my ideas.[23]

Jung found that evidence in two sources: alchemy and Gnosticism. Interpreted psychologically, both served as hoary counterparts to his brand of psychology and therefore as evidence of its objectivity:

> The experiences of the alchemists were, in a sense, my experiences, and their world was my world. This was, of course, a momentous discovery: I had stumbled upon the historical counterpart of my psychology of the unconscious. The possibility of a comparison with alchemy, and the uninterrupted intellectual chain back to Gnosticism, gave substance to my psychology.[24]

To be sure, Jung considered alchemy a more important prefiguration of his psychology than Gnosticism. Though he discusses both Gnosticism and alchemy throughout his writings, he devotes three whole volumes to alchemy[25] but only one essay to Gnosti-

---

[23] C. G. Jung, *Memories, Dreams, Reflections,* recorded and ed. Aniela Jaffé, trans. Richard and Clara Winston (New York: Vintage Books, 1962), 200. See also Jung, *Alchemical Studies,* Collected Works, ed. Sir Herbert Read et al., trans. R. F. C. Hull et al., vol. 13 (Princeton, N.J.: Princeton University Press, 1968), 3.

[24] Jung, *Memories, Dreams, Reflections,* 205.

[25] See Jung, *Psychology and Alchemy,* Collected Works, vol. 12, 2d ed. (Princeton, N.J.: Princeton University Press, 1968 [1944]); *Alchemical Studies; Mysterium Coniunctionis,* Collected Works, vol. 14, 2d ed. (Princeton, N.J.: Princeton University Press, 1970 [1955–56]). See also Jung, "The Psychology of the Transference," in his *The Practice of Psychotherapy,* Collected Works, vol. 16, 2d ed. (New York: Pantheon Books, 1966 [1954]), 163–323; "The Fish in Alchemy," "The Alchemical Interpretation of the Fish," and "Background to the Psychology of Christian Alchemical Symbolism," in his *Aion,* Collected Works, vol. 9, pt. 2, 2d ed. (Princeton, N.J.: Princeton University Press, 1968 [1951]), chaps. 10–12.

cism, and even this essay deals partly with parallels to alchemy.[26] Jung found Gnosticism too distant a phenomenon to be tied directly to modern psychology and saw alchemy as the medieval nexus between the two:

But the Gnostics were too remote for me to establish any link with them in regard to the questions that were confronting me. As far as I could see, the tradition that might have connected Gnosis with the present seemed to have been severed, and for a long time it proved impossible to find any bridge that led from Gnosticism—or neo-Platonism—to the contemporary world. But when I began to understand alchemy I realized that it represented the historical link with Gnosticism, and that a continuity

[26] See Jung, "Gnostic Symbols of the Self," *Aion*, chap. 13. See also Jung, "Christ, A Symbol of the Self," *Aion*, 41–42; "The Historical Significance of the Fish," *Aion*, 109–11; "Background to the Psychology of Christian Alchemical Symbolism," 173; "The Structure and Dynamics of the Self," *Aion*, chap. 14; "Archetypes of the Collective Unconscious," in his *The Archetypes and the Collective Unconscious*, Collected Works, vol. 9, pt. 1, 2d ed. (Princeton, N.J.: Princeton University Press, 1968 [1959]), 18; "The Psychology of the Child Archetype," *The Archetypes and the Collective Unconscious*, 173–77; "The Spiritual Problem of Modern Man," in his *Civilization in Transition*, Collected Works, vol. 10, 2d ed. (Princeton, N.J.: Princeton University Press, 1970 [1964]), 83–84; "Flying Saucers: A Modern Myth of Things Seen in the Skies," *Civilization in Transition*, 356–58; "On the Psychology of the Unconscious," in his *Two Essays on Analytical Psychology*, Collected Works, vol. 7, 2d ed. (Princeton, N.J.: Princeton University Press, 1966 [1953]), 77–78; "Psychology and Religion," in his *Psychology and Religion: West and East*, Collected Works, vol. 11, 2d ed. (Princeton, N.J.: Princeton University Press, 1969 [1958]), 96–102; "A Psychological Approach to the Dogma of the Trinity," *Psychology and Religion: West and East*, 169–70; "Transformation Symbolism in the Mass," *Psychology and Religion: West and East*, 284–90; Foreword to Victor White, *God and the Unconscious*, *Psychology and Religion: West and East*, 306–7; "Introduction to the Religious and Psychological Problems of Alchemy," *Psychology and Alchemy*, 24–25, 35; "Religious Ideas in Alchemy," *Psychology and Alchemy*, 299–302, 357, 372, 430, 449–52; "Commentary on 'The Secret of the Golden Flower'," *Alchemical Studies*, 3–4; "The Spirit Mercurius," *Alchemical Studies*, 204–5; "The Philosophical Tree," *Alchemical Studies*, 283, 334–39; "The Personification of the Opposites," *Mysterium Coniunctionis*, 102–4, 199–200, 243–44; "Rex and Regina," *Mysterium Coniunctionis*, 263–64, 373; "Religion and Philosophy: A Reply to Martin Buber," in his *The Symbolic Life*, Collected Works, vol. 18 (Princeton, N.J.: Princeton University Press, 1976), 663–70; "Jung and Religious Belief," *The Symbolic Life*, 727–30; Foreword to Erich Neumann, *Depth Psychology and a New Ethic*, *The Symbolic Life*, 621–22; Foreword to Gilles Quispel, *Tragic Christianity* [never published], *The Symbolic Life*, 651–53; "Address at the Presentation of the Jung Codex," *The Symbolic Life*, 671–72, 826–29; *Psychological Types*, Collected Works, vol. 6 (Princeton, N.J.: Princeton University Press, 1971 [1921]), 8–20, 241–42; "Richard Wilhelm: In Memoriam," in his *The Spirit in Man, Art, and Literature*, Collected Works, vol. 16 (Princeton, N.J.: Princeton University Press, 1966), 60; "The Houston Films," in his *C. G. Jung Speaking*, ed. William McGuire and R.F.C. Hull (Princeton, N.J.: Princeton University Press, 1977), 350–52; *Letters*, ed. Gerhard Adler and Aniela Jaffé, trans. R.F.C. Hull (Princeton, N.J.: Princeton University Press, 1973), vol. 1, 501–3, 552, 553–54, 574; vol. 2, 53–55, 61, 64–65, 147, 244–45, 254–56, 283, 570–73, 583–84, 602. Many of these writings are reprinted in *The Gnostic Jung*.

therefore existed between past and present. Grounded in the natural philosophy of the Middle Ages, alchemy formed the bridge on the one hand into the past, to Gnosticism, and on the other into the future, to the modern psychology of the unconscious.[27]

The remoteness of Gnosticism for Jung stemmed partly from the paucity of texts available to him. Working for most of his life before the discovery of Gnostic texts at Nag Hammadi, he was, as he says, dependent largely on the writings of the Gnostics' adversaries: "Since we possess only very few complete texts, and since most of what is known comes from the reports of Christian opponents, we have, to say the least, an inadequate knowledge of the history as well as the content of this strange and confused literature, which is so difficult to evaluate."[28]

Yet the remoteness of Gnosticism for Jung doubtless goes deeper. Gnosticism may for him be simply too otherworldly. Perhaps because alchemy combines the ancient, Gnostic focus on the immaterial and transcendent soul, or spark, with the modern, scientific-like focus on the transformation of worldly matter, it serves to connect the two.

Despite his professed closer kinship to alchemy, Jung interprets it and Gnosticism identically.[29] Indeed, he interprets alchemy as not just the link to Gnosticism but the outright continuation of it: "In spite of the suppression of the Gnostic heresy, it [the heresy] continued to flourish throughout the Middle Ages under the guise of alchemy."[30] For Jung, the alchemical process of extracting gold from base metals is a continuation of the Gnostic process of liberating fallen sparks from matter. Both processes are seemingly out-

[27] Jung, *Memories, Dreams, Reflections*, 201. See also Jung, "Commentary on 'The Secret of the Golden Flower'," 3–4; "The Houston Films," 350.

[28] Jung, "Commentary on 'The Secret of the Golden Flower'," 3. Jung gives an additional reason for the accessibility of alchemy: that "the Gnostic systems consist only in small part of immediate psychic experiences, the greater part being speculative and systematizing recensions" (ibid.). See also Jung, *Letters*, vol. 1, 553–54.

[29] See, for example, Jung, "Psychology and Religion," 98–102; "Transformation Symbolism in the Mass," 209; "Adam and Eve," *Mysterium Coniunctionis*, 437.

[30] Jung, "Psychology and Religion," 97. See also, for example, Jung, "Background to the Psychology of Christian Alchemical Symbolism," 173, 181; "The Structure and Dynamics of the Self," 232–33; "Religious Ideas in Alchemy," 372; "The Spirit Mercurius," 204–5, 220. On the influence of Gnosticism on alchemy see H. J. Sheppard, "Gnosticism and Alchemy," *Ambix* 6 (December 1957): 86–101.

ward, physical or metaphysical ones which in fact are inner, psychological ones. Both represent a progression from sheer ego consciousness to the ego's rediscovery of the unconscious and reintegration with it to forge the self.

In alchemy the progression is from base metals to the distillation of vapor out of them and the return of that vapor to the metals to form gold. In Gnosticism the progression is from the Gnostic's sheer bodily existence to the release of the immaterial spark within the Gnostic's body and the reunion of that spark with the godhead. In both cases the state truly sought lies within human beings—between the ego and the unconscious—rather than outside them—between the vapor and the metals or between the spark and the godhead. The human state is simply projected onto the external world.[31]

Jung's History of the Psyche

Tracing Jung's history of the psyche helps pinpoint the significance of Gnosticism for him. Jung divides the psychological history of humanity into four stages—primitive, ancient, modern, and contemporary—though he uses other terms for some of the stages.[32]

At birth, according to Jung, humans are entirely unconscious. Only slowly does consciousness emerge.[33] Because the initial human state is unconscious, unconsciousness is natural rather than, as for Freud, artificial. Where for Freud the unconscious arises

[31] On Jung's interpretation of alchemy see Walter Pagel, "Jung's Views on Alchemy," *Isis* 39 (May 1948): 44–48; Philip Mairet, "Dr. Jung and the Alchemists," *Fortnightly* 181 (January 1954): 55–61; Aniela Jaffé, *From the Life and Work of C. G. Jung*, trans. R.F.C. Hull (New York: Harper, 1971), chap. 2; Mircea Eliade, *The Forge and the Crucible*, trans. Stephen Corrin (New York: Harper Torchbooks, 1971), 156–66, 195–98, 221–26.

[32] Jung explicitly distinguishes the first three stages: see below, nn. 35, 42. See also Erich Neumann, *The Origins and History of Consciousness*, trans. R.F.C. Hull (Princeton, N.J.: Princeton University Press, 1970), passim. The distinction between "modern" and "contemporary" is only implicit, and unfortunately Jung uses the term "modern" for both.

[33] See, for example, Jung, "Analytical Psychology," *The Symbolic Life*, 8; *Memories, Dreams, Reflections*, 348–49; "The Stages of Life," in his *The Structure and Dynamics of the Psyche*, Collected Works, vol. 8, 2d ed. (Princeton, N.J.: Princeton University Press, 1969 [1960]), 387–91. See also Neumann, 3–127; M. Esther Harding, *The "I" and the "Not-I"* (Princeton, N.J.: Princeton University Press, 1965), chaps. 1–3; Gerhard Adler, *Studies in Analytical Psychology* (New York: Capricorn Books, 1969), 120–36.

out of consciousness, for Jung consciousness arises out of the unconscious.[34]

By "consciousness" Jung means awareness of oneself as a subject, or "I," distinct from both the external world and the unconscious. The first center of consciousness is the ego, so that the development of consciousness means at first the development of the ego.

Because the consciousness of humanity has developed slowly, the ego of primitives is weak.[35] Rather than differentiating themselves from their unconscious and the world, primitives project themselves onto the world and thereby encounter their unconscious rather than the world.[36] In projecting themselves, as personalities, onto the world, they create a religious world—a world ruled not by impersonal forces like atoms but by gods. Events in the world are not merely caused but willed.[37]

So weak is the primitive ego that primitives not only project themselves onto the world but also identify themselves with it. Like infants, of which they are for Jung the phylogenetic counterparts, primitives have scant sense of themselves "over against" the world. They do not distinguish between subjectivity and objectivity. They experience themselves objectively, as part of the world itself:

Thanks to our one-sided emphasis on so-called natural causes, we have learned to differentiate what is subjective and psychic from what is objective and "natural." For primitive man, on the contrary, the psychic and the objective coalesce in the external world. In the face of something extraordinary it is not he who is

[34] See Jung, "Analytical Psychology," 10.
[35] On primitives see above all Jung, "Archaic Man," *Civilization in Transition*, 50–73. Although Jung refers to primitives throughout his writings, this essay is his sole work on primitives in their own right. See also Jung, "Approaching the Unconscious," in Jung et al., *Man and His Symbols* (New York: Dell Laurel Editions, 1968), 6–8 (original version entitled "Symbols and the Interpretation of Dreams," *The Symbolic Life*, 183–264); "The Psychology of the Child Archetype," 153–54, 178. See also Adler, 127–29; Hans Schaer, *Religion and the Cure of Souls in Jung's Psychology*, trans. R.F.C. Hull (New York: Pantheon Books, 1950), 103–6; Harding, 38–40; Harding, *Psychic Energy*, 2d ed. (Princeton, N.J.: Princeton University Press, 1963), 332–33; Antonio Moreno, *Jung, Gods, and Modern Man* (Notre Dame, Ind.: University of Notre Dame Press, 1970), 9–14.
[36] On projection see Jung, "Analytical Psychology," 137–38. See also Harding, *Psychic Energy*, 331–34.
[37] See Jung, "Archaic Man," 55–68.

astonished, but rather the thing which is astonishing. . . . What we would call the powers of imagination and suggestion seem to him invisible forces which act on him from without. . . . Primitive man is unpsychological. Psychic happenings take place outside him in an objective way. Even the things he dreams about are real to him; that is his only reason for paying attention to dreams. . . . The simple truth is that primitive man is somewhat more given to projection than we because of the undifferentiated state of his mind and his consequent inability to criticize himself.[38]

In identifying themselves with the world, primitives identify themselves with the gods they have projected onto it. Humans and gods are therefore taken as one. Between humans and gods there exists what the philosopher Lucien Lévy-Bruhl, whom Jung regularly cites, terms *participation mystique*.

The world with which primitives identify themselves includes fellow primitives as well as gods. Because primitives identify themselves with one another, they have no sense of individuality either. Jung calls primitives "herd animals."[39]

The difference for Jung between ancients and primitives is that ancients have a sturdier ego. But even their ego is shaky, for ancients, too, project themselves onto the world in the form of gods. They do not, however, identify themselves with the world and therefore with the gods. They worship gods distinct from themselves. Like primitives, ancients experience the world through the unconscious and thus are not truly separated from either, but they nevertheless possess a budding sense of themselves vis-à-vis both.

My term "ancients," admittedly imprecise, refers to all humans between the primitive stage and the modern one. Ancients include Egyptians, Mesopotamians, Greeks, Romans, Jews, Christians, and Muslims.[40] Excluded are both Western and Eastern mystics, who for Jung are at a different psychological stage.

To the extent that ancients forge an ego, they create a split within themselves between their ego and their unconscious, from which it emerges. That split is not, however, antagonistic. In developing their ego, ancients do not forsake their unconscious. Like primi-

---

[38] Ibid., 63–65.
[39] See, for example, Jung, "The Spiritual Problem of Modern Man," 79.
[40] Jung devotes no single work to ancients, whom he discusses throughout his writings.

tives, ancients continue to tend to it through religion. As Jung says repeatedly: "Whenever there exists some external form, be it an ideal or a ritual, by which all the yearnings and hopes of the soul are adequately expressed—as for instance in a living religion—then we may say that the psyche is outside and that there is no psychic problem."[41]

The difference between moderns and ancients is that moderns possess a fully independent ego.[42] By withdrawing their projections from the world, they have demythicized it.[43] They thereby experience the world itself, unfiltered by their unconscious, and thus are differentiated from both.

Invariably, moderns do not merely separate themselves from their unconscious but reject it altogether. They thereby pit themselves—their ego—against their unconscious. Moderns consider themselves wholly rational, unemotional, scientific, and atheistic. Where earlier humanity had realized its unconscious through religion, moderns dismiss both religion and the unconscious as prescientific delusions. Instead, moderns proudly identify themselves with their ego and thereby boast of their omnipotence: "nowadays most people identify themselves almost exclusively with their consciousness, and imagine that they are only what they know about themselves. . . . Rationalism and doctrinairism are the disease of our time; they pretend to have all the answers."[44] Where primitives identify themselves with the world itself, moderns identify themselves with the part of them that controls the world: the ego.

The modern dismissal of the unconsciousness does not, however, eliminate it. Moderns still partly project their unconscious onto the world—for example, through superstitions,[45] which perpetuate participation mystique, and through the quintessentially modern belief in flying saucers.[46] Moreover, they continue to project their unconscious onto one another:

[41] Jung, "The Spiritual Problem of Modern Man," 79.

[42] On moderns see above all Jung, "Psychology and Religion," 3–105. See also Jung, "The Undiscovered Self," *Civilization in Transition*, 245–305. On the change from ancients to moderns see Adler, chap. 7.

[43] See, for example, Jung, "Psychology and Religion," 83; "Approaching the Unconscious," 85.

[44] Jung, *Memories, Dreams, Reflections*, 300.

[45] See, for example, Jung, "Approaching the Unconscious," 86.

[46] See Jung, "Flying Saucers," *Civilization in Transition*, 307–433. Jung deems flying saucers distinctively modern because they are technological rather than, like religion, supernatural phenomena and therefore fit the modern scientific self-image.

Modern science has subtilized its projections to an almost unrecognizable degree, but our ordinary life still swarms with them. You can find them spread out in the newspapers, in books, rumours, and ordinary social gossip. All gaps in our actual knowledge are still filled out with projections. We are still so sure we know what other people think or what their true character is. We are convinced that certain people have all the bad qualities we do not know in ourselves or that they practise all those vices which could, of course, never be our own. We must still be exceedingly careful not to project our own shadows too shamelessly; we are still swamped with projected illusions.[47]

As fully as moderns project their unconscious, merely expressing it inadvertently is not tending to it. The religiosity of primitives and ancients nurtures the unconscious, albeit in projected form. The atheism of moderns precludes any attention to the unconscious.

In desperation, the unconscious forces itself upon moderns in the form of neurosis:

When in the Babylonian epic Gilgamesh's arrogance and hybris defy the gods, they create a man equal in strength to Gilgamesh in order to check the hero's unlawful ambition. The very same thing has happened to our patient: he is a thinker who has settled, or is always going to settle, the world by the power of his intellect and reason. His ambition has at least succeeded in forging his own personal fate. He has forced everything under the inexorable law of his reason, but somewhere nature escaped and came back with a vengeance. . . . It was the worst blow that could be dealt to all his rational ideals and especially to his belief in the all-powerful human will. . . . Being highly rationalistic and intellectual he had found that his attitude of mind and his philosophy forsook him completely in the face of his neurosis and its demoralizing forces. He found nothing in his whole *Weltanschauung* that would help him gain sufficient control of himself.[48]

The difference between contemporaries and moderns is that contemporaries are conscious of their nonrational side, if not of its

[47] Jung, "Psychology and Religion," 83.
[48] Ibid., 16, 31–32.

unconscious source, and strive to tend to it.[49] Like moderns, who correspond crudely to nineteenth-century intellectuals, contemporaries—twentieth-century intellectuals—reject religion as a prescientific relic. Unlike moderns, however, they are not satisfied with the scruptulously rational life that they have inherited from moderns and yearn for the kind of fulfillment that religion once provided. They seek new, nonprojective outlets to replace the dead, projective ones of religion.[50] They do not, like moderns, boast of having transcended the need that religion once fulfilled:

> But the conscious, modern [i.e., contemporary] man can no longer refrain from acknowledging the might of the psyche, despite the most strenuous and dogged efforts at self-defence. This distinguishes our time from all others. We can no longer deny that the dark stirrings of the unconscious are active powers, that psychic forces exist which, for the present at least, cannot be fitted into our rational world order. . . . The revolution in our conscious outlook, brought about by the catastrophic results of the World War, shows itself in our inner life by the shattering of our faith in ourselves and our own worth. . . . The rapid and worldwide growth of a psychological interest over the last two decades shows unmistakably that modern man is turning his attention from outward material things to his own inner processes. . . . The psychological interest of the present time is an indication that modern man expects something from the psyche which the outer world has not given him: doubtless something which our religion ought to contain, but no longer does contain, at least for modern man.[51]

In identifying contemporaries with twentieth-century persons, Jung is deeming them not average but distinctive. Psychologically, most persons living in Jung's time are either moderns, and so oblivious to any nonrational needs, or ancients, and so satisfied

[49] On contemporaries see above all Jung, "The Spiritual Problem of Modern Man," 74–94. Despite the title this essay is Jung's chief work on contemporaries, not moderns. See also Jung, "Psychotherapists or the Clergy," *Psychology and Religion: West and East*, 327–47. On the distinction between contemporaries and moderns see Peter Homans, *Jung in Context* (Chicago: University of Chicago Press, 1979), 185–86.

[50] See, for example, Jung, "The Undiscovered Self," 303–4; "Flying Saucers," 414–15.

[51] Jung, "The Spiritual Problem of Modern Man," 80–83.

with traditional means of fulfilling them. Because contemporaries
are sensitive both to the existence of nonrational inclinations and to
the demise of past means of fulfilling them, they comprise a select
minority:

> the man we call modern [i.e., contemporary], the man who is
> aware of the immediate present, is by no means the average
> man. . . . The modern man—or, let us say again, the man of the
> immediate present—is rarely met with, for he must be conscious
> to a superlative degree. . . . Even in a civilized community the
> people who form, psychologically speaking, the lowest stratum
> live in a state of consciousness little different from that of primi-
> tives. Those of the succeeding strata [i.e., ancients] live on a level
> of consciousness which corresponds to the beginnings of human
> culture, while those of the highest stratum [i.e., moderns] have a
> consciousness that reflects the life of the last few centuries. Only
> the man who is modern in our meaning of the term really lives in
> the present; he alone has a present-day consciousness, and he
> alone finds that the ways of life on those earlier levels have begun
> to pall upon him. . . . [O]nly the man who has outgrown the
> stages of consciousness belonging to the past, and has amply
> fulfilled the duties appointed for him by his world, can achieve
> full consciousness of the present.[52]

Because contemporaries, unlike moderns, consciously experience rather than ignore their nonrational beckonings, they do not
suffer from ordinary neurosis, or threats to the ego from a spurned
unconscious. Rather, they suffer from emptiness or malaise. Like
moderns, contemporaries are severed from their unconscious, but
unlike moderns they are striving to overcome the divide. They
remain cut off not because, like moderns, they deny their nonrational side but because, as the heirs of moderns, they do not know
how to reconnect themselves to it: "Most of [my patients] already
have some form of psychotherapeutic treatment behind them, with
partial or negative results. About a third of my cases are not suffering from any clinically definable neurosis, but from the senseless-
ness and aimlessness of their lives. I should not object if this were

52 Ibid., 74–76.

called the general neurosis of our age."[53] As the quotation makes clear, distinctively Jungian patients, though by no means all of them, are contemporaries rather than, like Freudian patients, moderns.[54]

Gnostics and Contemporaries

The connection between this history of the psyche and Gnosticism is that for Jung Gnostics are the ancient counterparts to contemporaries and therefore to distinctively Jungian patients, who in turn are the contemporary counterparts to ancient Gnostics:

> The spiritual currents of our time have, in fact, a deep affinity with Gnosticism. . . . The most impressive movement numerically is undoubtedly Theosophy, together with its continental sister, Anthroposophy; these are pure Gnosticism in Hindu dress. . . . What is striking about these Gnostic systems is that they are based exclusively on the manifestations of the unconscious. . . . The passionate interest in these movements undoubtedly arises from psychic energy which can no longer be invested in obsolete religious forms.[55]

Like Gnostics, contemporaries feel alienated from their roots and are seeking to overcome the alienation. They are seeking new outlets for their unconscious. Where Gnostics feel cut off from the outer world, contemporaries feel cut off from the inner one. Contemporaries do not, like Gnostics, project their alienation onto the cosmos; through Jungian psychology they seek to discover their true selves within rather than outside themselves. They alone, then, have the chance fully to overcome their alienation.

Gnosticism for Jung is a wholly ancient, though certainly not

[53] Jung, "The Aims of Psychotherapy," *The Practice of Psychotherapy*, 41. See also Jung, "Approaching the Unconscious," 76–78, 84; *Memories, Dreams, Reflections*, 140, 143–44, 250–53, 340; "Psychotherapists or the Clergy," 330–31, 335–38; "Basic Postulates of Analytical Psychology," *The Structure and Dynamics of the Psyche*, 356. See also Schaer, 166–93; Aniela Jaffé, *The Myth of Meaning*, trans. R.F.C. Hull (New York: Penguin Books, 1975), 146–48; Barbara Hannah, *Jung* (New York: Putnam, 1976), 160–61.
[54] See Anthony Storr, *C. G. Jung*, Modern Masters Series (New York: Viking, 1973), 76–78.
[55] Jung, "The Spiritual Problem of Modern Man," 83–84. See also Jung, "On the Psychology of the Unconscious," 77–78.

wholly Christian, phenomenon. Jung thus pegs his psychology not as the contemporary *version* of Gnosticism but as the contemporary *counterpart* to it. At the same time he regards Gnosticism as the ancient version of something that itself is recurrent: alienation from the unconscious, which in Gnosticism is expressed in alienation from the immaterial essence.

Jung is not, to be sure, saying that this recurrent alienation is chronic. It still characterizes only a few persons and periods.[56] For by alienation Jung means the awareness, not merely the fact, of severance from the unconscious. He therefore excludes moderns from the camp of the alienated. Likewise neither primitives nor ancients are alienated, for religion links both to their unconscious, even if it does so indirectly through projection. Only Gnostics and contemporaries qualify, for they alone are both severed from their unconscious and aware of the fact.

A Jungian Interpretation of Gnostic Myths

The chief Gnostic myths are creation myths. Other Gnostic myths presuppose them. Understood in Jungian terms, Gnostic creation myths describe the development not of the world or even of human beings but of the human psyche. The literal account of the creation of the world must be made not merely human but, even more, psychological.[57] Cosmic terms must be translated into human ones and physical terms into mental ones.

The godhead symbolizes the unconscious. As a symbol of the unconscious, it is primordial. It is the source or agent of everything

[56] Jung does, however, say, albeit with typical snobbishness, that "Today we have a movement in the anonymous masses which is the exact psychological counterpart of the Gnostic movement nineteen hundred years ago" ("Richard Wilhelm: In Memoriam," 60).

[57] On Jung and Gnosticism, including Jungian interpretations of Gnosticism, see Gilles Quispel, "C. G. Jung und die Gnosis," *Eranos-Jahrbüch* 37 (1968): 277–98 (rpt. as "Hesse, Jung und die Gnosis" in Quispel, *Gnostic Studies*, vol. 2, ch. 29; herein 219–38); Quispel, "Gnosis and Psychology," in *The Rediscovery of Gnosticism*, vol. 1, 17–31 (herein 239–56); Quispel, *Gnosis als Weltreligion*, 2d ed. (Zurich: Origo, 1972 [1951]); Quispel, "Gnostic Man: The Doctrine of Basilides," in *Papers from the Eranos Yearbooks*, ed. Joseph Campbell, trans. Ralph Manheim, vol. 6 (Princeton, N.J.: Princeton University Press, 1968), 210–46 (rpt. Quispel, *Gnostic Studies*, vol. 1 [Istanbul: Nederlands Historisch-Archaeologisch Instituut, 1974], ch. 6; orig. "L'homme gnostique: La doctrine de Basilide," *Eranos-Jahrbuch* 16 [1948], 89–139); Victor White, "Some Notes on Gnosticism," *Spring* (1949), 40–56 (rpt. White, *God and the Unconscious* [London: Collins, 1952], chap. 11; herein 197–218); Marie-Louise von Franz, *Patterns of Creativity*

else. Prior to its emanating anything, it is whole, self-sufficient, perfect. The godhead thus symbolizes the unconscious before the emergence of the ego out of it.[58]

As a symbol of the all-encompassing unconscious, the godhead is appropriately androgynous rather than exclusively male or female.[59] For Jungians, the initially androgynous godhead ordinarily becomes a female god, whose bearing of a son symbolizes the emergence of the ego out of the primordial unconscious.[60]

The emergence of matter alongside the immaterial godhead symbolizes the beginning, but just the beginning, of the emergence of the ego out of the unconscious. Inert matter itself does not symbolize the ego, which requires a reflective entity conscious of itself as a subject distinct from the external world. The ego emerges not with the creation of either the Demiurge or Primal Man but only with the creation of individual human beings.[61]

Mirrored in Creation Myths (New York: Spring, 1972), 75–76, 124–30, 139–40, 195–97; von Franz, *C. G. Jung*, trans. William H. Kennedy (Boston: Little, Brown, 1977), 103–4, 123, 173, 183, 200, 230, 233, 271–72; Raschke, 143–53; Stephan A. Hoeller, *The Gnostic Jung and the Seven Sermons to the Dead* (Wheaton, Ill.: Theosophical Publishing House, 1982), 16–43; my *The Poimandres as Myth*, Religion and Reason Series, 33 (Berlin: Mouton de Gruyter, 1986), chap. 3; Ean Begg, "Gnosis and the Single Vision," in *In the Wake of Jung*, ed. Molly Tubb (London: Coventure, 1983), chap. 11; Jeff Dehing, "Jung and Knowledge: From Gnosis to Praxis," *Journal of Analytical Psychology* 35 (October 1990): 377–96; June Singer, "A Necessary Heresy," *Gnosis* (Summer/Spring 1987): 11–19; Singer, "The Invisible World," *Gnosis* (Winter 1989): 17–18; Singer, *Seeing Through the Visible World* (San Francisco: Harper, 1990), 97–102. For a brief quasi-Jungian interpretation of Gnosticism see F. C. Burkitt, *Church and Gnosis* (Cambridge: Cambridge University Press, 1932), 43–44. On this interpretation see C. H. Dodd, *The Interpretation of the Fourth Gospel* (Cambridge: Cambridge University Press, 1953), 107 n. 1.

Hans Jonas argues for a historical shift in Gnosticism from a projective, external, mythological phase to an internalized, philosophical one. But Jonas, in contrast to Jungians, not only is interpreting a mere phase of Gnosticism this way but by an internalized approach does not mean a psychological one: philosophical Gnosticism is still concerned with the relationship between humans and the external world. See Jonas, *Gnosis und spätantiker Geist*, vol. 2, chap. 4; "Myth and Mysticism: A Study of Objectification and Interiorization in Religious Thought," *Journal of Religion* 49 (October 1969): 315–29; "Delimitation of the Gnostic Phenomenon: Typological and Historical," in *Le Origini dello Gnosticismo*, 107.

[58] See Neumann, 5–9.

[59] Ibid., 13, 18.

[60] See Jung, *Symbols of Transformation*, Collected Works, vol. 5, 2d ed. (Princeton, N.J.: Princeton University Press, 1967 [1956]), pt. 2. See also Neumann, passim, esp. 125; Neumann, *The Great Mother*, trans. Ralph Manheim (Princeton, N.J.: Princeton University Press, 1972), passim. Neumann rightly contrasts this typical scenario to the Gnostic one, in which the androgynous godhead becomes male rather than female (*The Origins and History of Consciousness*, 119).

[61] To be sure, Jung himself interprets both the Demiurge and at times Primal Man as symbols of a full-fledged ego. See below, pp. 26–28.

The ego is symbolized not by the spark but by the thinking part of the human body—the unspecified center of human thoughts and actions vis-à-vis the external world. The spark, as the link to the forgotten godhead, symbolizes the unconscious. As long as one remains unaware of the spark, one remains an unrealized self. As long as one's values are material, one is merely an ego.

Insofar as a Jungian interpretation of myth is psychological, it collapses the literal distinction between the outer world and humanity. Both matter and the body symbolize the development of the ego—raw matter symbolizing the beginning of the process and the thinking portion of the body the end. Similarly, both the immaterial godhead and the spark symbolize the unconscious, if also at opposite stages of development.

The ego in Jungian psychology develops not just alongside the unconscious but also out of it. Those Gnostic myths in which matter originates out of the godhead thus express the dependence of the ego on the unconscious. Those myths in which matter is preexistent and merely comes into contact with the godhead express dissociation of the unconscious from the ego and thereby foreshadow the problems that dissociation spells.

For Jungians, the unconscious is naturally creative and spontaneously produces the ego. Gnostic myths depict the godhead as in part an impersonal principle, so that the creation of the material world and, if not preexistent, of matter itself is automatic rather than willed. The Jungian stress on the naturalness of creation abets the resolution of the key Gnostic paradox: why the godhead creates a world that it then seeks to undo.

A Jungian interpretation would ordinarily not account for the details of creation: what entities get created, with what characteristics, and with what importance. Still, the overall manner of creation—the division of matter—symbolizes the development of the mind, which proceeds by division, or differentiation.

The emergence of the ego is a gradual process. The long chains of emanations found in many Gnostic myths capture the gradualness of the task.[62] The emergence of the ego is a difficult process as well. If on the one hand the unconscious creates spontaneously, on the other hand it clings possessively to its progeny. The ego for its part

---

[62] See von Franz, *Patterns of Creativity*, chap. 11.

wants at once to be independent of the unconscious and to be sheltered by it.[63] In Gnostic myths the godhead freely and knowingly emanates parts of itself yet then strives to reclaim those parts. In turn, those parts commonly yearn both to create themselves and to be reabsorbed by the godhead. This mutually ambivalent relationship between the godhead and its emanations fits the relationship between the unconscious and the ego.

Once the ego becomes independent, it inevitably forgets, if not repudiates, its origins. As Marie-Louise von Franz says:

> We can only say that in every human being we meet with the same fact, namely, a pre-conscious totality in which everything is already contained, including consciousness, and at the same time something like an active tendency towards building up a separate consciousness, which, then, sometimes, in a Luciferian gesture, turns back to the pre-conscious totality and says: "I was not created by you, I made myself."[64]

Non-Gnostics, who for Jung ideally also possess a divine spark, are not only ignorant of their origin and the origin of the world but also smugly satisfied with the false, material nature of both. Their complacency makes them apt counterparts to moderns. Gnostics have also forgotten the true nature of themselves and the world, but they are nevertheless dissatisfied with the existing nature of both. Their dissatisfaction makes them suitable counterparts to contemporaries.

If ignorance alone, according to Gnostic orthodoxy, keeps humans tied to the material world, knowledge frees them from it. Because humans are ignorant, that knowledge must come from outside them. Because the powers of the material world are ignorant, too, that knowledge must come from beyond them as well: it can come only from the godhead. The dependence of humanity on the godhead matches the dependence of the ego on the unconscious to reveal itself.

The response of Gnostics to the revelation parallels that of contemporaries to their own discovery: gratitude. The disclosure of a heretofore unknown self and, for Gnostics, a heretofore unknown

---

[63] See Jung, *Symbols of Transformation*, 170–305, esp. 235–36, 271, 297–98, 303–4, 355–56. See also Neumann, *The Origins and History of Consciousness*, 39–191, esp. 114–15.
[64] Von Franz, *Patterns of Creativity*, 73.

world provides a fulfillment that amounts to salvation. As Jung says of contemporaries: "I do not believe that I am going too far when I say that modern [i.e., contemporary] man, in contrast to his nineteenth-century brother, turns to the psyche with very great expectations, and does so without reference to any traditional creed but rather with a view to Gnostic experience."[65] The response of non-Gnostics to the revelation parallels that of moderns to their own discovery: fear. The disclosure, which applies to non-Gnostics as well as to Gnostics, shatters the non-Gnostics' vaunted image of both human nature and the world.

Gnostic myths preach total identification with one's newly dis-covered divinity. Because that identification symbolizes the Gnos-tic's identification with the unconscious, Jungian psychology would consider it no less lopsided and dangerous than the non-Gnostic's identification with the ego—more precisely, with ego consciousness, or consciousness of the external world. Jungian psychology would say that non-Gnostics, like moderns, suffer from an exaggerated persona: their ego identifies itself wholly with the conscious, public personality. But Jungian psychology would equally say that Gnostics, whether or not contemporaries, suffer from an exaggerated, or inflated, ego, which, conversely, identifies itself wholly with the rediscovered unconscious.[66] Minimally, the consequence of inflation is excessive pride in the presumed unique-ness of one's unconscious. Maximally, the consequence is outright psychosis, or the dissolution of any consciousness of the external world: "the great psychic danger which is always connected with individuation, or the development of the self, lies in the identifica-tion of ego-consciousness with the self. This produces an inflation which threatens consciousness with dissolution."[67] The Jungian aim is no more to reject ego consciousness for the unconscious than, like the modern aim, to reject the unconscious for ego con-sciousness. The aim is, rather, to balance the two. This point will prove decisive.

In Gnosticism knowledge itself is liberating: the revelation of the existence of a higher reality automatically diminishes the hold of the lower one. Recognizing matter for what it is, Gnostics cease to

---

[65] Jung, "The Spiritual Problem of Modern Man," 84.

[66] On inflation see Jung, "The Relations between the Ego and the Unconscious," *Two Essays on Analytical Psychology*, 139–47.

[67] Jung, "Concerning Rebirth," *The Archetypes and the Collective Unconscious*, 145.

grant it the status they had till now, even when they had been discontented with it. The freedom from matter given them by the revelation symbolizes freedom from ego consciousness and parallels that given contemporaries by their self-discovery. With the revelation Gnostics are at last free, not to say obliged, to forsake the material world altogether. By contrast, with their self-discovery contemporaries are hardly obliged or even free to forsake ego consciousness: doing so would spell inflation. This continuing difference will, again, prove central.

In Jungian psychology the cultivation of the unconscious does involve a break with ego consciousness and a return to the unconscious. That break, however, is only temporary. The goal is not reversion to the original state of sheer unconsciousness but, on the contrary, the elevation of the unconscious—better, the symbols of it—to consciousness. One returns to the unconscious only to raise it to consciousness:

> Man's worst sin is unconsciousness, but it is indulged in with the greatest piety even by those who should serve mankind as teachers and examples. When shall we stop taking man for granted in this barbarous manner and in all seriousness seek ways and means to exorcize him, to rescue him from possession and unconsciousness, and make this the most vital task of civilization?[68]

As Jolande Jacobi says of the return to the unconscious:

> Once the psyche reaches the midpoint of life, the process of development demands a return to the beginning, a descent into the dark, hot depths of the unconscious. To sojourn in these depths, to withstand their dangers, is a journey to hell and "death." But he who comes through safe and sound, who is "reborn," will return, full of knowledge and wisdom, equipped for the outward and inward demands of life.[69]

---

[68] Jung, "The Phenomenology of the Spirit in Fairytales," *The Archetypes and the Collective Unconscious*, 253–54. See also Jung, " Jung and Religious Belief," 704–5.

[69] Jolande Jacobi, *Complex/Archetype/Symbol in the Psychology of C. G. Jung*, trans. Ralph Manheim (Princeton, N.J.: Princeton University Press, 1967), 186. See also 183–85. See also Jung, *Symbols of Transformation*, 347–48.

Humans should seek a unified state, as they possessed at birth, but now they should seek the integration of the unconscious with ego consciousness, not the restoration of pristine unconsciousness.[70] As Jung says of therapy: "Accordingly, the therapeutic method of complex psychology consists on the one hand in making as fully conscious as possible the constellated unconscious contents, and on the other hand in synthetizing them with consciousness through the act of recognition."[71]

The Gnostic goal, however, is the opposite: reversion to the incipient state of both humanity and the cosmos, not the transformation of either. The goal is a return to the state prior to the emergence of both the material world and humanity itself—the initial state of a total godhead. In Jungian terms, that goal is sheer unconsciousness. The state sought parallels not that of contemporaries but that of primitives—and, even earlier, the "uroboric" state before birth. In shedding both the body and material values, the Gnostic is shedding ego consciousness altogether.[72]

Accordingly, Gnostic myths do not urge humans to alter either their spark or the godhead, nor do they urge the enlightened to fuse their spark with their body or the godhead with the material world. Rather, they urge the escape of the spark from both the body and the material world and the restoration of both it and the godhead to their pristine state. That state *is* one of unity, but the unity is of all divinity, not of divinity with matter. In preaching both a return to the original state and a rejection of the present one, Gnosticism advocates the *opposite* of Jungian psychology.

What for Jung is only a means to an end—return to the unconscious—is for Gnosticism equivalent to the end itself. What for Jung is the end—the integration of the unconscious with ego consciousness—is for Gnosticism the present predicament: the association of divinity with matter. Conversely, what for Gnosticism is the end—the severance of the link between divinity and

---

[70] Thus if Jung praises the introverted East for its attention to the unconscious, he also faults it for one-sidedly seeking to revert to primordial unconsciousness: see *Psychology and Religion: West and East*, pt. 2, esp. 493.

[71] Jung, "Archetypes of the Collective Unconscious," 40.

[72] David Cox (*Jung and St. Paul* [London: Longmans, Green, 1959], 126–27) denies that Jungian psychology parallels Gnosticism on exactly the ground that where for Jung the shift from unconsciousness to even ego consciousness is positive, for Gnosticism even the shift from "pre-creation" to prefallen creation is negative.

matter—is the Jungian predicament: the dissociation of the unconscious from ego consciousness.

It is true that in at least the Gnostic *Hymn of the Pearl* the final state of the psyche, as symbolized there by the child, is different from the original one. The child does not merely change but matures: the robe he cast off at the beginning has grown by the end to accommodate his new size. His growth symbolizes the growth of his personality, which now ideally encompasses the raised unconscious as well as ego consciousness. But in few, if any, other Gnostic myths is there any permanent change in divinity.

It is true that in many Gnostic myths matter originates out of divinity. The Gnostic goal of reversion to the prelapsarian state of the cosmos might therefore seem to mean the reunification of divinity with matter rather than the divorce of the two—escape from the material world as the means to reunification somehow aside. But in fact matter is not originally part of divinity, which initially exists alone. Matter may emerge out of divinity, but it does not lie latent in divinity. Its emergence constitutes a paradox: that pure divinity produces matter and the material world, and does so despite its omniscience and omnipotence. Even in Gnostic myths which postulate primordial dualism, and thus the original independence of divinity from matter, a paradox remains: that divinity, still omniscient and omnipotent, succumbs to matter and produces the material world.

For Jungian psychology and Gnosticism alike, creation myths have a three-stage plot. Stage one for both postulates a preexistent monolith—for Jungian psychology, of unconsciousness; for Gnosticism, of either sheer divinity or else divinity isolated from matter. Stage two for both marks the beginning of creation and thereby of division—for Jungian psychology, into ego consciousness and unconsciousness; for Gnosticism, either into matter and divinity or, if matter is preexistent, into material world and divinity. Either immediately or eventually, the division becomes an opposition.

Stage three for both resolves the opposition, but in antithetical ways. For Gnosticism, there is a complete return to stage one, the time before the emergence of either matter or the material world. For Jungian psychology, however, there is, ideally, the establishment of a new state, one that completes rather than undoes the realization of consciousness begun in stage two. In sum, Jung's progressive ideal is at odds with the regressive one of Gnosticism.

Jung's Equations

In his essay on Gnosticism Jung makes the equations assumed so far: that divinity represents the unconscious and that matter— better, the unnamed thinking part of the human body—represents the ego.[73] To be sure, Jung singles out Primal Man rather than ordinary humanity as the symbol of the ego.

Jung first describes the primordial godhead:

> For instance, Epiphanius quotes an excerpt from one of the Valentinian letters, which says: "In the beginning the Autopator contained in himself everything that is, in a state of unconsciousness [lit., 'not-knowing': ἀγνωσία]." . . . So the "Father" is not only unconscious and without the quality of being, but also the *nirdvandva*, without opposites, lacking all qualities and therefore unknowable. This describes the state of the unconscious. . . . In him was ἔννοια, consciousness. . . . But the presence of ἔννοια does not prove that the Autopator himself is conscious, for the differentiation of consciousness results only from the syzygies and tetrads that follow afterwards, all of them symbolizing processes of conjunction and composition. Ἔννοια must be thought of here as the latent possibility of consciousness.[74]

Clearly, the godhead symbolizes the initial state of sheer unconsciousness.

Jung elsewhere uses the term "God" for this initial state, but more often he applies that term to the final state of integrated unconsciousness and ego consciousness. The godhead, which Jung takes to be a largely impersonal principle, embraces the whole psyche because it is not yet divided, or differentiated, into op-

---

[73] For these same equations see White, "Some Notes on Gnosticism," 44–51; Cox, 126–27; von Franz, *Patterns of Creativity*, 75–76. On the godhead as a symbol of the unconscious see Jung, "The Conjunction," *Mysterium Coniunctionis*, 462. See also Neumann, *The Origins and History of Consciousness*, 118–19.

[74] Jung, "Gnostic Symbols of the Self," 190–91.

posites. God, who for Jung is a full-fledged personality, encompasses the whole psyche because he mediates opposites within himself. He thereby symbolizes the ideal state of wholeness, selfhood, or individuation:

> these [Gnostic] symbols [of God] have the character of "wholeness" and therefore presumably *mean* wholeness. As a rule they are "uniting" symbols, representing the conjunction of a single or double pair of opposites, the result being either a dyad or a quaternion. They arise from the collision between the conscious and the unconscious. . . . The circle and quaternity symbolism appears at this point as a compensating principle of order, which depicts the union of warring opposites as already accomplished. . . . [T]his symbolism uses images or schemata which have always, in all the religions, expressed the universal "Ground," the Deity itself.[75]

Jung identifies the "Anthropos" ("Primal Man" or "Original Man"), "Christ," and the "Son" with God. The Anthropos begins as part of the unconscious godhead, emerges as an independent ego, eventually forgets his unconscious origin, must be reminded of it by the godhead, and then returns to it to form a unified self. Misleadingly identifying the Demiurge with the Anthropos, Jung says:

> The primordial image of the quaternity coalesces, for the Gnostics, with the figure of the demiurge or Anthropos. He is, as it were, the victim of his own creative act, for, when he descended into Physis, he was caught in her embrace. The image of the *anima mundi* or Original Man latent in the dark of matter expresses the presence of a transconscious centre which, because of its quaternary character and its roundness, must be regarded as a symbol of wholeness.[76]

As Jung says more clearly of Christ:

> This Gnostic Christ . . . symbolizes man's original unity and exalts it as the saving goal of his development. By "composing

[75] Ibid., 194–95.
[76] Ibid., 197–98.

the unstable," by bringing order into chaos, by resolving disharmonies and centring upon the mid-point, thus setting a "boundary" to the multitude and focusing attention upon the cross,
consciousness is reunited with the unconscious, the unconscious
man is made one with his centre . . . and in this wise the goal of
man's salvation and exaltation is reached.[77]

Just as Jung associates the godhead with the unconscious and
associates "God," "Anthropos," and "Christ" with the self, so he
ordinarily associates the Demiurge, together with the material side
of humanity, with the ego. Christ's toppling of the Demiurge as the
highest god symbolizes the toppling of the ego by the self as the
center of consciousness. Hence Gnostic texts compare Christ with a
magnet that "draws to itself those parts or substances in man that
are of divine origin . . . and carries them back to their heavenly
birthplace":[78] "This magnetic process revolutionizes the ego-
oriented psyche by setting up, in contradistinction to the ego,
another goal or centre. . . . The myth of the ignorant demiurge
who imagined he was the highest divinity illustrates the perplexity
of the ego when it can no longer hide from itself the knowledge that
it has been dethroned by a supraordinate authority."[79]

More accurately, the ego is in fact supplemented, not replaced,
by the self. For the aim of both Gnosticism and therapy is, once
again, the integration of ego consciousness with the unconscious,
not the rejection of either one for the other:

> When, in treating a case of neurosis, we try to supplement the
> inadequate attitude (or adaptedness) of the conscious mind by
> adding to it contents of the unconscious, our aim is to create a
> wider personality whose centre of gravity does not necessarily
> coincide with the ego, but which, on the contrary, as the patient's
> insights increase, may even thwart his [sheer] ego-tendencies.
> Like a magnet, the new centre [i.e., self] attracts to itself that
> which is proper to it.[80]

[77] Jung, "Transformation Symbolism in the Mass," 292.
[78] Jung, "Gnostic Symbols of the Self," 185–86.
[79] Ibid., 189. See also Jung, Foreword to Neumann, Depth Psychology and a New Ethic, 621–22.
[80] Jung, "Gnostic Symbols of the Self," 189–90.

As a magnet, Christ does not uproot sparks from their material state of ego consciousness and restore them to their primordial state of unconsciousness but instead integrates the two states. Even if the sparks return to "their heavenly birthplace," they return transformed. Having developed into egos through their sojourn on earth, they now become integrated wholes, or selves.

On the one hand Jung recognizes that the magnetized Gnostic spark is part of divinity and is therefore distinct from the material world in which it lies. What he overlooks is that the return of the spark to the godhead thereby signifies the abandonment of ego consciousness and a reversion to sheer unconsciousness—hardly the goal of Jungian therapy.

On the other hand Jung states that the goal of therapy is the development of a "wider personality," in which the unconscious supplements, not supplants, ego consciousness, even if the raised unconscious supplants the ego as the center of the psyche. What he overlooks here is that the spark is distinct from the matter in which it is embedded. Its escape from matter and return to the godhead therefore symbolize, again, the abandonment by the unconscious of ego consciousness, which the Demiurge and material humanity both symbolize, and a reversion to sheer unconsciousness—hardly the enlargement of personality.

Despite Jung's acknowledgment that the sparks lie trapped in matter, he fails to distinguish the two. He equates the awakened sparks as well as the threatened Demiurge with ego consciousness. Both may derive from the godhead, but they derive separately, and the return of the sparks means the rejection of everything material.

As long as the Demiurge, together with the material side of humanity, symbolizes ego consciousness, the final Gnostic state must spell the rejection of ego consciousness. Gnostics' recognition of their divinity entails their rejection of their materiality and its creator. Even those Gnostic myths that do not judge the Demiurge evil—for example, the *Poimandres*—still judge creation itself evil.[81]

---

[81] Jung himself views the Demiurge as, alternatively, good and evil: see my *The Poimandres as Myth*, 141–42.

The Difference Between Gnosticism and Alchemy

Perhaps Jung misinterprets Gnosticism because he interprets it as akin to alchemy. As noted, he considers the Gnostic process of liberating the immaterial sparks from matter the counterpart to the alchemical process of extracting gold from base metals. Where, however, gold is produced out of the metals, the sparks are scarcely produced out of matter, in which, on the contrary, they are presently imprisoned. Far from originating in matter, they have fallen into it and await release.

By contrast, gold originates in the metals. It lies not imprisoned in them but latent in them. It awaits not release but realization. Saying, then, that gold, like the sparks, is produced by extraction is most misleading. Gold is produced not by shedding but by transforming the metals.

Indeed, gold is produced not merely by the distillation of vapor out of the metals but by the return of that vapor to the metals. Rather than escaping from them, the vapor is fused with them. By contrast, the sparks, once liberated from matter, flee from it. They return not to matter but to the immaterial godhead, their true origin. A severance, not a fusion, occurs.[82]

For Jung, the base metals, like the thinking side of the Gnostic's body, symbolize ego consciousness. Similarly, the vapor, like the sparks, symbolizes the unconscious. Where, however, the fusion of the vapor with the metals symbolizes the forging of the self, the reunion of the sparks with the godhead symbolizes, or should symbolize, reversion to primordial unconsciousness.

The reunion of the Gnostic with the godhead constitutes the reunification of a piece of divinity with the rest of divinity, not of divinity with matter.[83] To say, alternatively, that not matter but the

---

[82] This difference is in effect noted by Colpe, "The Challenge of Gnostic Thought for Philosophy, Alchemy, and Literature," 42–45.

[83] It is not only Jung himself but also many Jungians and others who confuse Gnostic reunion with the reunion of divinity and matter. June Singer says that in Gnosticism "what is sought is not perfection, but wholeness. Wholeness or completion comes about symbolically in the mystical marriage between the Christ or Logos figure and the Sophia or Eros figure" (*Seeing Through the Visible World*, 149)—i.e., divinity and matter. Maurice Friedman calls Jung Gnostic because he espouses "the unification of good and evil" (*To Deny Our Nothingness* [New York: Delta Books, 1967], 149)—again, divinity and matter. Stephan Hoeller declares that "Jung, in his intuitive knowledge of the Gnosis, recognized that, not dualism, but the recognition of the ultimate necessity for the union of opposites

Gnostic spark symbolizes ego consciousness, which is then reintegrated with the unconscious, is to leave matter unexplained.

The equation of the godhead with ego consciousness and unconsciousness combined proves no more helpful. If at the outset the godhead is, as perfection, a fully realized self, then creation is psychologically superfluous. Moreover, the restoration of the pristine state of perfection still involves the rejection of matter, which remains unexplained. If, alternatively, the godhead is only unconscious at the outset and realizes itself through creation,[84] then, contrary to Gnostic teaching, the end is different from the beginning. Indeed, if the godhead must, psychologically, create the world in order to realize itself, then creation is necessary rather than superfluous, beneficial rather than harmful, and so laudable rather than lamentable—the reverse of the Gnostic view.

To say that Gnosticism, interpreted psychologically, violates rather than supports the Jungian ideal is scarcely to say that Jungian psychology cannot still interpret it. Gnosticism should simply be interpreted differently—as evincing inflation rather than individuation, as espousing the ego's rediscovery of the unconscious as an end in itself, not as a means to a different end.[85]

By interpreting the Gnostic's permanent return to the godhead as inflation, Jungian psychology would be able to make sense of the key Gnostic paradox: why an omniscient and omnipotent divinity creates a world that he then seeks to destroy. Jungian psychology would make not the creation but the dissolution of the world the mistake. Though it would admittedly thereby be evaluating Gnosticism by its own world-affirming rather than world-rejecting ideal, Jungian psychology would at least be able to make sense of creation. The unconscious, as symbolized by the godhead, would not be erring in creating the ego, as symbolized by the material side of humanity. The unconscious would truly be both omniscient and omnipotent. It is the ego which would be neither: lacking both the

---

[i.e., divinity and matter] was at the heart of the Gnostic attitude" (96). On Joseph Campbell's comparable celebration of Gnosticism see my *Joseph Campbell*, rev. ed. (New York: New American Library, 1990), 136–37.

[84] Jung interprets God this way in "Answer to Job," *Psychology and Religion: West and East*, 375–470.

[85] For a brief similar Jungian interpretation of Gnosticism see White, "Some Notes on Gnosticism," 45. At least once Jung himself characterizes the Gnostic state as inflated: see "Transformation Symbolism in the Mass," 286–87.

knowledge and the will to resist the spell of the unconscious, it would be returning of its own accord to the unconscious, which, to be sure, would be enticing it.

Though for most of his career Jung was working before the Nag Hammadi discovery, familiarity with its contents would likely not have altered his views. The discovery there of non-Christian Gnostic texts would only have confirmed the appropriateness of his broad definition of Gnosticism as radical dualism rather than as an exclusively Christian heresy. Surely his skewed interpretation of Gnosticism as the resolution of the dualism would not have changed. Other issues raised anew by Nag Hammadi—notably, that of the origin of Gnosticism—would not seem germane. Still, the discovery of so many primary Gnostic texts might have made Gnosticism more accessible to Jung and have thereby enabled him to use it even more fully than he does.

The Gnostics as Psychologists

Jung fails to make clear how psychologically sophisticated he thinks the Gnostics were. On the one hand he concedes that they, together with at least the early alchemists, were probably unaware of the psychological meaning of their beliefs: "It seems to me highly unlikely that they [Gnostics] had a psychological conception of [archetypal images]."[86] Gnostics thought that they were dealing with the cosmos as well as themselves: "The Gnostics projected their subjective inner perception . . . into a cosmogonic system and believed in the [metaphysical] reality of its psychological figures."[87]

On the other hand Jung says that his "enthusiasm" for the Gnostics "arose from the discovery that they were apparently the first thinkers to concern themselves (after their fashion) with the contents of the collective unconscious."[88] Jung declares that "Gnosis is undoubtedly a psychological knowledge whose contents derive

---

[86] Jung, *Memories, Dreams, Reflections*, 201. On alchemists as unconscious of their psychological activities see Jung, "Religious Ideas in Alchemy," 244–45; "The Psychology of the Transference," 208.

[87] Jung, *Psychological Types*, 19.

[88] Jung, "Psychology and Religion: A Reply to Martin Buber," 664.

from the unconscious"[89] and that "it is clear beyond a doubt that many of the Gnostics were nothing other than psychologists."[90] He thus denies that the existence of the unconscious is a recent discovery:

> Since all cognition is akin to recognition, it should not come as a surprise that what I have described as a gradual process of development had already been anticipated, and more or less prefigured, at the beginning of our era. We meet these images and ideas in Gnosticism. . . . The alchemists in their own way knew more about the nature of the individuation process than we moderns do. . . . The same knowledge, formulated differently to suit the age they lived in, was possessed by the Gnostics. The idea of an unconscious was not unknown to them.[91]

It is not easy to reconcile these two sets of statements. If, furthermore, the Gnostics were not psychologically self-conscious, it is not easy to see how they were psychologically superior to their peers and so on what grounds Jung toasts them.

Despite Jung's tribute to Gnostics for their psychological precocity, presumably he is not saying that they recognized the psychological meaning of their myths. His qualifying phrases "after their fashion" and "in their own way" suggest that for him the Gnostics were tending to the unconscious without knowing it. They *were* more psychologically savvy than other ancients, but not because they realized that they were projecting their psyches onto the cosmos. Rather, they felt unfulfilled and so, like their contemporary descendants, consciously sought new myths to provide the fulfillment that traditional ones no longer yielded:

> The psychological interest of the present time is an indication that modern [i.e., contemporary] man expects something from the psyche which the outer world has not given him: doubtless something which our religion ought to contain, but no longer does contain, at least for modern man. . . . That there is a gen-

---

[89] Jung, "The Structure and Dynamics of the Self," 223.
[90] Ibid., 222.
[91] Jung, "Gnostic Symbols of the Self," 184, 190. See also Jung, "Address at the Presentation of the Jung Codex," 672, 828–29; "On the Psychology of the Unconscious," 241–42; "The Spiritual Problem of Modern Man," 83–84. See also Schaer, 165–66, 182–83.

eral interest in these matters cannot be denied. . . . I am not thinking merely of the interest taken in psychology as a science, or of the still narrower interest in the psychoanalysis of Freud, but of the widespread and ever-growing interest in all sorts of psychic phenomena, including spiritualism, astrology, Theosophy, parapsychology, and so forth. The world has seen nothing like it since the end of the seventeenth century. We can compare it only to the flowering of Gnostic thought in the first and second centuries after Christ. . . . What is striking about these Gnostic systems is that they are based exclusively on the manifestations of the unconscious. . . . The passionate interest in these movements undoubtedly arises from psychic energy which can no longer be invested in obsolete religious forms.[92]

More specifically, Gnostics were seeking a mythology that recognized the reality of evil and the power of the feminine. Gnostics were also seeking a religion that provided experience and not just belief.

For Jung, non-Gnostics, by contrast, felt no discontent. Those non-Gnostics who were nonbelievers were like moderns: they scorned whatever conscious needs myth and religion fulfilled for believers. Those non-Gnostics who were believers were like ancients: their existing myths and religions satisfied the conscious needs they felt. They dismissed the reality of evil, minimized the significance of the feminine, and cultivated religious belief over religious experience.

Jung's Own Gnostic Myth

The most entrancing expression of Jung's attraction to Gnosticism is his own Gnostic myth, the "Seven Sermons to the Dead." As Jung recounts in his autobiography, he composed the piece in three evenings in 1916 in response to the most dramatic of his many parapsychological experiences:

Around five o'clock in the afternoon on Sunday the front doorbell began ringing frantically. It was a bright summer day; the

92 Jung, "The Spiritual Problem of Modern Man," 83–84.

two maids were in the kitchen, from which the open square outside the front door could be seen. Everyone immediately looked to see who was there, but there was no one in sight. I was sitting near the doorbell, and not only heard it but saw it moving. We all simply stared at one another. The atmosphere was thick, believe me! Then I knew that something had to happen. The whole house was filled as if there were a crowd present, crammed full of spirits. They were packed deep right up to the door, and the air was so thick it was scarcely possible to breathe. . . . Then they cried out in chorus, "We have come back from Jerusalem where we found not what we sought." That is the beginning of the *Septem Sermones*.[93]

The composition—or transcription—of the Seven Sermons was a response to Jung's "confrontation" with the collective unconscious. That confrontation, which followed his break with Freud in 1912, took the form of dreams, visions, and fantasies as well as the paranormal. Looking back, Jung says that "All my works, all my creative activity, has come from those initial fantasies and dreams which began in 1912, almost fifty years ago. Everything that I accomplished in later life was already contained in them, although at first only in the form of emotions and images."[94]

Yet Jung was embarrassed by the Seven Sermons, which he called "a sin of my youth."[95] At the least, he was embarrassed by the publication of the myth, which was first published privately and distributed only to friends. Yet he might have been abashed by the myth itself.[96] In any case only "for the sake of honesty" did he allow its inclusion in his memoirs.[97] He barred its inclusion in the Collected Works.

Included in Jung's experiences was a continuing "dialogue" with "Philemon," the most important of his personifications of the unconscious. Jung says that the Seven Sermons, which formally are attributed to the second-century Alexandrian Gnostic Basilides,

---

[93] Jung, *Memories, Dreams, Reflections*, 190–91.
[94] Ibid., 192. See also 199.
[95] Jung, "Religion and Psychology: A Reply to Martin Buber," 663.
[96] See, alternatively, Jaffé, headnote to *Memories, Dreams, Reflections*, 378; von Franz, *C. G. Jung*, 36, 121 n. 82; Hoeller, 8–9.
[97] Jung, quoted in Jaffé, headnote to *Memories, Dreams, Reflections*, 378.

"formulate and express what might have been said by Philemon."[98]
Indeed, Philemon himself was an imaginary Alexandrian Gnostic:
"Philemon was a pagan and brought with him an Egypto-Hellenistic
atmosphere with a Gnostic coloration."[99]

Jung's encounter with the "dead" must be understood both parapsychologically and psychologically.[100] Parapsychologically, the
dead of the Seven Sermons are the poltergeists occupying Jung's
house. They are the souls of dead Christians: "The dead now raised
a great tumult, for they were Christians" (Sermon II). The dead
had spent their lives under the spell of mainstream Christianity and
only posthumously discovered that their religion offered no answers to the questions they now faced. They are therefore beseech-
ing Jung for help. Remarkably, the dead are seeking out the living
rather than, as in standard parapsychology, the living seeking
out the dead. Either Jung is channeling Basilides, who is address-
ing the poltergeists, or Jung is using the channeled Basilides to
address the poltergeists himself.

Psychologically, it is not Basilides but Jung who is talking, and
the dead are not other persons but Jung's own unconscious. Yet
both of these equations need qualification. In the first place Jung
wrote the Seven Sermons while still immersed in his confrontation
with the unconscious. He was not yet, like Basilides, an individuated self. Basilides may, then, presage Jung's future state rather
than manifest his present one, much the way the spirit Ivenes
presaged the life of Jung's cousin Helly Preiswerk. After all, Jung
does credit the Seven Sermons with prefiguring his life's work.
Psychologically, then, Jung is channeling his own future self,
which only in the course of the rest of his life does he come fully to
develop.

In the second place Jung's unconscious, as collective, would for
him have been shaped by the experiences of both his familial and
his cultural ancestors. He continually castigated his father, a Prot-
estant minister, for failing to challenge the inadequacy of main-

[98] Ibid., 190.
[99] Ibid., 182. Still, E. M. Brenner may be going too far in saying that "Philemon was
merely a medium through whom the thoughts of Basilides were made manifest" ("Gnosticism and Psychology: Jung's Septem Sermones ad Mortuos," *Journal of Analytical Psychology* 35 [October 1990]: 398).
[100] On Jung and parapsychology see Jaffeé, *From the Life and Work of C. G. Jung*, chap. 1;
Stephan A. Hoeller, "Jung and the Occult," *Gnosis* (Winter 1989): 22–27.

stream Christian doctrine. [101] Jung's own unconscious would thus be pressing for the answers never secured by his progenitors during their lives: "I could well imagine that I might have lived in former centuries and there encountered questions I was not yet able to answer; that I had to be born again because I had not fulfilled the task that was given to me. . . . Perhaps it is a question which preoccupied my ancestors, and which they could not answer." [102] In Basilides' day it was Gnostics who tackled the questions either missed or ignored by others. Jung sees himself as a Basilides for the contemporary world: it is he and his patients who face the current questions either missed or ignored by others.

In other Gnostic myths the unconscious is seeking to reveal itself *to* ego consciousness. In the Seven Sermons the unconscious is seeking revelation *from* ego consciousness. The dead symbolize the unconscious: "the unconscious corresponds to the mythic land of the dead, the land of the ancestors." [103] The living symbolize ego consciousness. Jung speculates that, contrary to popular opinion, the dead are not "the possessors of great knowledge" but instead

"know" only what they knew at the moment of death, and nothing beyond that. Hence their endeavor to penetrate into life in order to share in the knowledge of men. . . . It seems to me as if they were dependent on the living for receiving answers to their questions, that is, on those who have survived them and exist in a world of change: as if omniscience or, as I might put it, omniconsciousness, were not at their disposal, but could flow only into the psyche of the living, into a soul bound to a body. [104]

Jung's Basilides preaches not to living Gnostics but to dead non-Gnostics. The dead are not incarnate souls awaiting revelation but disembodied souls that never secured any revelation during life. They are not, as in conventional Gnostic imagery, dead *to* a higher reality but are literally dead. [105] Far from dead to a deeper reality,

[101] On Jung's views of Christianity see Murray Stein, *Jung's Treatment of Christianity* (Wilmette, Ill.: Chiron, 1985).

[102] Jung, *Memories, Dreams, Reflections*, 318.

[103] Ibid., 191.

[104] Ibid., 308. See also 311, 315–16.

[105] Hoeller, citing standard Gnostic imagery, wrongly assumes the dead to be living Gnostics (*The Gnostic Jung and the Seven Sermons to the Dead*, 62–65). Brenner assumes the same (406).

they are clamoring for it. Rather than complacent, they are implacable. Psychologically, they symbolize not, like the subjects of other Gnostic myths, the state of ego consciousness severed from the unconscious but the state of undifferentiated unconsciousness itself. The goal remains the raising of the unconscious to consciousness, but now it is the unconscious which is imploring ego consciousness to raise it.

Having spent their lives in Jerusalem, the birthplace of mainstream Christianity, the dead "found not what they sought" (Sermon I). By contrast, the heterodox Basilides hails from Alexandria, the fabled Gnostic center "where the East toucheth the West."[106] The meeting of East and West is the meeting of the unconscious with ego consciousness—the Jungian ideal. In yoking the two spheres, Basilides epitomizes the individuated self.

The dead are pestering Basilides not only because orthodoxy never answered their questions but also because he, together with other Gnostic teachers, is the first person to be able to answer them. Psychologically, the collective unconscious is hounding Jung not only because it yearns for cultivation but also because Jung is the first person able to cultivate it. The wisdom he harbors is not, like Basilides', metaphysical but psychological. Indeed, the wisdom he harbors is *that* Gnostic metaphysics is really psychological exploration. In psychologizing Gnosticism, Jung is not, however, dismissing it, as he assumes Freud and other moderns would. Gnosticism remains wisdom, but now wisdom about humanity rather than about divinity.

In typical Gnostic fashion the wisdom imparted by Jung's Gnostic myth takes the form of a creation myth, or at least the outline of one.[107] In the beginning is the godhead, or pleroma, which stands for primordial unconsciousness. The pleroma is undifferentiated, so that none of the commonly assumed distinctions is yet made. For example, it is at once "nothingness and fullness" (Sermon I).

Out of the pleroma emerges "creatura," and likely out of creatura emerge individual "created beings." Creatura is the first god and likely corresponds to the Demiurge.[108] Just as the pleroma

---

[106] On Alexandria and Jerusalem see Hoeller, *The Gnostic Jung and the Seven Sermons to the Dead*, 61–62, 65–67.
[107] Brenner goes too far in saying that "Jung's treatise does not contain an intelligible Gnostic cosmology" (408).
[108] Quispel denies that the Seven Sermons has a Demiurge ("C. G. Jung und die Gnosis," 255).

stands for incipient unconsciousness, so creatura and the created beings stand for the ego. The development of created beings from or through creatura signifies the gradual development of the ego. The ambivalent relationship between created beings and the pleroma symbolizes the ambivalent relationship between the ego and the unconscious. On the one hand we created beings "are the pleroma itself" (Sermon I), for we never break wholly with our roots. On the other hand we "are from the pleroma infinitely removed" (Sermon I), for we do achieve autonomy. Psychological growth requires independence from the unconscious—the goal of the first half of life—yet reconnection with it—the goal of the second half.

In both halves growth involves differentiation: differentiation of the external world from the unconscious in the first half of life, differentiation of the parts of the unconscious in the second. In both halves the ego does the differentiating. As the Seven Sermons declare, "Distinctiveness [i.e., differentiation] is creatura. . . . Distinctiveness is its essence, and therefore it distinguisheth" (Sermon I). In saying that creatura, in contrast to the pleroma, "hath qualities," the Seven Sermons are saying the same. Differentiation is synonymous with individuation—the *"principium individuationis"* (Sermon I).

The Seven Sermons enumerate various pairs of opposites that lie undifferentiated in the pleroma and that it is the function of creatura to sort out. It is characteristic of Jung's rendition of Gnosticism that his pleroma contains, though undifferentiated, both sides of all opposites—notably, "force and matter" and "good and evil" (Sermon I). He might have added "masculine and feminine."

While the initial task of creatura is to separate out the sides of each opposite, the final goal is to integrate both sides of all opposites. Integration means neither effacing the differences between one side and the other nor, certainly, cultivating only one side. Integration means balance rather than either oneness or onesidedness. When, according to the Seven Sermons, "we strive after [only] the good or [only] the beautiful, we thereby forget our own nature, which is distinctiveness" (Sermon I). Jung's espousal of integration rather than onesidedness once again expresses the key difference between him and the Gnostics.

The god creatura has its own opposite: the devil. Both powers are "manifestations" of the pleroma (Sermon II), which again incorporates both good and evil. Like all other pairs of opposites, god and devil go hand in hand: "To god, therefore, always belongeth the devil" (Sermon II). Yet rather than cancelling each other out, as in the pleroma, they balance each other: "In so far as god and devil are [now both] creatura, they do not extinguish each other, but stand one against the other as effective opposites" (Sermon II). Contending that there are not just two but many gods, the text soberly prophesies "woe unto you, who replace these incompatible many by a single god" (Sermon IV)—the single, all-good deity of mainstream Christianity.

The god "Abraxas" encompasses both god and devil. For Jung, Abraxas is not, as for the historical Basilides, merely the Demiurge[109] but the highest god—in Gnostic jargon, "the god above god" (Sermon II). Similarly, for Jung the highest god is not, as for the historical Basilides, wholly good but evil as well as good.[110] Where the pleroma constitutes the undifferentiated totality, Abraxas for Jung constitutes the differentiated totality. The pleroma bespeaks the initial psychological state, Abraxas the final one.[111] Abraxas represents the self.

Read literally, the Seven Sermons postulate gods who exist independently of human beings. Rather than projections *of* human qualities, the gods manifest themselves *in* human qualities—above all in "spirituality" and "sexuality":

The world of the gods is made manifest in spirituality and in sexuality. The celestial ones appear in spirituality, the earthly in sexuality. Spirituality conceiveth and embraceth. It is womanlike and therefore we call it MATER COELESTIS, the celestial mother. Sexuality engendereth and createth. It is manlike, and therefore we call it PHALLOS, the earthly father. The sexuality

---

[109] Ibid., 288–89, 293–94. In defense of Jung see Hoeller, *The Gnostic Jung and the Seven Sermons to the Dead*, 90–91, 105. For a summary of the teachings of the historical Basilides see Rudolph, 309–12.

[110] Quispel rightly distinguishes Jung's incorporation of evil in the godhead from the Gnostic repudiation of evil from the godhead ("C. G. Jung und die Gnosis," 293–94). See also H. L. Philp, *Jung and the Problem of Evil* (London: Rockliff, 1958), 82–83.

[111] Judith Hubback oddly reverses these equations ("VII Sermones ad mortuous," *Journal of Analytical Psychology* 11 [July 1966]: 100–102).

of man is more of the earth, the sexuality of woman is more of the spirit. (Sermon V)

It is a Jungian commonplace for the Seven Sermons to associate spirituality, or immateriality, with the celestial gods and sexuality, or matter, with the diabolical ones. It is the reverse of Jungian convention for the myth in turn to associate spirituality with the feminine and sexuality with the masculine.[112] At the same time the text does distinguish between masculine and feminine spirituality and between masculine and feminine sexuality. The text opposes both the denial of either trait and the fusion of them. The insistence on the inclusion of sexuality alongside spirituality yet again differentiates the Jungian ideal from the Gnostic one.

The last sermon recounts the life of the soul, which psychologically means the psyche. The soul at first exists by itself, then is incarnate in a body, and finally leaves the body at death—perhaps to be reincarnated, as Jung speculates.[113] When the myth says that "Man is a gateway, through which from the outer world of gods, daemons, and souls ye pass into the inner world" (Sermon VII), it is referring to the transition from life in the body to life as a disembodied soul. At death "once again ye find yourselves in endless space, in the smaller or innermost infinity" (Sermon VII), for at death the soul reverts to its pristine, disembodied state, which psychologically means to unconsciousness.

The state of the soul at death depends on its accomplishments during life. The dead crying out to Basilides never found their "Star," or god, during life and are belatedly trying to find it now.[114] Having had no Basilides to abet their quest during life, they likely did not even seek their star till now. They thus face death not fulfilled but lost: "Now the dead howled and raged, for they were unperfected" (Sermon III). Psychologically, the unconscious during life had no ego to nurture it. An unconscious properly tended during life will become like Abraxas; one insufficiently tended will remain like the pleroma.

The Seven Sermons leave unclear the fate of the dead. Have they grasped Basilides' message? Can they act on it? We are told

[112] See Hoeller, *The Gnostic Jung and the Seven Sermons to the Dead,* 138–39.
[113] See Jung, *Memories, Dreams, Reflections,* 316–19.
[114] Ibid., 308–9.

only that the dead, now silent, ascended—to where it is not disclosed.[115] Jung never divulged the meaning of the closing anagram.[116]

Jung as Gnostic

It is one thing to maintain that Jung was entranced by Gnosticism. It is another to say that he was a Gnostic himself. Jung himself invokes this distinction[117] and vigorously, even bitterly, rejects the epithet "Gnostic"—not on the grounds that he disagrees with any Gnostic tenets but on the grounds that he is an empirical scientist rather than a metaphysician: "The designation of my 'system' as 'Gnostic' is an invention of my theological critics. . . . I am not a philosopher, merely an empiricist."[118] Jung continually professes *a*gnosticism rather than gnosticism:

> I would like to point out to my critic that I have in my time been regarded not only as a Gnostic and its opposite, but also as a theist and an atheist, a mystic and a materialist. . . . Anyone who does not know my work will certainly ask himself how it is that so many contrary opinions can be held about one and the same subject. The answer to this is that they are all thought up by "metaphysicians," that is, by people who for one reason or an-

---

[115] Brenner's comparison of the ascent with the ascent of disembodied souls at death (403–4) presupposes that prior to their ascent the dead are living Gnostics rather than dead non-Gnostics.

[116] For other Jungian interpretations of the Seven Sermons see Quispel, "C. G. Jung und die Gnosis," 277–98; Hubback, 95–111; James W. Heisig, "*The VII Sermones:* Play and Theory," *Spring* (1972): 206–18; Heisig, *Imago Dei* (Cranbury, N.J.: Bucknell University Press, 1979), 31–33; June Singer, *Boundaries of the Soul* (Garden City, N.Y.: Doubleday Anchor Books, 1972), 373–79; Brenner, 397–419; Miguel Serrano, *C. G. Jung and Hermann Hesse,* trans. Frank MacShane (New York: Schocken, 1966), 93–96; James Olney, *The Rhizome and the Flower* (Berkeley: University of California Press, 1980), 295–304; Robert S. Steele, *Freud and Jung* (London and Boston: Routledge & Kegan Paul, 1982), 287–90; Gerhard Wehr, *Jung,* trans. David M. Weeks (Boston: Shambhala, 1988), 192–96; above all Hoeller, *The Gnostic Jung and the Seven Sermons to the Dead,* 59–201. For a Freudian interpretation of the circumstances leading to the composition of the Seven Sermons see Nandor Fodor, "Jung's Sermons to the Dead," *Psychoanalytic Review* 51 (Spring 1964): 74–78.

[117] Jung, "Jung and Religious Belief," 730.

[118] Ibid., 727. See also 727–30; Foreword to White's, *God and the Unconscious,* 307; "Religion and Psychology: A Reply to Martin Buber," 663–70; *Memories, Dreams, Reflections,* 347–48; *Letters,* vol. 2, 53–55, 61, 64–65, 147, 244–45, 570–73, 583–84.

other think they know about unknowable things in the Beyond. I have never ventured to declare that such things do *not* exist; but neither have I ventured to suppose that any statement of mine could in any way touch them or even represent them correctly.[119]

Jung insists that God, Satan, angels, and demons are real psychologically, as manifestations of the human unconscious, but he insists equally strongly that their metaphysical status is beyond his scientific ken: "If, therefore, we speak of 'God' as an 'archetype,' we are saying nothing about His real nature but are letting it be known that 'God' already has a place in that part of our psyche which is pre-existent to consciousness and that He therefore cannot be considered an invention of consciousness."[120]

Despite Jung's epistemological disclaimers he has regularly been called a Gnostic. Sometimes the term is bestowed in praise, other times in condemnation. What the designation means varies from designator to designator. When the Jewish philosopher Martin Buber labels Jung Gnostic he means that Jung, in locating divinity within humanity, effaces the line between the one and the other. Gnosticism is therefore the flip side of atheism. Buber thus castigates Jung for reducing divinity to humanity—even amidst the Gnostic elevation of humanity to divinity: "In the place of that becoming one with the Self-contained [i.e., God], he [Jung] sets the 'Self,' which is also, as is well known, an originally mystical concept. In Jung, however, it is no longer a genuinely mystical concept but is transformed instead into a Gnostic one."[121]

Buber's objection is doubly off the mark, for no more than Jung do Gnostics reduce God to something merely human. Contrary to Buber, Gnostics *are* mystics: God and humanity are identical; God is not a mere projection of humanity. Jung's continual profession of agnosticism refutes Buber's accusation that Jung "oversteps with sovereign license the boundaries of psychology in its most essential point."[122] In short, Jung is no metaphysical Gnostic.

[119] Jung, "Religion and Psychology: A Reply to Martin Buber," 664.
[120] Jung, *Memories, Dreams, Reflections*, 347–48. See also Jung, "Religion and Psychology: A Reply to Martin Buber," 665.
[121] Martin Buber, *Eclipse of God*, trans. Maurice S. Friedman et al. (New York: Harper & Row, 1952), 84.
[122] Ibid., 78. On the exchange between Buber and Jung see also Buber's counterreply, in his *Eclipse of God*, chap. 9; Edward Whitmont, "Editorial Foreword to Jung's 'Reply to Buber'," *Spring* (1975): 1–3; Whitmont, "Prefatory Remarks to Jung's 'Reply to Buber'," *Spring* (1973): 188–95.

But is he a psychological one, as others who call him Gnostic maintain? Far from oblivious to the difference between metaphysical and psychological claims, Maurice Friedman, coincidentally the preeminent authority on Buber, states that "It would be a mistake to look on Jung as metaphysician or theologian, as he himself never tires of telling us."[123] In taking Gnostic myths "as symbols of unconscious psychic processes,"[124] Jung is not, for Friedman, overstepping the bounds of psychology.

Yet Friedman does not thereby accept at face value Jung's modest claim that "he is simply being empirical."[125] For Friedman, Jung is a Gnostic, not just a scientist, because he offers the psychological equivalent of salvation. Like an ancient Gnostic, Jung preaches salvation by self-knowledge, rejection of the external world for the inner world of the self, and the divinity of the self: "Like the ancient Gnostic, he sees the outer world as evil, and even the inner world that is accessible to man becomes good only when it comes into touch with that hidden divinity within the soul—the unconscious."[126]

But Jung is a contemporary Gnostic because he seeks salvation of an entirely psychological kind. He seeks it within the human self, not in any reunion with an independent deity:

> *Modern* Gnostic that he is, he turns to the unconscious with the same expectation of saving knowledge as the ancient Gnostic turned to the demiurge and the hidden God. . . . Jung sees no essential difference between modern man's relation to the inner self and ancient man's relation to the divine Other. . . . [T]he place of God is gradually taken by deified man. . . . Never has he stated so openly his goal of substituting for the Christian God-man the Modern Gnostic man-god who will achieve gnosis of the Divine through understanding himself.[127]

Not all of Friedman's characterizations of Jung as Gnostic are accurate. Jung does not, for example, solipsistically reject the outer world for the inner but on the contrary strives to straddle the two.

---

[123] Friedman, 148.
[124] Ibid.
[125] Ibid.
[126] Ibid., 150.
[127] Ibid., 148, 161–65.

Still, Friedman's general effort at making Jung a Gnostic of a non-metaphysical variety is plausible.

Like Friedman, Thomas Altizer, the theologian, labels Jung a contemporary Gnostic on the grounds that Jung is more than a scientist: "Despite his frequently repeated—and even compulsive—scientific claims, Jung has found his spiritual home in what he himself identifies as the Gnostic tradition."[128] But Altizer is much vaguer than Friedman about the nature of Gnosticism: "Gnosticism almost defies definition—but it might be defined as a violent reaction against the world of self-conscious and rational thinking evolved by Greek culture and an ecstatic return to the mythical world of the Oriental religious sensibility. To borrow Nietzsche's categories, it is a victory of the Dionysian over the Apollonian consciousness."[129]

It is not clear what for Altizer the difference is between ancient and contemporary antirationalism, so that it is unclear how Jung is a contemporary Gnostic or a Gnostic at all. Surely it is not only Gnostics, ancient or present, who purportedly rail against "self-conscious and rational thinking." Rather than matching specific Jungian tenets with Gnostic ones, Altizer proceeds to label Gnostic the alternative sources that he deems the true sources of Jung's ideas: German Romanticism and the East. His overall analysis is insufficiently precise or focused to prove his point.

Like Altizer, the Theosophist Stephan Hoeller sees Jung as part of a Gnostic tradition. For all his continual noting of Jung's psychologizing of ancient Gnostic teachings, Hoeller, like Buber, blurs any difference between ancient and current Gnosticism. Jung is merely the latest figure in a perennial line:

> This Pan-Sophic, or Theo-Sophic tradition was recognized by Jung to have taken many forms throughout the ages, but also to have been particularly manifest in the late nineteenth and early twentieth centuries within the movement of modern Theosophy, enunciated by the Russian noblewoman and world-traveler, Madame H. P. Blavatsky. . . . Jung clearly recognized modern Theosophy as an important contemporary manifestation of

[128] Thomas J. J. Altizer, "Science and Gnosis in Jung's Psychology," *Centennial Review* 3 (Summer 1959): 304.
[129] Ibid.

Gnosticism. . . . In short, Jung's insights need to be considered as one of the latest and greatest manifestations of the stream of alternative spirituality which descends from the Gnostics.[130]

For Hoeller, Jung offers not the psychological *equivalent* of ancient Gnosticism, as for Friedman and perhaps Altizer, but a psychological *updating* of it: Jung "knew that in his psychology he was putting forward an essentially Gnostic discipline of transformation in contemporary guise."[131] In fact, Hoeller maintains that Jung imbibes Gnosticism for its metaphysical insights—insights somehow translatable into psychological terms without thereby being denuded of their metaphysical clout.

Hoeller's appropriation of Jung is doubly tenuous. Not only, once again, does Jung formally profess to be a mere psychologist, but the outlook that Hoeller considers Theosophical and therefore Gnostic is in actuality Theosophical *rather than* Gnostic. Just as Jung reads Gnosticism through alchemical eyes and thereby reverses its world-rejecting ethos, so Hoeller reads Gnosticism through Theosophical eyes and thereby turns it on its world-rejecting head. For him, as for Jung, Gnostic wholeness means the reconciliation of immateriality with matter:

> The Gnostic effort . . . is directed toward individuation, the reintegration of differentiated and alienated consciousness with the unconscious. . . . Renaissance painters could joyously paint papal mistresses and aristocratic courtesans in the role of the madonna, not because they had lost their religious devotion, but because they recovered a spiritual orientation which gloried in the convergence of the opposites, and celebrated the intersection of time and eternity in human nature. Regrettably, this relatively brief burst of Gnosis during the Renaissance gave way to long centuries of increasing materialism and the trivialization of life.[132]

Needless to say, Gnostic wholeness does not mean the reunion of immateriality with matter. Nor, psychologically, does Gnostic

---

[130] Hoeller, *The Gnostic Jung and the Seven Sermons to the Dead*, 26, 32.
[131] Ibid., 26.
[132] Ibid., 101, 136.

wholeness quite mean the integration, let alone the fusion, of unconsciousness with ego consciousness.

Because Jung reads Gnosticism in the same world-affirming manner as Hoeller, Hoeller should really argue that Jung is a Theosophist *rather than* a Gnostic. Instead, Hoeller takes Jung's world-affirming outlook as identical with Hoeller's—as well as Jung's—notion of the Gnostic one:

> Like a true Gnostic, Carl Jung recognized that, even at best, [sheer] goodness is no substitute for wholeness; he frequently said that in the long run what matters is not goodness or obedience to moral laws, but only and simply the fullness of being. Gnostic psychology has always recognized that the artificial division or splitting apart of the fullness of being into the two halves of good and evil was a plot of the tyrannical forces bent upon keeping humanity in chains. . . . Jung, in his intuitive knowledge of the Gnosis, recognized that, not dualism, but the recognition of the ultimate necessity for the union of the opposites was at the heart of the Gnostic attitude.[133]

Is, then, Jung a Gnostic? If he qualifies, it is as a contemporary, not an ancient, Gnostic. Like ancient Gnostics, Jung seeks reconnection with the lost essence of human nature and treats reconnection as tantamount to salvation. For Jung, as for ancient Gnostics, reconnection is a lifelong process and typically requires the guidance of one who has already undertaken it—the therapist functioning as the Gnostic revealer. Knowledge for both Jung and ancient Gnostics is the key to the effort, and knowledge for both means above all self-knowledge. In these respects Jung can legitimately be typed a Gnostic. He is, however, a contemporary Gnostic because the rediscovered essence is entirely human, not divine, and lies entirely within oneself, not within divinity as well.

Victor White

Victor White (1902–1960) was an English Dominican priest and a Reader in Theology at Blackfriars, Oxford. He sought to reconcile

---

[133] Ibid., 42, 96.

religion with Jungian psychology, but without compromising his staunch Catholic convictions. It would be too much to say that he was to Jung as Oskar Pfister was to Freud, but he came closer to attaining that status than anyone else. White was a founding member of the Jung Institute in Zurich and lectured widely on Jungian psychology. But he was not, like Pfister, a lay analyst or even an analysand. His interest in Jungian psychology was theoretical, not clinical.

The relationship between White and Jung began in 1945 when White sent him some articles of his on psychology and religion. With Jung's response began an intense but often testy friendship that eventually tapered off yet nevertheless lasted until White's death. The two not only corresponded but also met at Jung's home in Bollingen.

White's letters to Jung have never been published. Jung's letters are to be found in the two-volume collection of his letters. Better known than the correspondence is Jung's long foreword to White's *God and the Unconscious*, a collection of articles and addresses on disparate theological and psychological topics. One chapter of the book is devoted to Gnosticism and, together with a portion of Jung's foreword, is reprinted here.

In his foreword Jung typically bemoans theological characterizations of him as an atheistic metaphysician rather than as an agnostic psychologist. Jung's single exception is White, who "has successfully undertaken to feel his way into the empiricist's manner of thinking as far as possible."[134] Ironically, the issue that Jung cites as evidence of the perennial misunderstanding of him by other theologians is the chief one that led to the break with White: the doctrine of *privatio boni*, or the Augustinian view of evil as the privation of good. Jung takes—or mistakes—that doctrine to be the denial of the reality of evil, which psychologically means the denial of the shadow side of human nature.[135] For Jung, theological recognition of evil requires inclusion of the devil in divinity. White maintains that Jung is thereby venturing beyond his self-imposed psychological boundary into theology and is in effect preaching heresy. Not coincidentally, Jung's own favorite term for this

---

[134] Jung, Foreword to White's *God and the Unconscious*, 307.
[135] See Victor White, *God and the Unconscious* (Cleveland: Meridian Books, 1961), 95–96; *Soul and Psyche* (London: Collins and Harvill Press, 1960), chap. 6 and appendix VIII.

"heresy" is "Gnosticism," which Jung celebrates for exactly its presumed incorporation of evil in the godhead.[136]

Gilles Quispel

Gilles Quispel (b. 1916), Professor of the History of the Early Church at the University of Utrecht, is a distinguished scholar of Gnosticism perhaps best known for his argument that the chief roots of Gnosticism are Jewish—a view that builds on the work of Gershom Scholem and Erik Peterson. Quispel is also conspicuous for his advocacy of a Jungian approach to Gnosticism. In 1947 he began lecturing at the Eranos Conference, where he became friends with Jung. Quispel's lectures at the Jung Institute in Zurich were published as *Gnosis als Weltreligion*, his best-known work. In honor of Jung, Quispel even bought for the Institute the Gnostic codex, Nag Hammadi I, subsequently known as "the Jung Codex."[137] Quispel's admiration for Jung is unblushing: Jung, he declares, "has done more for the interpretation of religion than any other living [i.e., present-day] person."[138]

At times Quispel, as a Jungian, seems to be reducing divinity to a projection of the human self. For example, he criticizes one conventional characterization of "the essence of all religion" as "the relationship between man and God" on the grounds that Gnostics "were not interested in God" but "only in the self."[139] But by the self Quispel does not mean something merely human. He means the mystical identity of the human with the divine: "Valentinus describes how the guardian angel, which is the self, gives the person gnosis, and is thus fatefully connected with him, because only

---

[136] On Jung and White see F. X. Charet, "A Dialogue Between Psychology and Theology: The Correspondence of C. G. Jung and Victor White," *Journal of Analytical Psychology* 35 (October 1990): 421–41; Stein, 5–8; Wehr, 349–50, 357–59, 394; Heisig, *Imago Dei*, 180–82, 185–89; Laurens van der Post, *Jung and the Story of Our Time* (New York: Vintage Books, 1977), 222–24; Charlene Schwartz, "Jung and Freud," *Integrity* 7 (July 1953): 20–24.

[137] See Gilles Quispel, "The Jung Codex and its Significance," in H. Ch. Puech, G. Quispel, and W. C. van Unnik, *The Jung Codex*, ed. and trans. F. L. Cross (London: Mowbray, 1955), 40–44 (rpt. Quispel, *Gnostic Studies*, vol. 1, chap. 1); "Gnosis and Psychology," 17–19.

[138] Quispel, interview with Christopher Farmer, *Gnosis* (Fall/Winter 1985): 28.

[139] Quispel, "C. G. Jung und die Gnosis," 296.

when the [human] I and the [divine] self are interconnected and in Dualitudo can they achieve perfection and eternity."[140] Quispel's objection to the standard characterization of religion is that it separates God from humanity, not that it postulates God.

Quispel does assert that "for Basilides the world and history were merely symbols referring to an inner process"—as if Quispel were, again, reducing the cosmic to the human. But by an "inner process" he means an inward "return of the soul to God" rather than an ascent "through the spheres of the external world."[141] He still means reunion with God, not reunion with only oneself.[142]

Quispel's brand of Jungian analysis of Gnosticism is, then, more metaphysical than psychological. Moreover, he berates those Jungians who reduce divinity to a projection of humanity. He argues for a synchronistic rather than a projective analysis:

> But students of Gnosis seem not to have observed that among the Jungians certain new views have been formulated which are relevant for our field. That is, the concept of synchronicity. . . . Up till that moment Jung had simply taken over from Freud the naive and unphilosophical view of projection, that man is just projecting his own illusions on the patient screen of eternity. . . . It is, however, the main associates of Jung who have drawn the consequences from "synchronicity" and who have thoroughly modified the old-time view of projection.[143]

What Quispel in fact proposes constitutes neither synchronicity nor projection but mysticism. Where synchronicity *parallels* the human with the cosmic,[144] Quispel *equates* the two. For example, he refers to the "*mysterium conjunctionis* between angel and man."[145] Since the fundamental Gnostic claim is that humanity and di-

---

[140] Ibid.

[141] Quispel, "Gnostic Man: The Doctrine of Basilides," 236.

[142] On Quispel's mystical interpretation of Gnosticism see his "Gnostic Man: The Doctrine of Basilides," 235–46; "Das ewige Ebenbild des Menschen: Zur Begegnung mit dem Selbst in der Gnosis," *Eranos-Jahrbüch* 36 (1967): 9–30 (rpt. Quispel, *Gnostic Studies*, vol. 1, chap. 8); "C. G. Jung und die Gnosis," 296–97; "Gnosis and Psychology," 23–31.

[143] Quispel, "Gnosis and Psychology," 23, 26.

[144] See Jung, "Synchronicity," *The Structure and Dynamics of the Psyche*, 417–531.

[145] Quispel, "Das ewige Ebenbild des Menschen: Zur Begegnung mit dem Selbst in der Gnosis," 22.

vinity are identical, it is hard to see what is distinctively Jungian, let alone Jungian at all, in Quispel's equation of them. Indeed, Quispel daringly speculates that Gnosticism may even be true metaphysically, not just psychologically:

> But they [Gnostics] did not agree that God is a projection of man. They rather expressed in their imaginative thinking that the world and man are a projection of God. . . . I suggest that this is a correct definition of the truth of imaginative thinking as revealed by the Gnostic symbols. The world and man are a projection of God. And the consummation of the historical process will consist in this: that man and the universe are taken back and reintegrated into their divine origin. . . . Certainly this is a plausible, spirited, and provocative hypothesis concerning the nature and end of the psyche, the universe, and ultimate reality.[146]

If Jung is deemed a contemporary Gnostic, Quispel hints at being an ancient one—a hint that fittingly matches Jung's own famous metaphysical, if not necessarily Gnostic, confession: "I know [that God exists]. I don't need to believe. I know."[147]

Robert A. Segal

[146] Quispel, "Gnosis and Psychology," 31.
[147] Jung, "The 'Face to Face' Interview," *C. G. Jung Speaking*, 428.

Part 1. Jung's Chief Writings on Gnosticism

Chapter 1. Jung's Main Psychological Interpretation of Gnosticism

While Jung discusses Gnosticism in passing throughout his writings, his one work devoted to Gnosticism is "Gnostic Symbols of the Self." This essay offers a psychological interpretation of such standard Gnostic symbols as the magnet, water, fish, the serpent, Logos, circle, the quaternity, androgyny, and marriage. More important, the essay interprets psychologically the plot and characters of Gnostic myths. The immaterial godhead symbolizes the unconscious in its primordial, undifferentiated state. The Demiurge, together with the differentiated matter over which he rules, symbolizes the ego. Anthropos ("Primal Man" or "Original Man"), Christ, the Son, and God all symbolize the self. The Gnostic cosmogony, according to which the Demiurge is created by the godhead, reigns confidently over the material world, and only eventually discovers that there is a god higher than he, symbolizes the emergence of the ego out of the unconscious, the forgetting of the unconscious by the ego, and the ego's eventual reconnection with the unconscious to form the self. See, in my introduction, the sections on "A Jungian Interpretation of Gnostic Myths" and "Jung's Equations."

"Gnostic Symbols of the Self," CW 9 ii, pars. 287–346

1

Since all cognition is akin to recognition, it should not come as a surprise to find that what I have described as a gradual process of development had already been anticipated, and more or less prefigured, at the beginning of our era. We meet these images and ideas in Gnosticism, to which we must now give our attention; for Gnosticism was, in the main, a product of cultural assimilation and is therefore of the greatest interest in elucidating and defining the contents constellated by prophecies about the Redeemer, or by his appearance in history, or by the synchronicity of the archetype.[1]

In the *Elenchos* of Hippolytus the attraction between the magnet and iron is mentioned, if I am not mistaken, three times. It first appears in the doctrine of the NAASSENES, who taught that the four rivers of Paradise correspond to the eye, the ear, the sense of smell, and the mouth. The mouth, through which prayers go out and food goes in, corresponds to the fourth river, the Euphrates. The well-known significance of the "fourth" helps to explain its connection with the "whole" man, for the fourth always makes a triad into a totality. The text says: "This is the water above the firmament,[2] of which, they say, the Saviour spoke: 'If you knew who it is that asks, you would have asked him, and he would have given you a spring of living water to drink.'[3] To this water comes every nature to choose its own substances, and from this water goes forth to every nature that which is proper to it, more [certainly] than iron to the Heracleian stone,"[4] etc.

As the reference to John 4:10 shows, the wonderful water of the Euphrates has the property of the *aqua doctrinae*, which perfects every nature in its individuality and thus makes man whole too. It does this by giving him a kind of magnetic power by which he can attract and integrate that which belongs to him. The Naassene doctrine is, plainly, a perfect parallel to the alchemical view already discussed: the doctrine is the magnet that makes possible the integration of man as well as the *lapis*.

In the PERATIC doctrine, so many ideas of this kind reappear that Hippolytus even uses the same metaphors, though the meaning is more subtle. No one, he says, can be saved without the Son:

---

[1] Unfortunately it is not possible for me to elucidate or even to document this statement here. But, as Rhine's ESP (extrasensory perception) experiments show, any intense emotional interest or fascination is accompanied by phenomena which can only be explained by a psychic relativity of time, space, and causality. Since the archetypes usually have a certain numinosity, they can arouse just that fascination which is accompanied by synchronistic phenomena. These consist in the *meaningful* coincidence of two or more causally unrelated facts. For details I would refer the reader to my "Synchronicity: An Acausal Connecting Principle."

[2] Genesis 1:7.

[3] Non-verbatim quotation from John 4:10.

[4] *Elenchos*, V, 9, 18f. (Cf. Legge trans., I, pp. 143f.) "Heracleian stone" = magnet.

But this is the serpent. For it is he who brought the signs of the Father down from above, and it is he who carries them back again after they have been awakened from sleep, transferring them thither from hence as substances proceeding from the Substanceless. This, they say, is [what is meant by] the saying, "I am the Door."[5] But they say he transfers them to those whose eyelids are closed,[6] as naphtha draws everywhere the fire to itself,[7] more than the Heracleian stone draws iron . . .[8] Thus, they say, the perfect race of men, made in the image [of the Father] and of the same substance [*homoousion*], is drawn from the world by the Serpent, even as it was sent down by him; but naught else [is so drawn].[9]

Here the magnetic attraction does not come from the doctrine or the water but from the "Son," who is symbolized by the serpent, as in John 3:14.[10] Christ is the magnet that draws to itself those parts or substances in man that are of divine origin, the πατρικοὶ χαρακτῆρες (signs of the Father), and carries them back to their heavenly birthplace. The serpent is an equivalent of the fish. The consensus of opinion interpreted the Redeemer equally as a fish and a serpent; he is a fish because he rose from the unknown depths, and a serpent because he came mysteriously out of the darkness. Fishes and snakes are favourite symbols for describing psychic happenings or experiences that suddenly dart out of the unconscious and have a frightening or redeeming effect. That is why they are so often expressed by the motif of helpful animals. The comparison of Christ with the serpent is more authentic than that with the fish, but, for all that, it was not so popular in primitive Christianity. The Gnostics favoured it because it was an old-established symbol for the "good" *genius loci*, the Agathodaimon,

---

[5] John 10:9: "I am the door. By me, if any man enter in, he shall be saved."

[6] I use the reading: καμμύουσιν ὀφθαλμοῦ βλέφαρον. Does this mean those who close their eyes to the world?

[7] The naphtha analogy reappears in the teachings of the Basilidians (*Elenchos*, VII, 24, 6f.). There it refers to the son of the highest archon, who comprehends the νοήματα ἀπὸ τῆς μακαρίας υἱότητος (idea of the blessed sonship). Hippolytus' exposition seems to be a trifle confused at this point.

[8] Several more metaphors now follow, and it should be noted that they are the same as in the passage previously quoted (V, 9, 19).

[9] *Elenchos*, V, 17, 8ff. (Cf. Legge trans., I, pp. 158f.)

[10] "And as Moses lifted up the serpent in the wilderness, even so must the Son of man be lifted up."

and also for their beloved Nous. Both symbols are of inestimable value when it comes to the natural, instinctive interpretation of the Christ-figure. Theriomorphic symbols are very common in dreams and other manifestations of the unconscious. They express the psychic level of the content in question; that is to say, such contents are at a stage of unconsciousness that is as far from human consciousness as the psyche of an animal. Warm-blooded or cold-blooded vertebrates of all kinds, or even invertebrates, thus indicate the degree of unconsciousness. It is important for psychopathologists to know this, because these contents can produce, at all levels, symptoms that correspond to the physiological functions and are localized accordingly. For instance, the symptoms may be distinctly correlated with the cerebrospinal and the sympathetic nervous system. The Sethians may have guessed something of this sort, for Hippolytus mentions, in connection with the serpent, that they compared the "Father" with the cerebrum (ἐγκέφαλον) and the "Son" with the cerebellum and spinal cord (παρελκεφαλίς δρακοντοειδής). The snake does in fact symbolize "cold-blooded," inhuman contents and tendencies of an abstractly intellectual as well as a concretely animal nature: in a word, the extra-human quality in man.

The third reference to the magnet is to be found in Hippolytus' account of the SETHIAN doctrine. This has remarkable analogies with the alchemical doctrines of the Middle Ages, though no direct transmission can be proved. It expounds, in Hippolytus' words, a theory of "composition and mixture": the ray of light from above mingles with the dark waters below in the form of a minute spark. At the death of the individual, and also at his figurative death as a mystical experience, the two substances unmix themselves. This mystical experience is the *divisio* and *separatio* of the composite (τὸ διχάσαι καὶ χωρίσαι τὰ συγκεκραμένα). I purposely give the Latin terms used in medieval alchemy, because they denote essentially the same thing as do the Gnostic concepts. The separation or unmixing enables the alchemist to extract the *anima* or *spiritus* from the *prima materia*. During this operation the helpful Mercurius appears with the dividing sword (used also by the adept!), which the Sethians refer to Matthew 10:34: "I came not to send peace, but a sword." The result of the unmixing is that what was previously mixed up with the "other" is now drawn to "its own place" and to that which is "proper" or "akin" to it, "like iron to the magnet" (ὡς σίδηρος [πρὸς] ᾽Ηράκλειον λίθον).[11] In the same way, the spark or ray of light, "having received from the teaching and learning its proper place, hastens to the Logos, which comes from above in the form of a slave . . . more [quickly] than iron [flies] to the magnet."[12]

Here the magnetic attraction comes from the Logos. This denotes a thought or idea that has been formulated and articulated, hence a content and a product of consciousness. Consequently the Logos is very like the *aqua doctrinae*, but whereas the Logos has the advantage of being an autonomous personality, the latter is merely a passive object of human action. The Logos is nearer to the historical Christ-figure, just as the "water" is nearer to the magical water used in ritual (ablution, aspersion, baptism). Our three examples of magnetic action suggest three different forms of magnetic agent:

1. The agent is an inanimate and in itself passive substance, *water*. It is drawn from the depths of the well, handled by human hands, and used according to man's needs. It signifies the visible doctrine, the *aqua doctrinae* or the Logos, communicated to others by word of mouth and by ritual.

2. The agent is an animate, autonomous being, the *serpent*. It appears spontaneously or comes as a surprise; it fascinates; its glance is staring, fixed, unrelated; its blood cold, and it is a stranger to man: it crawls over the sleeper, he finds it in a shoe or in his pocket. It expresses his fear of everything inhuman and his awe of the sublime, of what is beyond human ken. It is the lowest (devil) and the highest (son of God, Logos, Nous, Agathodaimon). The snake's presence is frightening, one finds it in unexpected places at unexpected moments. Like the fish, it represents and personifies the dark and unfathomable, the watery deep, the forest, the night,

---

[11] Here, as in the previous passages about the magnet, mention is made of *electron* (amber) and the sea-hawk, emphasis being laid on the bird's *centre*.

[12] *Elenchos*, V, 21, 8 (Legge trans., I, p. 168). The ray of light (*radius*) plays an analogous role in alchemy. Dorn (*Theatr. chem.*, I, p. 276) speaks of the "invisible rays of heaven meeting together at the centre of the earth," and there, as Michael Maier says, shining with a "heavenly light like a carbuncle" (*Symbola aureae mensae*, 1617, p. 377). The arcane substance is extracted from the ray, and constitutes its "shadow" (*umbra*), as the "Tractatus aureus" says (*Ars chemica*, 1566, p. 15). The *aqua permanens* is extracted from the rays of the sun and moon by the magnet (Mylius, *Philosophia reformata*, p. 314), or the rays of the sun are united in the "silver water" (Beatus, "Aurelia occulta," *Theatr. chem.*, IV, p. 563).

the cave. When a primitive says "snake," he means an experience of something extrahuman. The snake is not an allegory or metaphor, for its own peculiar form is symbolic in itself, and it is essential to note that the "Son" has the form of a snake and not the other way round: the snake does not signify the "Son."

3. The agent is the *Logos*, a philosophical idea and abstraction of the bodily and personal son of God on the one hand, and on the other the dynamic power of thoughts and words.

It is clear that these three symbols seek to describe the unknowable essence of the incarnate God. But it is equally clear that they are hypostatized to a high degree: it is real water, and not figurative water, that is used in ritual. The Logos was in the beginning, and God was the Logos, long before the Incarnation. The emphasis falls so much on the "serpent" that the Ophites celebrated their eucharistic feast with a live snake, no less realistic than the Aesculapian snake at Epidaurus. Similarly, the "fish" is not just the secret language of the mystery, but, as the monuments show, it meant something in itself. Moreover, it acquired its meaning in primitive Christianity without any real support from the written tradition, whereas the serpent can at least be referred back to an authentic logion.

All three symbols are phenomena of assimilation that are in themselves of a numinous nature and therefore have a certain degree of autonomy. Indeed, had they never made their appearance, it would have meant that the annunciation of the Christ-figure was ineffective. These phenomena not only prove the effectiveness of the annunciation, but provide the necessary conditions in which the annunciation can take effect. In other words, the symbols represent the prototypes of the Christ-figure that were slumbering in man's unconscious and were then called awake by his actual appearance in history and, so to speak, magnetically attracted. That is why Meister Eckhart uses the same symbolism to describe Adam's relation to the Creator on the one hand and to the lower creatures on the other.[13]

---

[13] "And therefore the highest power, seeing her stability in God, communicates it to the lowest, that they may discern good and evil. In this union Adam dwelt, and while this union lasted he had all the power of creatures in his highest power. As when a lodestone exerts its power upon a needle and draws it to itself, the needle receives sufficient power to pass on to all the needles beneath, which it raises and attaches to the lodestone." (Meister Eckhart, trans. by Evans, I, p. 274, slightly modified.)

This magnetic process revolutionizes the ego-oriented psyche by setting up, in contradistinction to the ego, another goal or centre which is characterized by all manner of names and symbols: fish, serpent, centre of the sea-hawk,[14] point, monad, cross, paradise, and so on. The myth of the ignorant demiurge who imagined he was the highest divinity illustrates the perplexity of the ego when it can no longer hide from itself the knowledge that it has been dethroned by a supraordinate authority. The "thousand names" of the *lapis philosophorum* correspond to the innumerable Gnostic designations for the Anthropos, which make it quite obvious what is meant: the greater, more comprehensive Man, that indescribable whole consisting of the sum of conscious and unconscious processes. This objective whole, the antithesis of the subjective ego-psyche, is what I have called the self, and this corresponds exactly to the idea of the Anthropos.

2

When, in treating a case of neurosis, we try to supplement the inadequate attitude (or adaptedness) of the conscious mind by adding to it contents of the unconscious, our aim is to create a wider personality whose centre of gravity does not necessarily coincide with the ego, but which, on the contrary, as the patient's insights increase, may even thwart his ego-tendencies. Like a magnet, the new centre attracts to itself that which is proper to it, the "signs of the Father," i.e., everything that pertains to the original and unalterable character of the individual ground-plan. All this is older than the ego and acts towards it as the "blessed, nonexistent God" of the Basilidians acted towards the archon of the Ogdoad, the demiurge, and—paradoxically enough—as the son of the demiurge acted towards his father. The son proves superior in that he has knowledge of the message from above and can therefore tell his father that he is not the highest God. This apparent contradiction resolves itself when we consider the underlying psychological experience. On the one hand, in the products of the unconscious the self appears as it were *a priori*, that is, in well-known circle and quaternity symbols which may already have occurred in the earliest dreams of childhood, long before there was any possibility of con-

[14] [Cf. n. 11, supra.]

sciousness or understanding. On the other hand, only patient and painstaking work on the contents of the unconscious, and the resultant synthesis of conscious and unconscious data, can lead to a "totality," which once more uses circle and quaternity symbols for purposes of self-description.[15] In this phase, too, the original dreams of childhood are remembered and understood. The alchemists, who in their own way knew more about the nature of the individuation process than we moderns do, expressed this paradox through the symbol of the uroboros, the snake that bites its own tail.

The same knowledge, formulated differently to suit the age they lived in, was possessed by the Gnostics. The idea of an unconscious was not unknown to them. For instance, Epiphanius quotes an excerpt from one of the Valentinian letters, which says: "In the beginning the Autopator contained in himself everything that is, in a state of unconsciousness [lit., 'not-knowing': ἀγνωσία]."[16] It was Professor G. Quispel who kindly drew my attention to this passage. He also points out the passage in Hippolytus: ὁ Πατὴρ . . . ὁ ἀνεννόητος καὶ ἀνούσιος, ὁ μήτε ἄρρεν μήτε θῆλυ, which he translates: "le Père . . . qui est dépourvu de conscience et de substance, celui qui est ni masculin, ni féminin."[17] So the "Father" is not only unconscious and without the quality of being, but also *nirdvandva*, without opposites, lacking all qualities and therefore unknowable. This describes the state of the unconscious. The Valentinian text gives the Autopator more positive qualities: "Some called him the ageless Aeon, eternally young, male and female, who contains everything in himself and is [himself] contained by nothing." In him was ἔννοια, consciousness, which "conveys the treasures of the greatness to those who come from the greatness." But the presence of ἔννοια does not prove that the Autopator himself is conscious, for the differentiation of consciousness results only from the syzygies and tetrads that follow afterwards, all of them symbolizing processes of conjunction and composition. Ἔννοια must be thought of here as the latent possi-

---

[15] Cf. *Psychology and Alchemy*, pars. 127ff., and "A Study in the Process of Individuation," in Part I of vol. 9.

[16] Ἐξ ἀρξῆς ὁ Αὐτοπάτωρ αὐτὸς ἐν ἐαυτῷ περιεῖχε τὰ πάντα ὄντα ἐν ἐαυτῷ ἐν ἀγνωσίᾳ κτλ. *Panarium*, XXXI, cap. V (Oehler edn., I, p. 314).

[17] *Elenchos*, VI, 42, 4; Quispel, "Note sur 'Basilide,'" p. 115.

bility of consciousness. Oehler translates it as *mens*, Cornarius as *intelligentia* and *notio*.

St. Paul's concept of ἄγνοια (*ignorantia*) may not be too far removed from ἀγνωσία, since both mean the initial, unconscious condition of man. When God "looked down" on the times of ignorance, the Greek word used here, ὑπεριδών (Vulgate: *despiciens*) has the connotation 'to disdain, despise.'[18] At all events, Gnostic tradition says that when the highest God saw what miserable, unconscious creatures these human beings were whom the demiurge had created, who were not even able to walk upright, he immediately got the work of redemption under way.[19] And in the same passage in the Acts, Paul reminds the Athenians that they were "God's offspring,"[20] and that God, looking back disapprovingly on "the times of ignorance," had sent the message to mankind, commanding "all men everywhere to repent." Because that earlier condition seemed to be altogether too wretched, the μετάνοια (transformation of mind) took on the moral character of repentance of sins, with the result that the Vulgate could translate it as "poenitentiam agere."[21] The sin to be repented, of course, is ἄγνοια or ἀγνωσία, unconsciousness.[22] As we have seen, it is not only man who is in this condition, but also, according to the Gnostics, the ἀνεννόητος, the God without consciousness. This idea is more or less in line with the traditional Christian view that God was transformed during the passage from the Old Testament to the New, and, from being the God of wrath, changed into the God of Love—a thought that is expressed very clearly by Nicolaus Caussin in the seventeenth century.[23]

In this connection I must mention the results of Riwkah Schärf's examination of the figure of Satan in the Old Testament.[24] With the

[18] Acts 17:30.

[19] Cf. Scott, *Hermetica* (I, pp. 150f.) where there is a description of the *krater* filled with Nous which God sent down to earth. Those whose hearts strive after consciousness (γνωρίζουσα ἐπὶ τὶ γέγονας) can "baptize" themselves in the *krater* and thereby obtain Nous. "God says that the man filled with Nous should know himself" (pp. 126f.).

[20] Γένος οὖν ὑπάρχοντες τοῦ Θεοῦ (Acts 17:29).

[21] Likewise the μετανοεῖτε of the Baptist (Matt. 3:2).

[22] Cf. the τὸ τῆς ἀγνοίας ἁμάρτημα, 'sin of unconsciousness' in pseudo-Clement (*Homilies* XIX, cap. XXII), referring to the man who was born blind (John 9:1).

[23] *Polyhistor symbolicus*, p. 348: "God, formerly the God of vengeance, who with thunders and lightnings brought the world to disorder, took his rest in the lap of a Virgin, nay, in her womb, and was made captive by love."

[24] "Die Gestalt des Satans im Alten Testament."

historical transformation of the concept of Satan the image of Yahweh changes too, so that one can well say that there was a differentiation of the God-image even in the Old Testament, not to speak of the New. The idea that the world-creating Deity is not conscious, but may be dreaming, is found also in Hindu literature:

> Who knows how it was, and who shall declare
> Whence it was born and whence it came?
> The gods are later than this creation;
> Who knows, then, whence it has sprung?

> Whence this created world came,
> And whether he made it or not,
> He alone who sees all in the highest heaven
> Knows—or does not know.[25]

Meister Eckhart's theology knows a "Godhead" of which no qualities, except unity and being,[26] can be predicated;[27] it "is becoming," it is not yet Lord of itself, and it represents an absolute coincidence of opposites: "But its simple nature is of forms formless; of becoming becomingless; of beings beingless; of things thingless," etc.[28] Union of opposites is equivalent to unconsciousness, so far as human logic goes, for consciousness presupposes a differentiation into subject and object and a relation between them. Where there is no "other," or it does not yet exist, all possibility of consciousness ceases. Only the Father, the God "welling" out of the Godhead, "notices himself," becomes "beknown to himself," and "confronts himself as a Person." So, from the Father, comes the Son, as the Father's thought of his own being. In his original unity "he knows nothing" except the "suprareal" One which he *is*. As the Godhead is essentially unconscious,[29] so too is the man who lives in God. In his sermon on "The Poor in Spirit" (Matt. 5:3), the Meister

[25] *Rig-Veda*, X, 129. (Cf. NacNicol trans., *Hindu Scriptures*, p. 37.)
[26] "Being" is controversial. The Masters says: "God in the Godhead is a spiritual substance, so unfathomable that we can say nothing about it except that it is naught [*niht ensi*]. To say it is aught [*iht*] were more lying than true." (Cf. Evans trans., I, p. 354.)
[27] "To this end there is no way, it is beyond all ways." (Cf. ibid., p. 211).
[28] ". . . von formen formelôs, von werdenne werdelôs, von wesenne weselôs und ist von sachen sachelôs." (Cf. ibid., p. 352.)
[29] "[The will] is the nobler in that it plunges into unknowing, which is God." Cf. ibid., p. 351. Cf. also n. 16, supra: ἀγνωσία.

says: "The man who has this poverty has everything he was when he lived not in any wise, neither in himself, nor in truth, nor in God. He is so quit and empty of all knowing that no knowledge of God is alive in him; for while he stood in the eternal nature of God, there lived in him not another: what lived there was himself. And so we say this man is as empty of his own knowledge as he was when he was not anything; he lets God work what he will, and he stands empty as when he came from God."[30] Therefore he should love God in the following way: "Love him as he is: a not-God, a not-spirit, a not-person, a not-image; as a sheer, pure, clear One, which he is, sundered from all secondness; and in this One let us sink eternally, from nothing to nothing. So help us God. Amen."[31]

The world-embracing spirit of Meister Eckhart knew, without discursive knowledge, the primordial mystical experience of India as well as of the Gnostics, and was itself the finest flower on the tree of the "Free Spirit" that flourished at the beginning of the eleventh century. Well might the writings of this Master lie buried for six hundred years, for "his time was not yet come." Only in the nineteenth century did he find a public at all capable of appreciating the grandeur of his mind.

These utterances on the nature of the Deity express transformations of the God-image which run parallel with changes in human consciousness, though one would be at a loss to say which is the cause of the other. The God-image is not something *invented*, it is an *experience* that comes upon man spontaneously—as anyone can see for himself unless he is blinded to the truth by theories and prejudices. The unconscious God-image can therefore alter the state of consciousness, just as the latter can modify the God-image once it has become conscious. This, obviously, has nothing to do with the "prime truth," the unknown God—at least, nothing that could be verified. Psychologically, however, the idea of God's ἀγνωσία, or of the ἀνεννόητος θεός, is of the utmost importance, because it identifies the Deity with the numinosity of the unconscious. The *atman/purusha* philosophy of the East and, as we have seen, Meister Eckhart in the West both bear witness to this.

Now if psychology is to lay hold of this phenomenon, it can only do so if it expressly refrains from passing metaphysical judgments,

---

[30] Evans, I, p. 219.
[31] End of the sermon "Renovamini spiritu" (Eph. 4:23). Ibid., pp. 247f.

and if it does not presume to profess convictions to which it is ostensibly entitled on the ground of scientific experience. But of this there can be no question whatever. The one and only thing that psychology can establish is the presence of pictorial symbols, whose interpretation is in no sense fixed beforehand. It can make out, with some certainty, that these symbols have the character of "wholeness" and therefore presumably *mean* wholeness. As a rule they are "uniting" symbols, representing the conjunction of a single or double pair of opposites, the result being either a dyad or a quaternion. They arise from the collision between the conscious and the unconscious and from the confusion which this causes (known in alchemy as "chaos" or "nigredo"). Empirically, this confusion takes the form of restlessness and disorientation. The circle and quaternity symbolism appears at this point as a compensating principle of order, which depicts the union of warring opposites as already accomplished, and thus eases the way to a healthier and quieter state ("salvation"). For the present, it is not possible for psychology to establish more than that the symbols of wholeness mean the wholeness of the individual.[32] On the other hand, it has to admit, most emphatically, that this symbolism uses images or schemata which have always, in all the religions, expressed the universal "Ground," the Deity itself. Thus the circle is a well-known symbol for God; and so (in a certain sense) is the cross, the quaternity in all its forms, e.g., Ezekiel's vision, the *Rex gloriae* with the four evangelists, the Gnostic Barbelo ("God in four") and Kolorbas ("all four"); the duality (*tao*, hermaphrodite, father-mother); and finally, the human form (child, son, anthropos) and the individual personality (Christ and Buddha), to name only the most important of the motifs here used.

All these images are found, empirically, to be expressions for the unified wholeness of man. The fact that this goal goes by the name of "God" proves that it has a numinous character; and indeed, experiences, dreams, and visions of this kind do have a fascinating and impressive quality which can be spontaneously felt even by people who are not prejudiced in their favour by prior psychologi-

---

[32] There are people who, oddly enough, think it a weakness in me that I refrain from metaphysical judgments. A scientist's conscience does not permit him to assert things he cannot prove or at least show to be probable. No assertion has ever yet brought anything corresponding to it into existence. "What he says, is" is a prerogative exclusive to God.

cal knowledge. So it is no wonder that naïve minds make no distinction between God and the image they have experienced. Wherever, therefore, we find symbols indicative of psychic wholeness, we encounter the naïve idea that they stand for God. In the case of those quite common Romanesque pictures of the Son of Man accompanied by three angels with animal heads and one with a human head, for example, it would be simpler to assume that the Son of Man meant the ordinary man and that the problem of one against three referred to the well-known psychological schema of one differentiated and three undifferentiated functions. But this interpretation would, according to the traditional view, devalue the symbol, for it means the second Person of the Godhead in its universal, fourfold aspect. Psychology cannot of course adopt this view as its own; it can only establish the existence of such statements and point out, by way of comparison, that essentially the same symbols, in particular the dilemma of one and three, often appear in the spontaneous products of the unconscious, where they demonstrably refer to the psychic totality of the individual. They indicate the presence of an archetype of like nature, one of whose derivates would seem to be the quaternity of functions that orient consciousness. But, since this totality exceeds the individual's consciousness to an indefinite and indeterminable extent, it invariably includes the unconscious in its orbit and hence the totality of all archetypes. But the archetypes are complementary equivalents of the "outside world" and therefore possess a "cosmic" character. This explains their numinosity and "godlikeness."

3

To make my exposition more complete, I would like to mention some of the Gnostic symbols for the universal "Ground" or arcanum, and especially those synonyms which signify the "Ground." Psychology takes this idea as an image of the unconscious background and begetter of consciousness. The most important of these images is the figure of the demiurge. The Gnostics have a vast number of symbols for the source or origin, the centre of being, the Creator, and the divine substance hidden in the creature. Lest the reader be confused by this wealth of images, he should always remember that each new image is simply another aspect of the divine mystery immanent in all creatures. My list of Gnostic symbols is no more than an amplification of a single transcendental idea, which is so comprehensive and so difficult to visualize in itself that a great many different expressions are required in order to bring out its various aspects.

According to Irenaeus, the Gnostics held that Sophia represents the world of the Ogdoad,[33] which is a double quaternity. In the form of a dove, she descended into the water and begot Saturn, who is identical with Yahweh. Saturn, as we have already mentioned, is the "other sun," the *sol niger* of alchemy. Here he is the "primus Anthropus." He created the first man, who could only crawl like a worm.[34] Among the Naassenes, the demiurge Esaldaios, "a fiery god, the fourth by number," is set up against the Trinity of Father, Mother, and Son. The highest is the Father, the Archanthropos, who is without qualities and is called the higher Adam. In various systems Sophia takes the place of the Protanthropos.[35] Epiphanius mentions the Ebionite teaching that Adam, the original man, is identical with Christ.[36] In Theodor Bar-Kuni the original man is the five elements (i.e., $4 + 1$).[37] In the Acts of Thomas, the dragon

---

[33] *Adversus haereses*, I, 30, 3. In the system of Barbelo-Gnosis (ibid., 29, 4) the equivalent of Sophia is Προύνιχος, who "sinks into the lower regions." The name Prunicus (προύνεικος) means both 'carrying a burden' and 'lewd.' The latter connotation is more probable, because this Gnostic sect believed that, through the sexual act, they could recharge Barbelo with the pneuma that was lost in the world. In Simon Magus it is Helen, the μήτηρ and ἔννοια, who "descended to the lower regions . . . and generated the inferior powers, angels, and firmaments." She was forcibly held captive by the lower powers (Irenaeus, I, 27, 1–4). She corresponds to the much later alchemical idea of the "soul in fetters" (cf. Dorn, *Theatr. chem.*, I, pp. 298, 497; Mylius, *Phil. ref.*, p. 262; *Rosarium philosophorum* in *Art. aurif.*, II, p. 284; "Platonis liber quartorum," *Theatr. chem.*, V, pp. 185f.; Vigenère, *Theatr. chem.*, VI, p. 19). The idea derives from Greek alchemy and can be found in Zosimos (Berthelot, *Alch. grecs*, III, xlix, 7; trans. in *Psychology and Alchemy*, pars. 456ff.). In the "Liber quartorum" it is of Sabaean origin. See Chwolsohn, *Die Ssabier und der Ssabismus* (II, p. 494): "The soul once turned towards matter, fell in love with it, and, burning with desire to experience bodily pleasures, was no longer willing to tear herself away from it. So was the world born." Among the Valentinians, Sophia Achamoth is the Ogdoad. In *Pistis Sophia* (trans. by Mead, p. 362) she is the daughter of Barbelo. Deluded by the false light of the demon Authades, she falls into imprisonment in chaos. Irenaeus (I, 5, 2) calls the demiurge the Heptad, but Achamoth the Ogdoad. In I, 7, 2 he says that the Saviour is compounded of four things in repetition of the first Tetrad. A copy of the Four is the quaternity of elements (I, 17, 1), and so are the four lights that stand round the Autogenes of Barbelo-Gnosis (I, 29, 2).

[34] *Adv. haer.*, I, 24, 1.

[35] Bousset, *Hauptprobleme der Gnosis*, p. 170.

[36] *Panarium*, XXX, 3.

[37] Theodor Bar-Kuni, *Inscriptiones mandaïtes des coupes de Khouabir*, Part 2, p. 185.

says of itself: "I am the son . . . of him that hurt and smote the four brethren which stood upright."[38]

The primordial image of the quaternity coalesces, for the Gnostics, with the figure of the demiurge or Anthropos. He is, as it were, the victim of his own creative act, for, when he descended into Physis, he was caught in her embrace.[39] The image of the *anima mundi* or Original Man latent in the dark of matter expresses the presence of a transconscious centre which, because of its quaternary character and its roundness, must be regarded as a symbol of wholeness. We may assume, with due caution, that some kind of psychic wholeness is meant (for instance, conscious + unconscious), though the history of the symbol shows that it was always used as a God-image. Psychology, as I have said, is not in a position to make metaphysical statements. It can only establish that the symbolism of psychic wholeness coincides with the God-image, but it can never prove that the God-image is God himself, or that the self takes the place of God.

This coincidence comes out very clearly in the ancient Egyptian Heb-Sed festival, of which Colin Campbell gives the following description: "The king comes out of an apartment called the sanctuary, then he ascends into a pavilion open at the four sides, with four staircases leading up to it. Carrying the emblems of Osiris, he takes his seat on a throne, and turns to the four cardinal points in succession. . . . It is a kind of second enthronement . . . and sometimes the king acts as a priest, making offerings to himself. This last act may be regarded as the climax of the deification of the king."[40]

All kingship is rooted in this psychology, and therefore, for the anonymous individual of the populace, every king carries the symbol of the self. All his insignia—crown, mantle, orb, sceptre, starry orders, etc.—show him as the cosmic Anthropos, who not only begets, but himself is, the world. He is the *homo maximus*, whom we meet again in Swedenborg's speculations. The Gnostics, too, constantly endeavoured to give visible form and a suitable conceptual dress to this being, suspecting that he was the matrix and organizing principle of consciousness. As the "Phrygians"

[38] *The Apocryphal New Testament*, ed. James, p. 379.
[39] Bousset, pp. 114ff.
[40] *The Miraculous Birth of King Amon-Hotep III*, p. 81.

(Naasenes) say in Hippolytus,[41] he is the "undivided point," the "grain of mustard seed" that grows into the kingdom of God. This point is "present in the body." But this is known only to the πνευματικοί, the "spiritual" men as opposed to the ψυχικοί and the ὑλικοί ("material" men). He is τὸ ῥῆμα τοῦ θεοῦ, the utterance of God (*sermo Dei*), and the "matrix of the Aeons, Powers, Intelligences, Gods, Angels, and Emissary Spirits, of Being and Non-Being, of Begotten and Unbegotten, of the Non-Intelligible Intelligible, of the Years, Moons, Days, Hours. . . ." This point, "being nothing and consisting of nothing," becomes a "certain magnitude incomprehensible by thought." Hippolytus accuses the Naassenes of bundling everything into their thought like the syncretists, for he obviously cannot quite understand how the point, the "utterance of God," can have a human form. The Naassenes, he complains, also call him the "polymorphous Attis," the young dying son of the Great Mother, or, as the hymn cited by Hippolytus says, τὸ κατέφες ἄκουσμα ῾Ρέας, the 'dark rumour of Rhea.' In the hymn he has the synonyms Adonis, Osiris, Adam, Korybas, Pan, Bacchus, and ποιμὴν λευκῶν ἀστρῶν, 'shepherd of white stars.'

The Naassenes themselves considered Naas, the serpent, to be their central deity, and they explained it as the "moist substance," in agreement with Thales of Miletus, who said water was the prime substance on which all life depended. Similarly, all living things depend on the Naas; "it contains within itself, like the horn of the one-horned bull, the beauty of all things." It "pervades everything, like the water that flows out of Eden and divides into four sources" (ἄρχας). "This Eden, they say, is the brain." Three of the rivers of Paradise are sensory functions (Pison = sight, Gihon = hearing, Tigris = smell), but the fourth, the Euphrates, is the mouth, "the seat of prayer and the entrance of food." As the fourth function it has a double significance,[42] denoting on the one hand the purely material activity of bodily nourishment, while on the other hand it "gladdens,"[43] feeds, and forms [χαρακτηρίζει] the spiritual, perfect [τέλειον] man."[44] The "fourth" is something special, ambivalent—a daimonion. A good example of this is in Daniel

---

[41] *Elenchos*, V, 9, 5f. (Legge trans., I, pp. 140f.).

[42] *Psychology and Alchemy*, index, s.v. "Axiom of Maria." Cf. infra, pars. 395ff.

[43] εὐφραίνει, a play on the word εὐφραθής, 'well-speaking.'

[44] *Elenchos*, V, 9, 15ff. [Cf. Legge, I, p. 143.]

3:24f., where the three men in the burning fiery furnace are joined by a fourth, whose form was "like a son of God."

The water of the Euphrates is the "water above the firmament," the "living water of which the Saviour spoke,"[45] and possessing, as we have seen, magnetic properties. It is that miraculous water from which the olive draws its oil and the grape the wine. "That man," continues Hippolytus, as though still speaking of the water of the Euphrates, "is without honour in the world."[46] This is an allusion to the τέλειος ἄνθρωπος. Indeed, this water *is* the "perfect man," the ῥῆμα θεοῦ, the Word sent by God. "From the living water we spiritual men choose that which is ours,"[47] for every nature, when dipped in this water, "chooses its own substances . . . and from this water goes forth to every nature that which is proper to it."[48] The water or, as we could say, this Christ is a sort of panspermia, a matrix of all possibilities, from which the πνευματικός chooses "his Osob," his idiosyncrasy,[49] that "flies to him more [quickly] than iron to the magnet." But the "spiritual men" attain their proper nature by entering in through the "true door," Jesus Makarios (the blessed), and thus obtaining knowledge of their own wholeness, i.e., of the complete man. This man, unhonoured in the world, is obviously the inner, spiritual man, who becomes conscious for those who enter in through Christ, the door to life, and are illuminated by him. Two images are blended here: the image of the "strait gate,"[50] and that of John 14:6: "I am the way, and the truth, and the life. No one comes to the Father but through me."[51] They represent an integration process that is characteristic of psychological individuation. As formulated, the water symbol continually coalesces with Christ and Christ with the inner man. This, it seems to me, is not a confusion of thought but a psychologically correct formulation of the facts, since Christ as the "Word" is indeed the "living water" and at the same time the symbol of the inner "complete" man, the self.

---

[45] An allusion to John 4:10.
[46] Legge, I, p. 144.
[47] *Elenchos*, V, 9, 21.
[48] V, 9, 19 (Legge trans., p. 144).
[49] This means the integration of the self, which is also referred to in very similar words in the Bogomil document discussed above (pars. 225ff.), concerning the devil as world creator. He too finds what is "proper" (ἴδιον) to him.
[50] Matt. 7:14: "Strait is the gate, and narrow is the way, which leadeth unto life."
[51] The passage discussed here is in *Elenchos*, V, 9, 4ff. (Legge trans., I, p. 140).

For the Naassenes, the universal "Ground" is the Original Man, Adam, and knowledge of him is regarded as the beginning of perfection and the bridge to knowledge of God.[52] He is male/female; from him come "father and mother";[53] he consists of three parts: the rational (νοερόν), the psychic, and the earthly (χοικόν). These three "came down together into one man, Jesus," and "these three men spoke together, each of them from his own substance to his own," i.e., from the rational to the rational, etc. Through this doctrine Jesus is related to the Original Man (Christ as second Adam). His soul is "of three parts and (yet) one"—a Trinity.[54] As examples of the Original Man the text mentions the Cabiros[55] and Oannes. The latter had a soul capable of suffering, so that the "figure (πλάσμα) of the great, most beautiful and perfect man, humbled to a slave," might suffer punishment. He is the "blessed nature, at once hidden and revealed, of everything that has come to be and will be," "the kingdom of heaven which is to be sought within man" (ἐντός ἀνθρώπου), even "in children of seven years."[56] For the Naassenes, says Hippolytus, place the "procreative nature of the Whole in the procreative seed."[57] On the face of it, this looks like the beginnings of a "sexual theory" concerning the underlying psychic substance, reminiscent of certain modern attempts in the same vein. But one should not overlook the fact that in reality man's procreative power is only a special instance of the "procreative nature of the Whole." "This, for them, is the hidden and mystical Logos," which, in the text that follows, is likened to the phallus of Osiris—"and they say Osiris is water." Although the substance of this seed is the cause of all things, it does not partake of their nature. They say therefore: "I become what I will, and I am what I am." For he who moves everything is himself unmoved. "He, they say, is alone good."[58] A further synonym is the ithyphallic Hermes Kyllenios. "For they say Hermes is the Logos,

---

[52] *Elenchos*, V, 6, 6: Θεοῦ δὲ γνῶσις ἀπηρτισμένη τελείωσις ("Knowledge of God is perfect wholeness").

[53] V, 6, 5 (Legge trans., I, p. 120).

[54] V, 6, 6f. (p. 121).

[55] Nicknamed καλλίπαις, 'with beautiful children' or 'the beautiful child.' (*Elenchos*, V, 7, 4.)

[56] According to Hippocrates, a boy at seven years old is half a father. (*Elenchos*, V, 7, 21.)

[57] τὴν ἀρχέγονων φύσιν τῶν ὅλων ἐν ἀρξέγονῳ σπέρματι. Archegonos is the tribal father.

[58] With express reference to Matt. 19:17: "One is good, God."

the interpreter and fashioner of what has been, is, and will be." That is why he is worshipped as the phallus, because he, like the male organ, "has an urge [ὁρμήν] from below upwards."[59]

4

The fact that not only the Gnostic Logos but Christ himself was drawn into the orbit of sexual symbolism is corroborated by the fragment from the *Interrogationes maiores Mariae*, quoted by Epiphanius.[60] It is related there that Christ took this Mary with him on to a mountain, where he produced a woman from his side and began to have intercourse with her: ". . . seminis sui defluxum assumpsisset, indicasse illi, quod oporteat sic facere, ut vivamus."[61] It is understandable that this crude symbolism should offend our modern feelings. But it also appeared shocking to Christians of the third and fourth centuries; and when, in addition, the symbolism became associated with a concretistic misunderstanding, as appeared to be the case in certain sects, it could only be rejected. That the author of the *Interrogationes* was by no means ignorant of some such reaction is evident from the text itself. It says that Mary received such a shock that she fell to the ground. Christ then said to her: "Wherefore do you doubt me, O you of little faith?" This was meant as a reference to John 3:12: "If I have told you earthly things and you do not believe, how can you believe if I tell you heavenly things?" and also to John 6:53: "Unless you eat the flesh of the Son of man and drink his blood, you have no life in you" (RSV).

This symbolism may well have been based, originally, on some visionary experience, such as happens not uncommonly today during psychological treatment. For the medical psychologist there is nothing very lurid about it. The context itself points the way to the right interpretation. The image expresses a psychologem that can hardly be formulated in rational terms and has, therefore, to make use of a concrete symbol, just as a dream must when a more or less "abstract" thought comes up during the *abaissement du niveau mental* that occurs in sleep. These "shocking" surprises, of which there

[59] Cf. Legge trans., p. 128.
[60] *Panarium*, XXVI, cap. VIII.
[61] ". . . partaking of his flowing semen, showed that this was to be done, that we might have life."

is certainly no lack in dreams, should always be taken "as-if," even though they clothe themselves in sensual imagery that stops at no scurrility and no obscenity. They are unconcerned with offensiveness because they do not really mean it. It is as if they were stammering in their efforts to express the elusive meaning that grips the dreamer's attention.[62]

The context of the vision (John 3:12) makes it clear that the image should be taken not concretistically but symbolically; for Christ speaks not of earthly things but of a heavenly or spiritual mystery—a "mystery" not because he is hiding something or making a secret of it (indeed, nothing could be more blatant than the naked obscenity of the vision!) but because its meaning is still hidden from consciousness. The modern method of dream-analysis and interpretation follows this heuristic rule.[63] If we apply it to the vision, we arrive at the following result:

1. The MOUNTAIN means ascent, particularly the mystical, spiritual ascent to the heights, to the place of revelation where the spirit is present. This motif is so well known that there is no need to document it.[64]

2. The central significance of the CHRIST-FIGURE for that epoch has been abundantly proved. In Christian Gnosticism it was a visualization of God as the Archanthropos (Original Man = Adam), and therefore the epitome of man as such: "Man and the Son of Man." Christ is the inner man who is reached by the path of self-knowledge, "the kingdom of heaven within you." As the Anthropos he corresponds to what is empirically the most important archetype and, as judge of the living and the dead and king of glory,

---

[62] On the other hand, I cannot rid myself of the impression that dreams do occasionally twist things in a scurrilous way. This may have led Freud to the singular assumption that they disguise and distort for so-called "moral" reasons. However, this view is contradicted by the fact that dreams just as often do the exact opposite. I therefore incline to the alchemical view that Mercurius—the unconscious Nous—is a "trickster." [Cf. "The Spirit Mercurius" and "The Psychology of the Trickster Figure."—EDITORS.]

[63] But not the Freudian, "psychoanalytical" method, which dismisses the manifest dream-content as a mere "façade," on the ground that the psychopathology of hysteria leads one to suspect incompatible wishes as dream-motifs. The fact that the dream as well as consciousness rest on an instinctual foundation has nothing to do either with the meaning of the dream-figures or with that of the conscious contents, for the essential thing in both cases is *what the psyche has made of the instinctual impulse*. The remarkable thing about the Parthenon is not that it consists of stone and was built to gratify the ambitions of the Athenians, but that it is—the Parthenon.

[64] Cf. "Phenomenology of the Spirit in Fairytales," par. 403.

to the real organizing principle of the unconscious, the quaternity, or squared circle of the self.[65] In saying this I have not done violence to anything; my views are based on the experience that mandala structures have the meaning and function of a centre of the unconscious personality.[66] The quaternity of Christ, which must be borne in mind in this vision, is exemplified by the cross symbol, the *rex gloriae*, and Christ as the year.

3. The production of the WOMAN from his side suggests that he is interpreted as the second Adam. Bringing forth a woman means that he is playing the role of the Creator-god in Genesis.[67] Just as Adam, before the creation of Eve, was supposed by various traditions to be male/female,[68] so Christ here demonstrates his androgyny in a drastic way.[69] The Original Man is usually hermaphroditic; in Vedic tradition too he produces his own feminine half and unites with her. In Christian allegory the woman sprung from Christ's side signifies the Church as the Bride of the Lamb.

The splitting of the Original Man into husband and wife expresses an act of nascent consciousness; it gives birth to a pair of opposites, thereby making consciousness possible. For the beholder of the miracle, Mary, the vision was the spontaneous visualization or projection of an unconscious process in herself. Experience shows that unconscious processes are compensatory to a definite conscious situation. The splitting in the vision would therefore suggest that it is compensating a conscious condition of unity. This unity probably refers in the first place to the figure of the Anthropos, the incarnate God, who was then in the forefront of religious interest. He was, in Origen's words, the "Vir Unus,"[70] the One Man. It was with this figure that Mary was confronted in her vision. If we assume that the recipient of the vision was in reality a woman—an assumption that is not altogether without

---

[65] "The Psychology of Eastern Meditation," pars. 942f.

[66] Cf. "A Study in the Process of Individuation."

[67] This is consistent with his nature as the Logos and second Person of the Trinity.

[68] Naturally this view is rejected by the Church.

[69] Three different interpretations of Christ are combined here. Such contaminations are characteristic not only of Gnostic thinking but of all unconscious image-formation.

[70] Gregory the Great, *Expositions in librum I Regum*, Lib. I, cap. I (Migne, *P.L.*, vol. 79, col. 23): "For God and man is one Christ. Therefore in that he is called one, he is shown to be incomparable." In accordance with the spirit of the age, his incomparability or uniqueness is explained by the "excellence of his virtue." It is, however, significant in itself.

grounds—then what she had been missing in the pure, deified masculinity of Christ was the counterbalancing femininity. Therefore it was revealed to her: "I am both, man and woman." This psychologem is still incorporated today in the Catholic conception of Christ's androgyny as the "Virgo de Virgine," though this is more a *sententia communis* than a *conclusio*. Medieval iconography sometimes shows Christ with breasts, in accordance with Song of Solomon 1:1: "For thy breasts are better than wine" (DV). In Mechthild of Magdeburg, the soul remarks that when the Lord kissed her,[71] he had, contrary to expectation, no beard. The tokens of masculinity were lacking. Mechthild had a vision similar to Mary's, dealing with the same problem from a different angle: she saw herself transported to a "rocky mountain" where the Blessed Virgin sat, awaiting the birth of the divine child. When it was born, she embraced it and kissed it three times. As the text points out, the mountain is an allegory of the "spiritualis habitus," or spiritual attitude. "Through divine inspiration she knew how the Son is the innermost core [*medulla*] of the Father's heart." This *medulla* is "strengthening, healing, and most sweet"; God's "strength and greatest sweetness" are given to us through the Son, the "Saviour and strongest, sweetest Comforter," but "the innermost [core] of the soul is that sweetest thing."[72] From this it is clear that Mechthild equates the "medulla" with the Father's heart, the Son, and the inner man. Psychologically speaking, "that sweetest thing" corresponds to the self, which is indistinguishable from the God-image.

There is a significant difference between the two visions. The antique revelation depicts the birth of Eve from Adam on the spiritual level of the second Adam (Christ), from whose side the feminine pneuma, or second Eve, i.e., the soul, appears as Christ's daughter. As already mentioned, in the Christian view the soul is interpreted as the Church: she is the woman who "embraces the man"[73] and anoints the Lord's feet. Mechthild's vision is a continuation of the sacred myth: the daughter-bride has become a mother and bears the Father in the shape of the Son. That the Son is

---

[71] "He offered her his rosy [sic!] mouth to kiss" (*Liber gratiae spiritualis*, fol. J iv^v).

[72] "Medulla vero animae est illud dulcissimum." Ibid., fol. B.

[73] Gregory the Great; Migne, *P.L.*, vol. 79, col. 23. Cf. Jerem. 31:22: "A woman shall compass a man" (AV).

closely akin to the self is evident from the emphasis laid on the quaternary nature of Christ: he has a "fourfold voice" (*quadruplex vox*),[74] his heart has four kinds of pulse,[75] and from his countenance go forth four rays of light.[76] In this image a new millennium is speaking. Meister Eckhart, using a different formulation, says that "God is born from the soul," and when we come to the *Cherubinic Wanderer*[77] of Angelus Silesius, God and the self coincide absolutely. The times have undergone a profound change: the procreative power no longer proceeds from God, rather is God born from the soul. The mythologem of the young dying god has taken on psychological form—a sign of further assimilation and conscious realization.

4. But to turn back to the first vision: the bringing forth of the woman is followed by COPULATION. The *hieros gamos* on the mountain is a well-known motif,[78] just as, in the old alchemical pictures, the hermaphrodite has a fondness for elevated places. The alchemists likewise speak of an Adam who always carries his Eve around with him. Their *coniunctio* is an incestuous act, performed not by father and daughter but, in accordance with the changed times, by brother and sister or mother and son. The latter variant corresponds to the ancient Egyptian mythologem of Amen as Ka-mutef, which means 'husband of his mother,' or of Mut, who is the "mother of her father and daughter of her son."[79] The idea of self-copulation is a recurrent theme in descriptions of the world creator: for instance, God splits into his masculine and feminine halves,[80] or he fertilizes himself in a manner that could easily have served as a model for the *Interrogationes* vision, if literary antecedents must be conjectured. Thus the relevant passage in the Heliopolitan story of the Creation runs: "I, even I, had union with my clenched hand, I joined myself in an embrace with my shadow, I poured seed into my

---

[74] *Liber gratiae spiritualis*, fol. A vii^r. The quaternity refers to the four gospels.

[75] Ibid., fol. B ii^v.

[76] Ibid., fol. B vii^v.

[77] Cf. Flitch, *Angelus Silesius*, pp. 128ff.

[78] For instance, the *hieros gamos* of Zeus and Hera on "the heights of Gargaros," *Iliad*, XIV, 246ff. (Cf. Rieu trans., p. 266.)

[79] Brugsch, *Religion und Mythologie der alten Ägypter*, p. 94.

[80] In the ancient Egyptian view God is "Father and Mother," and "begets and gives birth to himself" (Brugsch, p. 97). The Indian Prajapati has intercourse with his own split-off feminine half.

mouth, my own, I sent forth issue in the form of Shu, I sent forth moisture in the form of Tefnut."[81]

Although the idea of self-fertilization is not touched on in our vision, there can be no doubt that there is a close connection between this and the idea of the cosmogonic self-creator. Here, however, world creation gives place to spiritual renewal. That is why no visible creature arises from the taking in of seed; it means a nourishing of life, "that we may live." And because, as the text itself shows, the vision should be understood on the "heavenly" or spiritual plane, the pouring out (ἀπόρροια) refers to a λόγος σπερματικός, which in the language of the gospels means a living water "springing up into eternal life." The whole vision reminds one very much of the related alchemical symbolisms. Its drastic naturalism, unpleasantly obtrusive in comparison with the reticence of ecclesiastical language, points back on the one hand to archaic forms of religion whose ideas and modes of expression had long since been superseded, but forwards, on the other, to a still crude observation of Nature that was just beginning to assimilate the archetype of man. This attempt continued right up to the seventeenth century, when Johannes Kepler recognized the Trinity as underlying the structure of the universe—in other words, when he assimilated this archetype into the astronomer's picture of the world.[82]

5

After this digression on the phallic synonyms for the Original Man, we will turn back to Hippolytus' account of the central symbols of the Naassenes and continue with a list of statements about Hermes.

Hermes is a conjurer of spirits (ψυχαγωγός), a guide of souls (ψυχοπομπός), and a begetter of souls (ψυχῶν αἴτιος). But the souls were "brought down from the blessed Man on high, the archman Adamas, . . . into the form of clay, that they might serve the demiurge of this creation, Esaldaios, a fiery god, the fourth by number."[83] Esaldaios corresponds to Ialdabaoth, the highest

---

[81] Budge, *Gods of the Egyptians*, I, pp. 310f.

[82] I owe this idea to a lecture delivered by Professor W. Pauli, in Zurich, on the archetypal foundations of Kepler's astronomy. Cf. his "The Influence of Archetypal Ideas" etc.

[83] *Elenchos*, V, 7, 30f. (Cf. Legge trans., I, p. 128.)

archon, and also to Saturn.[84] The "fourth" refers to the fourth Person—the devil—who is opposed to the Trinity. Ialdabaoth means "child of chaos"; hence when Goethe, borrowing from alchemical terminology, calls the devil the "strange son of chaos," the name is a very apt one.

Hermes is equipped with the golden wand.[85] With it he "drops sleep on the eyes of the dead and wakes up the sleepers." The Naassenes referred this to Ephesians 5:14: "Awake, O sleeper, and arise from the dead, and Christ shall give you light." Just as the alchemists took the well-known allegory of Christ, the *lapis angularis* or cornerstone, for their *lapis philosophorum*, so the Naassenes took it as symbolizing their Protanthropos Adam, or more precisely, the "inner man," who is a rock or stone, since he came from the πέτρη τοῦ Ἀδάμαντος, "fallen from Adamas the arch-man on high."[86] The alchemists said their stone was "cut from the mountain without hands,"[87] and the Naassenes say the same thing of the inner man, who was brought down "into the form of oblivion."[88] In Epiphanius the mountain is the Archanthropos Christ, from whom the stone or inner man was cut. As Epiphanius interprets it, this means that the inner man is begotten "without human seed," "a small stone that becomes a great mountain."[89]

The Archanthropos is the Logos, whom the souls follow "twittering," as the bats follow Hermes in the *nekyia*. He leads them to Oceanus and—in the immortal words of Homer—to "the doors of Helios and the land of dreams." "He [Hermes] is Oceanus, the begetter of gods and men, ever ebbing and flowing, now forth, now back." Men are born from the ebb, and gods from the flow. "It is this, they say, that stands written: 'I have said, you are gods, and all of you the sons of the most High.' "[90] Here the affinity or identity of

---

[84] Bousset, *Hauptprobleme der Gnosis*, pp. 352f.

[85] Here Hippolytus cites the text of *Odyssey*, XXIV, 2.

[86] *Elenchos*, V, 7, 36 (Legge trans., I, pp. 129f.).

[87] Daniel 2:34: "Thus thou sawest, till a stone was cut out of a mountain without hands" (DV). This was the stone that broke in pieces the clay and iron feet of the statue.

[88] Εἰς τὸ πλάσμα τῆς λήθης, i.e., *lethargia*, the state of forgetfulness and sleep resembling that of the dead. The "inner man" is as if buried in the somatic man. He is the "soul in fetters" or "in the prison of the body," as the alchemists say. *Lēthē* corresponds to the modern concept of the unconscious.

[89] *Ancoratus*, 40. Cf. Daniel 2:35: "But the stone that struck the statue became a great mountain and filled the whole earth" (DV).

[90] *Elenchos*, V, 7, 37 (Legge trans., I, p. 130). Cf. Psalm 82 (Vulg. 81): 6, to which reference is made in Luke 6:35 and John 10:34.

God and man is explicit, in the Holy Scriptures no less than in the Naassene teachings.

6

The Naassenes, as Hippolytus says,[91] derived all things from a triad, which consists firstly of the "blessed nature of the blessed Man on high, Adamas," secondly of the mortal nature of the lower man, and thirdly of the "kingless race begotten from above," to which belong "Mariam the sought-for one, and Jothor[92] the great wise one, and Sephora[93] the seer, and Moses whose generation was not in Egypt."[94] Together these four form a marriage *quaternio*[95] of the classic type:

Their synonyms are:

MOTHER	— FATHER
QUEEN	— KING
THE UNKNOWN WOMAN	— THE DISTANT LOVER
ANIMA	— ANIMUS

Moses corresponds to the husband, Sephora to the wife; Mariam (Miriam) is the sister of Moses; Jothor (Jethro) is the archetype of the wise old man and corresponds to the father-animus, if the *quaternio* is that of a woman. But the fact that Jothor is called "the great wise one" suggests that the *quaternio* is a man's. In the case of a woman the accent that falls here on the wise man would fall on Mariam, who would then have the significance of the Great Mother. At all events our *quaternio* lacks the incestuous brother-sister relationship, otherwise very common. Instead, Miriam has something of a mother significance for Moses (cf. Exodus 2:4ff.).

---

[91] V, 8, 2 (ibid., p. 131).
[92] Ἰοθώρ = Jethro, the priest-king of Midian and the father-in-law of Moses.
[93] Zipporah, the wife of Moses.
[94] This is probably an allusion to the pneumatic nature of the "generation" produced by Moses, for, according to *Elenchos*, V, 7, 41, "Egypt is the body" (Legge trans., I, p. 130).
[95] The marriage *quaternio* is the archetype to which the cross-cousin marriage corresponds on a primitive level. I have given a detailed account of it in "The Psychology of the Transference," pars. 425ff.

As a prophetess (Exodus 15:20f.) she is a "magical" personality. When Moses took a Moor to wife—the "Ethiopian woman"—this incensed Miriam so much that she was smitten with leprosy and became "as white as snow" (Numbers 12:10). Miriam is therefore not altogether unsuited to play the role of the anima. The best-known anima-figure in the Old Testament, the Shulamite, says: "I am black, but comely" (Song of Songs 1:5). In the *Chymical Wedding* of Christian Rosenkreutz, the royal bride is the concubine of the Moorish king. Negroes, and especially Ethiopians, play a considerable role in alchemy as synonyms of the *caput corvi* and the *nigredo*.[96] They appear in the Passion of St. Perpetua[97] as representatives of the sinful pagan world.

The triad is characterized by various names that may be onomatopoetic: Kaulakau, Saulasau, Zeesar.[98] Kaulakau means the higher Adam, Saulasau the lower, mortal man, and Zeesar is named the "upwards-flowing Jordan." The Jordan was caused by Jesus to flow up-stream; it is the rising flood and this, as already mentioned, is the begetter of gods. "This, they say, is the human hermaphrodite in all creatures, whom the ignorant call 'Geryon of the threefold body' [that is, ὡς ἐκ γῆς ῥέοντα, 'flowing from the earth']; but the Greeks name it the celestial horn of the moon." The text defines the above-mentioned *quaternio*, which is identical with Zeesar, the upwards-flowing Jordan, the hermaphrodite, Geryon of the threefold body, and the horn of the moon, as the cosmogonic Logos (John 1:1ff.), and the "life that was in him" (John 1:4) as a "generation of perfect men" (τέλειοι ἀνθρώποι).[99]

This Logos or quaternity is "the cup from which the king, drinking, draws his omens,"[100] or the beaker of Anacreon. The cup leads Hippolytus on to the wine miracle at Cana, which, he says, "showed forth the kingdom of heaven"; for the kingdom of heaven lies within us, like the wine in the cup. Further parallels of the cup are the ithyphallic gods of Samothrace and the Kyllenic Hermes,

---

[96] Cf. *Psychology and Alchemy*, par. 484.

[97] See the study by Marie-Louise von Franz.

[98] These words occur in the Hebrew of Isaiah 28:10, where they describe what "men with stammering lips and alien tongue" speak to the people. [The Hebrew runs: "tsaw latsaw, tsaw latsaw, kaw lakaw, kaw lakaw, zeer sham, zeer sham."—EDITORS.] AV: "For precept must be upon precept, precept upon precept, line upon line, line upon line; here a little and there a little."

[99] Cf. *Psychology and Alchemy*, pars. 550f. [Cf. Legge trans., I, p. 131.]

[100] Cf. Genesis 44:5.

who signify the Original Man as well as the spiritual man who is reborn. This last is "in every respect consubstantial" with the Original Man symbolized by Hermes. For this reason, says Hippolytus, Christ said that one must eat of his flesh and drink of his blood, for he was conscious of the *individual nature* of each of his disciples, and also of the need of each "to come to his own special nature."[101]

Another synonym is Korybas, who was descended from the crown of the head and from the unformed (ἀχαραχτηρίστον) brain, like the Euphrates from Eden, and permeates all things. His image exists—unrecognized—"in earthly form." He is the god who *dwells in the flood.* I need not describe this symbol here, as I have already discussed it at some length in one of my Paracelsus studies.[102] So far as Korybas is concerned, the parallel between him and the Protanthropos is explained by the ancient view that the corybants were the original men.[103] The name "Korybas" does not denote a particular personality, but rather the anonymous member of a collectivity, such as the Curetes, Cabiri, Dactyls, etc. Etymologically, it has been brought into connection with χορυφή (crown of the head), though this is not certain.[104] Korybas seems in our text to be the name of a single personality—the Kyllenian Hermes, who appears here as synonymous with the Cabiri of Samothrace. With reference to this Hermes the text says: "Him the Thracians . . . call Korybas."[105] I have suggested in an earlier publication[106] that this unusual single personality may perhaps be a product of contamination with Korybas, known to us from the Dionysus legend, because he too seems to have been a phallic being, as we learn from a scholium to Lucian's *De dea Syria.*[107]

From the centre of the "perfect man" flows the ocean (where, as we have said, the god dwells). The "perfect" man is, as Jesus says, the "true door," through which the "perfect" man must go in order to be reborn. Here the problem of how to translate "teleios" be-

---

[101] *Elenchos*, V, 8, 12 (Legge trans., I, p. 133).

[102] "Paracelsus as a Spiritual Phenomenon," pars. 181ff.

[103] Roscher, *Lexikon*, II, part 1, col. 1608, s.v. "Kuretes."

[104] Ibid., col. 1607. The descent from the brain may be an allusion to the ancient idea that the sperm was conducted down from the head to the genitals, through the spinal cord. [Cf. Onians, *The Origins of European Thought*, p. 234.—EDITORS.]

[105] *Elenchos*, V, 8, 13 (Legge trans., I, p. 133).

[106] "The Spirit Mercurius," par. 278.

[107] Roscher, col. 1392, s.v. "Korybos," where the text is given in full.

comes crucial; for—we must ask—why should anyone who is "perfect" need renewal through rebirth?[108] One can only conclude that the perfect man was not so perfected that no further improvement was possible. We encounter a similar difficulty in Philippians 3:12, where Paul says: "Not that I . . . am already perfect (τετελείωμαι). But three verses further on he writes: "Let us then, as many as are perfect (τέλειοι) be of this mind." The Gnostic use of τέλειος obviously agrees with Paul's. The word has only an approximate meaning and amounts to much the same thing as πνευματικός, 'spiritual,'[109] which is not connected with any conception of a definite degree of perfection or spirituality. The word "perfect" gives the sense of the Greek τέλειος correctly only when it refers to God. But when it applies to a man, who in addition is in need of rebirth, it can at most mean "whole" or "complete," especially if, as our text says, the complete man cannot even be saved unless he passes through this door.[110]

The father of the "perfectus" is the higher man or Protanthropos, who is "not clearly formed" and "without qualities." Hippolytus goes on to say that he is called Papa (Attis) by the Phrygians. He is a bringer of peace and quells "the war of the elements" in the human body,[111] a statement we meet again word for word in medieval alchemy, where the *filius philosophorum* "makes peace between enemies or the elements."[112] This "Papa" is

---

[108] The alchemists say very aptly: "Perfectum non perficitur" (that which is perfect is not perfected).

[109] *Elenchos*, V, 8, 22, describes the πνευματικοί as "perfect men endowed with reason," from which it is clear that the possession of an *anima rationalis* is what makes the "spiritual" man.

[110] *Elenchos*, V. 8, 21 (Legge trans., I, p. 134). Cramer (*Bibl.-theol. Wörterbuch der Neutestamentlichen Gräzität*) gives as the meaning of τέλειος 'complete, perfect, lacking nothing, having reached the destined goal.' Bauer (*Griech.-deutsch. Wörterbuch zu den Schriften des Neuen Testaments*, col. 1344) has, with reference to age, 'mature, full-grown,' and with reference to the mysteries, 'initiated.' Lightfoot (*Notes on the Epistles of St Paul*, p. 173) says: "*Τέλειος* is properly that of which the parts are fully developed, as distinguished from ὁλόκληρος, that in which none of the parts are wanting, 'full-grown,' as opposed to νήπιος, 'childish,' or παιδία, 'childhood.'" *Teleios* is the man who has received Nous: he has gnosis (knowledge). Cf. Guignebert, "Quelques remarques sur la perfection (τελείωσις) et ses voies dans le mystère paulinien," p. 419. Weiss (*The History of Primitive Christianity*, II, p. 576) declares that it is just the "consciousness of imperfection and the will to progress that is the sign of perfection." He bases this on Epictetus (*Enchiridion*, 51, 1f.), where it says that he who has resolved to progress (προκόπτειν) is, by anticipation, already "perfect."

[111] First mentioned at V, 8, 19. [Cf. Legge, I, p. 134.]

[112] *Hermetis Trismegisti Tractatus vere Aureus cum scholiis* (1610), p. 44.

also called νέκυς (cadaver), because he is buried in the body like a mummy in a tomb. A similar idea is found in Paracelsus; his treatise *De vita longa* opens with the words: "Life, verily, is naught but a kind of embalmed mummy, which preserves the mortal body from the mortal worms."[113] The body lives only from the "Mumia," through which the "peregrinus microcosmus," the wandering microcosm (corresponding to the macrocosm), rules the physical body.[114] His synonyms are the Adech, Archeus, Protothoma, Ides, Idechtrum, etc. He is the "Protoplast" (the first-created), and, as Ides, "the door whence all created things have come."[115] (Cf. the "true door" above!) The Mumia is born together with the body and sustains it,[116] though not to the degree that the "supercelestial Mumia" does.[117] The latter would correspond to the higher Adam of the Naassenes. Of the Ideus or Ides Paracelsus says that in it "there is but One Man . . . and he is the Protoplast."[118]

The Paracelsian Mumia therefore corresponds in every way to the Original Man, who forms the microcosm in the mortal man and, as such, shares all the powers of the macrocosm. Since it is often a question of cabalistic influences in Paracelsus, it may not be superfluous in this connection to recall the figure of the cabalistic *Metatron*. In the *Zohar* the Messiah is described as the "central column" (i.e., of the Sephiroth system), and of this column it is said: "The column of the centre is Metatron, whose name is like that of the Lord. It is created and constituted to be his image and likeness, and it includes all gradations from Above to Below and from Below to Above, and binds [them] together in the centre."[119]

The dead man, Hippolytus continues, will rise again by passing through the "door of heaven." Jacob saw the gate of heaven on his

---

[113] Published 1562 by Adam von Bodenstein. In *Paracelsus Sämtliche Werke*, ed. Sudhoff, III, p. 249. [Cf. "Paracelsus the Physician," par. 21.]

[114] *De origine Morborum invisibilium*, beginning of Book IV, says of the Mumia: "All the power of herbs and of trees is found in the Mumia; not only the power of the plants grown of earth, but also of water, all the properties of metals, all the qualities of marcasites, all the essence of precious stones. How should I count all these things, and name them? They are all within man, no fewer and no less, as strong and as powerful, in the Mumia." (*Volumen Paramirum*, pp. 291ff.)

[115] *Fragmentarische Ausarbeitungen zur Anatomie* (Sudhoff, III, p. 462).

[116] The Mumia is, accordingly, an alexipharmic. (*De mumia libellus;* ibid., p. 375.)

[117] *De vita longa*, Lib. IV, cap. VII (ibid., p. 284).

[118] "Paracelsus as a Spiritual Phenomenon," par. 168.

[119] *Zohar*, cited in Schoettgen, *Horae Hebraicae et Talmudicae*, II, p. 16.

way to Mesopotamia, "but they say Mesopotamia is the stream of
the great ocean that flows from the midst of the perfect man." This
is the gate of heaven of which Jacob said: "How terrible is this
place! This is no other but the house of God, and the gate of
heaven."[120] The stream that flows out of the Original Man (the gate
of heaven) is interpreted here as the flood-tide of Oceanus, which,
as we have seen, generates the gods. The passage quoted by Hippolytus probably refers to John 7:38 or to an apocryphal source common to both. The passage in John—"He who believes in me, as the
scripture has said, Out of his belly shall flow rivers of living
water"—refers to a nonbiblical source, which, however, seemed
scriptural to the author. Whoever drinks of this water, in him it
shall be a fountain of water springing up into eternal life, says
Origen.[121] This water is the "higher" water, the *aqua doctrinae*, the
rivers from the belly of Christ, and the divine life as contrasted with
the "lower" water, the *aqua abyssi*, where the darknesses are, and
where dwell the Prince of this world and the deceiving dragon and
his angels.[122] The river of water is the "Saviour" himself.[123] Christ
is the river that pours into the world through the four gospels,[124]
like the rivers of Paradise. I have purposely cited the ecclesiastical
allegories in greater detail here, so that the reader can see how
saturated Gnostic symbolism is in the language of the Church, and
how, on the other hand, particularly in Origen, the liveliness of his
amplifications and interpretations has much in common with
Gnostic views. Thus, to him as to many of his contemporaries and
successors, the idea of the cosmic correspondence of the "spiritual

---

[120] Gen. 28:17 (DV).

[121] *In Genesim hom.* XI, 3 (Migne, *P.G.*, vol. 12, col. 224): "And that ye may see the well
of vision, and take from it the living water, which shall be in you a fountain of water
springing up unto eternal life."

[122] Ibid., I, 2 (col. 148).

[123] *In Numeros hom.* XVII, 4 (Migne, *P.G.*, vol. 12, cols. 707f.): "For these paradises
upon the waters are like and akin to that paradise in which is the tree of life. And the
waters we may take to be either the writings of the apostles and evangelists, or the aid
given by the angels and celestial powers to such souls; for by these they are watered and
inundated, and nourished unto all knowledge and understanding of heavenly things;
although our Saviour also is the river which maketh glad the city of God; and the Holy
Spirit not only is himself that river, but out of those to whom he is given, rivers proceed
from their belly."

[124] See the valuable compilation of patristic allegories in Rahner, "Flumina de ventre
Christi," pp. 269ff. The above reference is on p. 370 and comes from Hippolytus' *Commentary on Daniel*, I, 17 (*Werke*, I, pp. 28f.).

inner man" was something quite familiar: in his first Homily on Genesis he says that God first created heaven, the whole spiritual substance, and that the counterpart of this is "our mind, which is itself a spirit, that is, it is our spiritual inner man which sees and knows God."[125]

These examples of Christian parallels to the partly pagan views of the Gnostics may suffice to give the reader a picture of the mentality of the first two centuries of our era, and to show how closely the religious teachings of that age were connected with psychic facts.

7

Now let us come back to the symbols listed by Hippolytus. The Original Man in his *latent state*—so we could interpret the term ἀχαραχτηριστός—is named *Aipolos*, "not because he feeds he-goats and she-goats," but because he is ἀειπόλος, the Pole that turns the cosmos round.[126] This recalls the parallel ideas of the alchemists, previously mentioned, about Mercurius, who is found at the North Pole. Similarly the Naassenes named Aipolos—in the language of the Odyssey—*Proteus*. Hippolytus quotes Homer as follows: "This place is frequented by the Old Man of the Sea, immortal Proteus the Egyptian . . . who always tells the truth . . ."[127] Homer then continues: ". . . who owes allegiance to Poseidon and knows the sea in all its depths."[128] Proteus is evidently a personification of the unconscious:[129] it is difficult to "catch this mysterious old being . . . he might see me first, or know I am there and keep away." One must seize him quickly and hold him fast, in order to force him to speak. Though he lives in the sea, he comes to the lonely shore at the sacred noon-tide hour, like an amphibian, and lies down to sleep among his seals. These, it must be remembered, are warm-blooded—that is to say, they can be thought of as contents of the unconscious that are capable of becoming conscious, and at certain times they appear spon-

---

[125] *In Genesim hom.* I, 2 (Migne, *P.G.*, vol. 12, col. 147).
[126] *Elenchos*, V, 8, 34 (Legge, I, p. 137). This is a play on the words αἰπόλος (from αἰγοπόλος), 'goat-herd,' and ἀειπόλος (from ἀεὶ πολεῖν, 'ever turning'). Hence πόλος = the earth's axis, the Pole.
[127] *Odyssey*, trans. by Rouse, p. 65.
[128] Ibid., trans. by Rieu, p. 74.
[129] He has something of the character of the "trickster" (cf. n. 62, supra).

taneously in the light and airy world of consciousness. From Proteus the wandering hero learns how he may make his way homewards "over the fish-giving sea," and thus the Old Man proves to be a psychopomp.[130] Οὐ πιπρασκέται, Hippolytus says of him, which can best be translated by the French colloquialism "il ne se laisse pas rouler." "But," the text goes on, "he spins round himself and changes his shape." He behaves, therefore, like a revolving image that cannot be grasped. What he says is νημερτής, 'in sooth,' infallible; he is a "soothsayer." So it is not for nothing that the Naassenes say that "knowledge of the complete man is deep indeed and hard to comprehend."

Subsequently, Proteus is likened to the green ear of corn in the Eleusinian mysteries. To him is addressed the cry of the celebrants: "The Mistress has borne the divine boy, Brimo has borne Brimos!" A "lower" correspondence to the high Eleusinian initiations, says Hippolytus, is the dark path of Persephone, who was abducted by the god of the underworld; it leads "to the grove of adored Aphrodite, who rouses the sickness of love." Men should keep to this lower path in order to be initiated "into the great and heavenly" mysteries.[131] For this mystery is "the gate of heaven" and the "house of God," where alone the good God dwells, who is destined only for the spiritual men. They should put off their garments and all become νυμφίοι, 'bridegrooms,' "robbed of their virility by the

---

[130] Proteus has much in common with Hermes: above all, the gift of second sight and the power of shape-shifting. In *Faust* (Part II, Act 5) he tells the Homunculus how and where to begin his labours.

[131] When I visited the ancient pagoda at Turukalukundram, southern India, a local pundit explained to me that the old temples were purposely covered on the outside, from top to bottom, with obscene sculptures, in order to remind ordinary people of their sexuality. The spirit, he said, was a great danger, because Yama, the god of death, would instantly carry off these people (the "imperfecti") if they trod the spiritual path directly, without preparation. The erotic sculptures were meant to remind them of their *dharma* (law), which bids them fulfil their ordinary lives. Only when they have fulfilled their *dharma* can they tread the spiritual path. The obscenities were intended to arouse the erotic curiosity of visitors to the temples, so that they should not forget their *dharma*; otherwise they would not fulfil it. Only the man who was qualified by his *karma* (the fate earned through works in previous existences), and who was destined for the life of the spirit, could ignore this injunction with impunity, for to him these obscenities mean nothing. That was also why the two seductresses stood at the entrance of the temple, luring the people to fulfil their *dharma*, because only in this way could the ordinary man attain to higher spiritual development. And since the temple represented the whole world, all human activities were portrayed in it; and because most people are always thinking of sex anyway, the great majority of the temple sculptures were of an erotic nature. For this reason too, he said, the *lingam* (phallus) stands in the sacred cavity of the adyton (Holy of Holies), in the *garbha griha* (house of the womb). This pundit was a Tantrist (scholastic; *tantra* = 'book').

virgin spirit."¹³² This is an allusion to Revelation 14:4: ". . . for they are virgins. These . . . follow the Lamb withersoever he goeth."¹³³

8

Among the objective symbols of the self I have already mentioned the Naassene conception of the ἀμέριστος στιγμή, the indivisible point. This conception fully accords with that of the "Monad" and "Son of Man" in Monoïmos. Hippolytus says:

> Monoïmos . . . thinks that there is some such Man as Oceanus, of whom the poet speaks somewhat as follows: Oceanus, the origin of gods and of men.¹³⁴ Putting this into other words, he says that the Man is All, the source of the universe, unbegotten, incorruptible, everlasting; and that there is a Son of the aforesaid Man, who is begotten and capable of suffering, and whose birth is outside time, neither willed nor predetermined . . . This Man is a single Monad, uncompounded [and] indivisible, [yet] compounded [and] divisible; loving and at peace with all things [yet] warring with all things and at war with itself in all things; unlike and like [itself], as it were a musical harmony containing all things . . . showing forth all things and giving birth to all things. It is its own mother, its own father, the two immortal names. The emblem of the perfect Man, says Monoïmos, is the jot or tittle.¹³⁵ This one tittle is the uncompounded, simple, unmixed Monad, having its composition from nothing whatsoever, yet composed of many forms, of many parts. That single, indivisible jot is the many-faced, thousand-eyed and thousand-named, the jot of the iota. This is the emblem of that perfect and indivisible Man. . . . The Son of the Man is the one iota, the one jot flowing from on high, full and filling all things, containing in

---

¹³² Their prototypes are the emasculated Attis and the priests of Eleusis, who, before celebrating the *hieros gamos*, were made impotent with a draught of hemlock.

¹³³ Cf. Matt. 5:8: "Blessed are the pure in heart, for they shall see God."

¹³⁴ A condensation of *Iliad*, XIV, 200f. and 246: "I am going to the ends of the fruitful earth to visit Ocean, the forbear of the gods, and Mother Tethys . . . even Ocean Stream himself, who is the forbear of them all." (Rieu trans., pp. 262f.)

¹³⁵ The iota (τὴν μίαν κεραίαν), the smallest Greek character, corresponding to our "dot" (which did not exist in Greek). Cf. Luke 16:17: "And it is easier for heaven and earth to pass than one tittle of the law to fall." Also Matt. 5:18. This may well be the origin of the iota symbolism, as Irenaeus (*Adv. haer.*, I, 3, 2) suggests.

himself everything that is in the Man, the Father of the Son of Man.[136]

This paradoxical idea of the Monad in Monoïmos describes the psychological nature of the self as conceived by a thinker of the second century under the influence of the Christian message.

A parallel conception is to be found in Plotinus, who lived a little later (c. 205–70). He says in the *Enneads:* "Self-knowledge reveals the fact that the soul's natural movement is not in a straight line, unless indeed it have undergone some deviation. On the contrary, it circles around something interior, around a centre. Now the centre is that from which proceeds the circle, that is, the soul. The soul will therefore move around the centre, that is, around the principle from which she proceeds; and, trending towards it, she will attach herself to it, as indeed all souls should do. The souls of the divinities ever direct themselves towards it, and that is the secret of their divinity; for divinity consists in being attached to the centre. . . . Anyone who withdraws from it is a man who has remained un-unified, or who is a brute."[137]

Here the point is the centre of a circle that is created, so to speak, by the circumambulation of the soul. But this point is the "centre of all things," a God-image. This is an idea that still underlies the mandala-symbols in modern dreams.[138]

Of equal significance is the idea, also common among the Gnostics, of the σπινθήρ or spark.[139] It corresponds to the *scintilla vitae*, the "little spark of the soul," in Meister Eckhart,[140] which we meet with rather early in the teachings of Saturninus.[141] Similarly Her-

---

[136] *Elenchos*, VIII, 12, 5ff. (Legge, pp. 107ff.). All this is a Gnostic paraphrase of John 1 and at the same time a meaningful exposition of the psychological self. The relationship of the ι to the self is the same as that of the Hebrew Letter Yod (ʼ) to the *lapis* in the cabala. The Original Man, Adam, signifies the small hook at the top of the letter Yod. (*Shaare Kedusha*, III, 1.)

[137] Ennead, VI, 9, 8 (Guthrie trans., p. 163, slightly mod.).

[138] See "A Study in the Process of Individuation" and "Concerning Mandala Symbolism."

[139] Bousset, *Hauptprobleme der Gnosis*, p. 321, says: "[The Gnostics believed] that human beings, or at any rate some human beings, carry within them from the beginning a higher element [the *spinther*] deriving from the world of light, which enables them to rise above the world of the Seven into the upper world of light, where dwell the unknown Father and the heavenly Mother."

[140] Meerpohl, "Meister Eckharts Lehre vom Seelenfünklein."

[141] Irenaeus, *Adv. haer.*, I, 24. The *pneumatikoi* contain a small part of the Pleroma (II,

aclitus, "the physicist," is said to have conceived the soul as a "spark of stellar essence."[142] Hippolytus says that in the doctrine of the Sethians the darkness held "the brightness and the spark of light in thrall,"[143] and that this "very small spark" was finely mingled in the dark waters[144] below.[145] Simon Magus[146] likewise teaches that in semen and milk there is a very small spark which "increases and becomes a power boundless and immutable."[147]

The symbol of the point is found also in alchemy, where it stands for the arcane substance; in Michael Maier[148] it signifies "the purity or homogeneity of the essence." It is the "punctum solis"[149] in the egg-yolk, which grows into a chick. In Khunrath it represents Sapientia in the form of the "salt-point";[150] in Maier it symbolizes gold.[151] To the scholiast of the "Tractatus aureus" it is the midpoint, the "circulus exiguus" and "mediator" which reconciles the hostile elements and "by persistent rotation changes the angular form of the square into a circular one like itself."[152] For Dorn the

---

29). Cf. the doctrine of Satorneilos in Hippolytus, *Elenchos*, VII, 28, 3 (Legge trans., II, pp. 80f.).

[142] Macrobius, *Commentarium in Somnium Scipionis*, XIV, 19.

[143] *Elenchos*, V, 19, 7: Ἵνα ἔχῃ τὸν σπινθῆρα δουλεύοντα.

[144] This idea reappears in alchemy in numerous variations. Cf. Michael Maier, *Symbola aureae mensae*, p. 380, and *Scrutinium chymicum*, Emblema XXXI: "The King swimming in the sea, and crying with a loud voice: Whosoever shall bring me out, shall have a great reward." Also *Aurora Consurgens* (ed. von Franz), p. 57: "For this cause have I laboured night by night with crying, my jaws become hoarse; who is the man that liveth, knowing and understanding, delivering my soul from the hand of hell?"

[145] *Elenchos*, V, 21, 1: Τὸν σπινθῆρα τὸν ἐλάχιστον ἐν τοῖς σκοτεινοῖς ὕδασι κάτω καταμεμίχθαι λεπτῶς.

[146] *Elenchos*, VI, 17, 7. Cf. "Transformation Symbolism in the Mass," par. 359.

[147] Cf. the vision reported by Wickes, *The Inner World of Man*, p. 245. It is a typical piece of individuation symbolism: "Then I saw that on the shaft there hung a human figure that held within itself all the loneliness of the world and of the spaces. Alone, and hoping for nothing, the One hung and gazed down into the void. For long the One gazed, drawing all solitude unto itself. Then deep in the fathomless dark was born an infinitesimal spark. Slowly it rose from the bottomless depth, and as it rose it grew until it became a star. And the star hung in space just opposite the figure, and the white light streamed upon the Lonely One." Conversely, it is related of Zoroaster that he drew down sparks from a star, which scorched him. (Bousset, p. 146.)

[148] Maier, *De circulo physico quadrato* (1616), p. 27.

[149] Or *punctus solis*. "In the egg therefore are four things: earth, water, air, and fire; but the 'punctum solis' is apart from these four, in the midst of the yolk (which) is the chick." (*Turba*, Sermo IV.) Ruska (*Turba philosophorum*, p. 51) puts "saliens" instead of "solis" ("springing point" instead of "sun-point"), in the belief that all the copyists repeated the same error. I am not so sure of this.

[150] *Von hylealischen Chaos*, p. 194.

[151] *De circulo quadrato*, p. 27.

[152] *Theatr. chem.*, IV, p. 691.

"punctum vix intelligibile" is the starting point of creation.[153] Similarly John Dee says that all things originated from the point and the monad.[154] Indeed, God himself is simultaneously both the centre and the circumference. In Mylius the point is called the bird of Hermes.[155] In the "Novum lumen" it is spirit and fire, the life of the arcane substance, similar to the spark.[156] This conception of the point is more or less the same as that of the Gnostics.

From these citations we can see how Christ was assimilated to symbols that also meant the kingdom of God, for instance the grain of mustard-seed, the hidden treasure, and the pearl of great price. He and his kingdom have the same meaning. Objections have always been made to this dissolution of Christ's personality, but what has not been realized is that it represents at the same time an assimilation and integration of Christ into the human psyche.[157] The result is seen in the growth of the human personality and in the development of consciousness. These specific attainments are now gravely threatened in our anti-christian age, not only by the sociopolitical delusional systems, but above all by the rationalistic hybris which is tearing our consciousness from its transcendent roots and holding before it immanent goals.

From "Foreward to Neumann: *Depth Psychology and a New Ethic,*" CW 18, par. 1419

Such being the behaviour of the unconscious, the process of coming to terms with it, in the ethical sense, acquires a special character. The process does not consist in dealing with a given "material," but in negotiating with a psychic minority (or majority, as the case may be) that has equal rights. For this reason the author compares the relation to the unconscious with a parliamentary democracy, whereas the old ethic unconsciously imitates, or actually prefers, the procedure of an absolute monarchy or a tyrannical

---

[153] "Physica genesis," *Theatr. chem.*, I, p. 382.

[154] *Monas hieroglyphica* (first edn., 1564). Also in *Theatr. chem.* (1602), II, p. 218.

[155] *Phil. ref.*, p. 131.

[156] *Mus. herm.*, p. 559.

[157] Here I would like to cite a theological opinion: "Jesus is a synthesis and a growth, and the resultant form is one which tells of a hundred forces which went to its making. But the interesting thing is that the process did not end with the closing of the canon. Jesus is still in the making." Roberts, "Jesus or Christ?—A Reply," p. 124.

one-party system. Through the new ethic, the ego-consciousness is ousted from its central position in a psyche organized on the lines of a monarchy or totalitarian state, its place being taken by *wholeness* or the *self*, which is now recognized as central. The self was of course always at the centre, and always acted as the hidden director. Gnosticism long ago projected this state of affairs into the heavens, in the form of a metaphysical drama: ego-consciosness appearing as the vain demiurge, who fancies himself the sole creator of the world, and the self as the highest, unknowable God, whose emanation the demiurge is. The union of conscious and unconscious in the individuation process, the real core of the ethical problem, was projected in the form of a drama of redemption and, in some Gnostic systems, consisted in the demiurge's discovery and recognition of the highest God.

Chapter 2. Jung's Alternative Psychological Interpretation of Gnosticism

In "Gnostic Symbols of the Self" Jung equates the godhead with the unconscious and differentiated matter with the ego or ego consciousness, but in his brief discussion of the Gnostic Hymn of the Pearl *he reverses himself. Matter, here in its raw rather than differentiated state, now symbolizes the unconscious and the godhead the ego or ego consciousness. Jung stresses that the* Hymn *obliges human beings to descend to the material world in order to realize their divine, immaterial nature. Clearly, the descent refers not, as in "Gnostic Symbols of the Self," to the birth of the ego out of the unconscious but, on the contrary, to the re-entry of the ego into the unconscious for the purpose of raising it to consciousness. The birth of the ego described in "Gnostic Symbols of the Self" is now presupposed and constitutes the beginning rather than the end of the journey. Matter now not only already exists rather than emerges but also symbolizes the unconscious rather than the ego, which is now symbolized by the godhead.*

These new equations only reverse, not solve, the problems the original ones posed. First, the return of the newly independent ego to the unconscious should be for the purpose of raising it to consciousness, but in fact the descent of the savior is for the purpose of extricating the divine sparks ensnared in matter. Rather than getting raised to consciousness, the unconscious is instead symbolically abandoned. Jung conflates the pearl, which symbolizes the sparks, with the matter in which it is trapped, so that for him the retrieval of the pearl means the retrieval of matter. In actuality, the pearl and matter are antagonists, so that the retrieval of the pearl means the rejection of matter. The return of the child to his parents is the equivalent of the reunion of the ego with itself, not of the unconscious with the ego.

Second, the return of the child savior in the Hymn *may involve his transformation rather than his mere restoration, but in other Gnostic myths the return of the savior does not. The rejection of the ego aside, the end in those myths cannot therefore represent the establishment of a new state of the psyche.*

From "**Archetypes of the Collective Unconscious**," CW 9 i, pars. 37–41

We must surely go the way of the waters, which always tend downward, if we would raise up the treasure, the precious heritage of the father. In the Gnostic hymn to the soul,[1] the son is sent forth by his parents to seek the pearl that fell from the King's crown. It lies at the bottom of a deep well, guarded by a dragon, in the land of the Egyptians—that land of fleshpots and drunkenness with all its material and spiritual riches. The son and heir sets out to fetch the jewel, but forgets himself and his task in the orgies of Egyptian worldliness, until a letter from his father reminds him what his duty is. He then sets out for the water and plunges into the dark depths of the well, where he finds the pearl on the bottom, and in the end offers it to the highest divinity.

This hymn, ascribed to Bardesanes, dates from an age that resembled ours in more than one respect. Mankind looked and waited, and it was a *fish*—"levatus de profundo" (drawn from the deep)[2]—that became the symbol of the saviour, the bringer of healing.

As I wrote these lines, I received a letter from Vancouver, from a person unknown to me. The writer is puzzled by his dreams, which are always about water: "Almost every time I dream it is about water: *either I am having a bath, or the water-closet is overflowing, or a pipe is bursting, or my home has drifted down to the water's edge, or I see an acquaintance about to sink into water, or I am trying to get out of water, or I am having a bath and the tub is about to overflow,*" etc.

Water is the commonest symbol for the unconscious. The lake in the valley is the unconscious, which lies, as it were, underneath

[1] James, *Apocryphal New Testament*, pp. 411–15.
[2] Augustine, *Confessions*, Lib. XIII, cap. XXI.

consciousness, so that it is often referred to as the "subconscious," usually with the pejorative connotation of an inferior consciousness. Water is the "valley spirit," the water dragon of Tao, whose nature resembles water—a *yang* embraced in the *yin*. Psychologically, therefore, water means spirit that has become unconscious. So the dream of the theologian is quite right in telling him that down by the water he could experience the working of the living spirit like a miracle of healing in the pool of Bethesda. The descent into the depths always seems to precede the ascent. Thus another theologian[3] dreamed that *he saw on a mountain a kind of Castle of the Grail. He went along a road that seemed to lead straight to the foot of the mountain and up it. But as he drew nearer he discovered to his great disappointment that a chasm separated him from the mountain, a deep, darksome gorge with underworldly water rushing along the bottom. A steep path led downwards and toilsomely climbed up again on the other side. But the prospect looked uninviting,* and the dreamer awoke. Here again the dreamer, thirsting for the shining heights, had first to descend into the dark depths, and this proves to be the indispensable condition for climbing any higher. The prudent man avoids the danger lurking in these depths, but he also throws away the good which a bold but imprudent venture might bring.

The statement made by the dream meets with violent resistance from the conscious mind, which knows "spirit" only as something to be found in the heights. "Spirit" always seems to come from above, while from below comes everything that is sordid and worthless. For people who think in this way, spirit means highest freedom, a soaring over the depths, deliverance from the prison of the chthonic world, and hence a refuge for all those timorous souls who do not want to become anything different. But water is earthy and tangible, it is also the fluid of the instinct-driven body, blood and the flowing of blood, the odour of the beast, carnality heavy with passion. The unconscious is the psyche that reaches down from the daylight of mentally and morally lucid consciousness into the nervous system that for ages has been known as the "sympathetic." This does not govern perception and muscular activity like

[3] The fact that it was another theologian who dreamed this dream is not so surprising, since priests and clergymen have a professional interest in the motif of "ascent." They have to speak of it so often that the question naturally arises as to what they are doing about their own spiritual ascent.

the cerebrospinal system, and thus control the environment; but, though functioning without sense-organs, it maintains the balance of life and, through the mystericus paths of sympathetic excitation, not only gives us knowledge of the innermost life of other beings but also has an inner effect upon them. In this sense it is an extremely collective system, the operative basis of all *participation mystique*, whereas the cerebrospinal function reaches its high point in separating off the specific qualities of the ego, and only apprehends surfaces and externals—always through the medium of space. It experiences everything as an outside, whereas the sympathetic system experiences everything as an inside.

From "**The Personification of the Opposites**," CW 14, par. 257

We must also mention the Peratic interpretation of the Red Sea. The Red Sea drowned the Egyptians, but the Egyptians were all "non-knowers" (οἱ ἀγνοοῦντες). The exodus from Egypt signifies the exodus from the body, which is Egypt in miniature, being the incarnation of sinfulness, and the crossing (περᾶσαι)[1] of the Red Sea is the crossing of the water of corruption, which is Kronos. The other side of the Red Sea is the other side of Creation. The arrival in the desert is a "genesis outside of generation" (ἔξω γενέσεως γενέσθαι). There the "gods of destruction" and the "god of salvation" are all together.[2] The Red Sea is a water of death for those that are "unconscious," but for those that are "conscious" it is a baptismal water of rebirth and transcendence.[3] By "unconscious" are meant those who have no gnosis, i.e., are not enlightened as to the nature and destiny of man in the cosmos. In modern language it would be those who have no knowledge of the contents of the personal and collective unconscious. The personal unconscious is the shadow and the inferior function,[4] in Gnostic terms the sinful-

[1] Whence the designation "Peratics," a Gnostic sect. (Cf. *Aion*, pp. 185f.) They were the "trans-scendentalists."

[2] Hippolytus, *Elenchos*, V, 16, 4f.

[3] There exists a level or threshold of consciousness which is characteristic of a definite time-period or stratum of society, and which might be compared to a water-level. The unconscious level rises whenever the conscious level falls, and vice versa. Anything that is not in the conscious field of vision remains invisible and forms a content of the unconscious.

[4] Cf. *Psychological Types*, def. 30.

ness and impurity that must be washed away by baptism. The collective unconscious expresses itself in the mythological teachings, characteristic of most mystery religions, which reveal the secret knowledge concerning the origin of all things and the way to salvation. "Unconscious" people who attempt to cross the sea without being purified and without the guidance of enlightenment are drowned; they get stuck in the unconscious and suffer a spiritual death in so far as they cannot get beyond their one-sidedness. To do this they would have to be more conscious of what is unconscious to them and their age, above all of the inner opposite, namely those contents to which the prevailing views are in any way opposed. This continual process of getting to know the counterposition in the unconscious I have called the "transcendent function,"[5] because the confrontation of conscious (rational) data with those that are unconscious (irrational) necessarily results in a modification of standpoint. But an alteration is possible only if the existence of the "other" is admitted, at least to the point of taking conscious cognizance of it. A Christian of today, for instance, no longer ought to cling obstinately to a one-sided credo, but should face the fact that Christianity has been in a state of schism for four hundred years, with the result that every single Christian has a split in his psyche. Naturally this lesion cannot be treated or healed if everyone insists on his own standpoint. Behind those barriers he can rejoice in his absolute and consistent convictions and deem himself above the conflict, but outside them he keeps the conflict alive by his intransigence and continues to deplore the pig-headedness and stiffneckedness of everybody else. It seems as if Christianity had been from the outset the religion of chronic squabblers, and even now it does everything in its power never to let the squabbles rest. Remarkably enough, it never stops preaching the gospel of neighbourly love.

[5] Ibid., def. 51 (especially par. 828). See also my "The Transcendent Function."

Chapter 3. Gnosticism as a Psychological Phenomenon

Jung's interpretation of Gnosticism is doubly psychological. Not only does he psychologize the meaning of Gnostic myths, but he also credits Gnostics with being psychologists themselves. Yet for all his praise of the psychological astuteness of Gnostics he also stresses that they projected themselves onto the cosmos through Gnostic metaphysics. See, in my introduction, the section on "The Gnostics as Psychologists."

"Address at the Presentation of the Jung Codex,"[1] CW 18, pars. 1826–34

Mr. President, Mr. Minister, viri magnifici, Ladies and Gentlemen!
It gives me much pleasure to accept this precious gift in the name of our Institute. For this I thank you, and also for the surprising and undeserved honour you have done me in baptising the Codex

---

[1] [(Translation revised and augmented by L. R.) The text of this address given above, pars. 1514–1517 (q.v.), was obtained by the Editors from the Jung archives at Küsnacht in the early 1960's and was assigned to R.F.C. Hull for translation on the assumption that it represented the text that Jung read at the convocation in Zurich, 15 Nov. 1953. In 1975, when the present vol. was in page proof, a considerably augmented version was published (in German) by Professor Gilles Quispel as an appendix to the volume. *C. G. Jung: een mens voor deze tijd* (Rotterdam), consisting of essays (in Dutch) on Jung's work by Quispel ("Jung and Gnosis"), C. Aalders, and J. H. Plokker. Quispel had obtained this text of the Address some years earlier from one of the persons who had arranged the convocation. Subsequently, Professor C. A. Meier provided an even fuller version of Jung's actual remarks, and that is translated here (the added material being indicated by a vertical line in the left margin). Jung had first written the shorter version, then had expanded it prior to the occasion, but the shorter version had been circulated.

George H. Page, of Switzerland, donated funds that enabled the Jung Institute to purchase the Codex from the estate of Albert Eid, a Belgian dealer in antiquities who had acquired it in Egypt. Professor Meier, then director of the Institute, had played the leading role in tracing and negotiating for the Codex. In accordance with the original agreement, the Codex was eventually given to the Coptic Museum in Cairo.]

with my name. I would like to express my special thanks both to Mr. Page, who through generous financial assistance made the purchase of the papyrus possible, and to Dr. Meier, who through unflagging efforts has given it a home.

Dr. Meier has asked me to say a few words to you about the psychological significance of Gnostic texts. Of the four tracts contained in this codex, I should like to single out especially the *Evangelium Veritatis*, an important Valentinian text that affords us some insight into the mentality of the second century A.D. "The Gospel of Truth" is less a gospel than a highly interesting commentary on the Christian message. It belongs therefore to the series of numerous "phenomena of assimilation," its purpose being to assimilate this strange and hardly understandable message to the Hellenistic-Egyptian world of thought. It is evident that the author was appealing to the intellectual understanding of his reader, as if in remembrance of the words: "We preach Christ crucified, unto the Jews a stumbling-block, and unto the Greeks foolishness" (I Cor. 1.23). For him Christ was primarily a metaphysical figure, a light-bringer, who went forth from the Father in order to illuminate the stupidity, darkness, and unconsciousness of mankind and to lead the individual back to his origins through self-knowledge. This deliverance from *agnosia* relates the text to the accounts which Hippolytus, in his *Elenchos*, has left of the Gnostics, and of the Naassenes and Peratics in particular. There we also find most of what I call the "phenomena of assimilation." By this term I mean to delineate those specifically psychic reactions aroused by the impact that the figure and message of Christ had on the pagan world, most prominently those allegories and symbols such as fish, snake, lion, peacock, etc., characteristic of the first Christian centuries, but also those much more extensive amplifications due to Gnosticism, which clearly were meant to illuminate and render more comprehensible the metaphysical role of the Saviour. For the modern mind this accumulation of symbols, parables, and synonyms has just the opposite effect, since it only deepens the darkness and entangles the light-bringer in a network of barely intelligible analogies.

Gnostic amplification, as we encounter it in Hippolytus, has a character in part hymn-like, in part dream-like, which one invariably finds where an aroused imagination is trying to clarify an as yet

cause in most cases he has long since forgotten this basic problem of Christianity: the moral and intellectual *agnosia* of the merely natural man. Christianity, considered as a psychological phenomenon, contributed a great deal to the development of consciousness, and wherever this dialectical process has not come to a standstill we find new evidence of assimilation. Even in medieval Judaism a parallel process took place over the centuries, independently of the Christian one, in the Kabbala. Its nearest analogy in the Christian sphere was philosophical alchemy, whose psychological affinities with Gnosticism can easily be demonstrated.

The urgent therapeutic necessity of confronting the individual with his own dark side is a secular continuation of the Christian development of consciousness and leads to phenomena of assimilation similar to those found in Gnosticism, the Kabbala, and Hermetic philosophy.

The reactions of the matrix that we observe these days are not only comparable, both in form and in content, with Gnostic and medieval symbols, but presumably are also of the same sort, and have the same purpose as well, in that they make the figure of *Hyios tou anthropou*, Son of Man, the innermost concern of the individual, and also expand it into a magnitude comparable with that of the Indian *purusha-atman*, the *anima mundi*. At this time, however, I would prefer not to go any further into these modern tendencies, which indeed were developing among the Gnostics.

Since comparison with these earlier historical stages is of the greatest importance in interpreting the modern phenomena, the discovery of authentic Gnostic texts is, especially for the direction our research is taking, of the greatest interest, all the more so in that it is not only of a theoretical but also of a practical nature. If we seek genuine psychological understanding of the human being of our own time, we must know his spiritual history absolutely. We cannot reduce him to mere biological data, since he is not by nature merely biological but is a product also of spiritual presuppositions.

I must unfortunately content myself with these bare outlines in attempting to explain our interest in a Gnostic text. Further proof of our interest in Gnosticism and detailed explanations may be found in a number of studies that have already been published.

From "**The Structure and Dynamics of the Self,**" CW 9ii, pars. 347–50

1

The examples given in the previous chapter should be sufficient to describe the progressive assimilation and amplification of the archetype that underlies ego-consciousness. Rather than add to their number unnecessarily, I will try to summarize them so that an over-all picture results. From various hints dropped by Hippolytus, it is clear beyond a doubt that many of the Gnostics were nothing other than psychologists. Thus he reports them as saying that "the soul is very hard to find and to comprehend,"¹ and that knowledge of the whole man is just as difficult. "For knowledge of man is the beginning of wholeness (τελείωσις), but knowledge of God is perfect wholeness (ἀπηρτισμένη τελείωσις)." Clement of Alexandria says in the *Paedagogus* (III, 1): "Therefore, as it seems, it is the greatest of all disciplines to know oneself; for when a man knows himself, he knows God." And Monoïmos, in his letter to Theophrastus, writes: "Seek him from out thyself, and learn who it is that taketh possession of everything in thee, saying: *my* god, *my* spirit, *my* understanding, *my* soul, *my* body; and learn whence is sorrow and joy, and love and hate, and waking though one would not, and sleeping though one would not, and getting angry though one would not, and falling in love though one would not. And if thou shouldst closely investigate these things, thou wilt find Him in thyself, the One and the Many, like to that little point [κεραία], for it is in thee that he hath his origin and his deliverance."²

One cannot help being reminded, in reading this text, of the Indian idea of the Self as brahman and atman, for instance in the Kena Upanishad: "By whom willed and directed does the mind fly forth? By whom commanded does the first breath move? Who sends forth the speech we utter here? What god is it that stirs the eye and ear? The hearing of the ear, the thinking of the mind, the speaking of the speech . . . That which speech cannot express, by which speech is expressed . . . which the mind cannot think, by which the mind thinks, know that as Brahman."³

¹ *Elenchos*, V, 7, 8 (Legge trans., I, p. 123).
² *Elenchos*, VIII, 15, 1ff. Cf. Legge trans., II, p. 10.
³ Based on Radhakrishnan, *The Principal Upanishads*, pp. 581f.

Yajñyavalkya defines it in indirect form in the Brihadāranyaka Upanishad: "He who dwells in all beings, yet is apart from all beings, whom no beings know, whose body is all beings, who controls all beings from within, he is your Self, the inner controller, the immortal. . . . There is no other seer but he, no other hearer but he, no other perceiver but he, no other knower but he. He is your Self, the inner controller, the immortal. All else is of sorrow."[4]

In Monoïmos, who was called "the Arab," Indian influences are not impossible. His statement is significant because it shows that even in the second century[5] the ego was considered the exponent of an all-embracing totality, the self—a thought that by no means all psychologists are familiar with even today. These insights, in the Near East as in India, are the product of intense introspective observation that can only be psychological. *Gnosis is undoubtedly a psychological knowledge whose contents derive from the unconscious.* It reached its insights by concentrating on the "subjective factor,"[6] which consists empirically in the demonstrable influence that the collective unconscious exerts on the conscious mind. This would explain the astonishing parallelism between Gnostic symbolism and the findings of the psychology of the unconscious.

Foreword to Quispel: *Tragic Christianity,*[1] CW 18, pars. 1478–82

The author of this essay has asked me to start off his book with a few introductory words. Although I am not a philologist, I gladly accede to this request because Dr. Quispel has devoted particular attention to a field of work which is familiar also to me from the psychological standpoint. Gnosticism is still an obscure affair and in need of explanation, despite the fact that sundry personages have already approached it from the most diverse angles and tried their hands at explanations with doubtful success. One even has the

---

[4] Ibid., pp. 228f.

[5] Hippolytus lived *c.* A.D. 230. Monoïmos must therefore antedate him.

[6] *Psychological Types,* pars. 620ff.

[1] [According to information from Gilles Quispel (professor of ancient church history, Utrecht University, Netherlands), in 1949 he planned to publish in Bollingen Series a volume of his lectures given at the Eranos conferences. The projected title was *Tragic Christianity,* and Jung consented to write this foreword. The book was never published.]

impression that the ban on heresy still hangs over this wide domain, or at least the disparagement which specialists are accustomed to feel for annoying incomprehensibilities. We have an equivalent of this situation in psychiatry, which has ostentatiously neglected the psychology of the psychoses and shows pronounced resistances to all attempts in this direction. This fact, though astonishing in itself, is, however, comprehensible when one considers the difficulties to be overcome once one tries to fathom the psychology of delusional ideas. We can understand mental illness only if we have some understanding of the mind in general. Delusional ideas cannot be explained in terms of themselves, but only in terms of our knowledge of the normal mind. Here the only phenomenological method that promises success, as opposed to philosophical and religious prejudice, has made next to no headway, indeed it has still not even been understood. The fundamental reason for this is that the doctor, to whom alone psychopathological experiences are accessible, seldom or never has the necessary epistemological premises at his command. Instead of which, if he reflects at all and does not merely observe and register, he has usually succumbed to a philosophical or religious conviction and fills out the gaps in his knowledge with professions of faith.

What is true of psychopathology can—*mutatis mutandis*—be applied directly to the treatment which Gnosticism has undergone. Its peculiar mental products demand the same psychological understanding as do psychotic delusional formations. But the philologist or theologian who concerns himself with Gnosticism generally possesses not a shred of psychiatric knowledge, which must always be called upon in explaining extraordinary mental phenomena. The explanation of Gnostic ideas "in terms of themselves," i.e., in terms of their historical foundations, is futile, for in that way they are reduced only to their less developed forestages but not understood in their actual significance.

We find a similar state of affairs in the psychopathology of the neuroses, where, for instance, Freud's psychoanalysis reduces the neurotic symptomatology only to its infantile forestages and completely overlooks its functional, that is, its *symbolic* value. So long as we know only the causality or the historical development of a normal biological or psychic phenomenon, but not its functional development, i.e., its purposive significance, it is not really under-

still unconscious content. These are, on the one hand, intellectual, philosophical—or rather, theosophical—speculations, and, on the other, analogies, synonyms, and symbols whose psychological nature is immediately convincing. The phenomenon of assimilation mainly represents the reaction of the psychic matrix, i.e., the unconscious, which becomes agitated and responds with archetypal images, thereby demonstrating to what degree the message has penetrated into the depths of the psyche and how the unconscious interprets the phenomenon of Christ.

It is not likely that the Gnostic attempts at elucidation met with success in the pagan world, quite aside from the fact that the Church very soon opposed them and whenever possible suppressed them. Luckily during this process some of the best pieces (to judge by their content) were preserved for posterity, so that today we are in a position to see in what way the Christian message was taken up by the unconscious of that age. These assimilation phenomena are naturally of especial significance for psychologists and psychiatrists, who are professionally concerned with the psychic background, and this is the reason why our Institute is so interested in acquiring and translating authentic Gnostic texts.

Although suppressed and forgotten, the process of assimilation that began with Gnosticism continued all through the Middle Ages, and it can still be observed in modern times whenever individual consciousness is confronted with its own shadow, or the inferior part of the personality. This aspect of human personality, which is most often repressed owing to its incompatibility with one's self-image, does not consist only of inferior characteristics but represents the entire unconscious; that is, it is almost always the first form in which unconsciousness brings itself to the attention of consciousness. Freud's psychology occupied itself exclusively, so to speak, with this aspect. Behind the shadow, however, the deeper layers of the unconscious come forward, those which, so far as we are able to ascertain, consist of archetypal, sometimes instinctive, structures, so-called "patterns of behaviour." Under the influence of extraordinary psychic situations, especially life crises, these archetypal forms or images may spontaneously invade consciousness, in the case of sick persons just as in the case of healthy ones. The general rule, however, is that modern man needs expert help to become conscious of his darkness, be-

stood. The same is true of Gnostic ideas: they are not mere symptoms of a certain historical development, but creative new configurations which were of the utmost significance for the further development of Western consciousness. One has only to think of the Jewish-Gnostic presuppositions in Paul's writings and of the immense influence of the "gnostic" gospel of John. Apart also from these important witnesses, and in spite of being persecuted, branded as heresy, and pronounced dead within the realm of the Church, Gnosticism did not die out at once by any means. Its philosophical and psychological aspects went on developing in alchemy up to the time of Goethe, and the Jewish syncretism of the age of Philo[2] found its continuation within orthodox Judaism in the Kabbala. Both these trends, if not exactly forestages of the modern psychology of the unconscious, are at all events well-nigh inexhaustible sources of knowledge for the psychologist. This is no accident inasmuch as parallel phenomena to the empirically established contents of the collective unconscious underlie the earliest Gnostic systems. The archetypal motifs of the unconscious are the psychic source of Gnostic ideas, of delusional ideas (especially of the paranoid schizophrenic forms), of symbol-formation in dreams, and of active imagination in the course of an analytical treatment of neurosis.

In the light of these reflections, I regard Dr. Quispel's quotations from the Gnostics, that the "Autopator contained in himself all things, in [a state of] unconsciousness (ἐν ἀγνωσία)"[3] and that "The Father was devoid of consciousness (ἀνεννόητος),"[4] as a fundamental discovery for the psychology of Gnosticism. It means nothing less than that the Gnostics in question derived the knowable ὑπερκόσμια from the unconscious, i.e., that these represented unconscious contents. This discovery results not only in the possibility but also in the necessity of supplementing the historical method of explanation by one that is based on a scientific psychology.

---

[2] [Philo Judaeus (fl. A.D. 39), Graeco-Judaic philosopher of Alexandria. His works include commentaries on the Old Testament, which he interpreted allegorically, finding in it the source of the main doctrines of Plato, Aristotle, and other Greek philosophers.]
[3] Epiphanius, *Panarium*, XXXI, cap V. [The quotation is here abbreviated; for Jung's fuller version of the Greek text see *Aion* (C.W., vol. 9, ii), par. 298 and n. 16.]
[4] Hippolytus, *Elenchos*, VI, 42, 4. [This quotation, also abbreviated here, comes immediately after the one from Epiphanius in *Aion*, par. 298, where Jung cites Quispel's French trans. of the Greek text.]

Psychology is indebted to the author for his endeavors to facilitate the understanding of Gnosticism, not merely because we psychologists have made it our task to explain Gnosticism, but because we see in it a *tertium comparationis* which affords us the most valuable help in the practical understanding of modern individual symbol-formation.

May 1949

From "**The Type Problem in Poetry,**" CW 6, par. 409

The fact that three of the greatest minds of Germany should fasten on early medieval psychology in their most important works is proof, it seems to me, that that age has left behind a question which still remains to be answered. It may be well, therefore, to examine this question a little more closely. I have the impression that the mysterious something that inspired the knightly orders (the Templars, for instance), and that seems to have found expression in the Grail legend, may possibly have been the germ of a new orientation to life, in other words, a nascent symbol. The non-Christian or Gnostic character of the Grail symbol takes us back to the early Christian heresies, those germinating points in which a whole world of audacious and brilliant ideas lay hidden. In Gnosticism we see man's unconscious psychology in full flower, almost perverse in its luxuriance; it contained the very thing that most strongly resisted the *regula fidei*, that Promethean and creative spirit which will bow only to the individual soul and to no collective ruling. Although in crude form, we find in Gnosticism what was lacking in the centuries that followed: a belief in the efficacy of individual revelation and individual knowledge. This belief was rooted in the proud feeling of man's affinity with the gods, subject to no human law, and so overmastering that it may even subdue the gods by the sheer power of Gnosis. In Gnosis are to be found the beginnings of the path that led to the intuitions of German mysticism, so important psychologically, which came to flower at the time of which we are speaking.

Chapter 4. Gnosticism as Dealing with Evil

In Jungian psychology the ideal state involves the acceptance of moral opposites: human beings must accept the evil as well as the good side of their own personality. Jung usually identifies the evil side of the personality with the shadow archetype. Hence he deems the devil, or the Antichrist, the projection of the shadow of Christ and then deems both figures projections of, respectively, the shadow and the persona archetypes of God the Father. Jung castigates mainstream Christianity for denying the devil a place in the pantheon. The devil, he argues, is the missing quarter of divinity, which consequently gets represented by only a Trinity. By contrast, Jung lauds Gnosticism for granting evil a place in the godhead.

Whether or not mainstream Christianity in fact ignores evil, Gnosticism scarcely incorporates it in the godhead. Gnostic myths do attribute the creation of either matter itself or the material world to the godhead, but that attribution poses the central unresolved paradox: that the godhead, which is wholly immaterial and therefore good, willfully and knowingly produces either matter or the material world, both of which are incontestably evil. Far from conceding the evilness of divinity, Gnosticism emphatically denies it and thereby faces the problem of accounting for evil. Mainstream Christianity may likewise deny any evilness in divinity, but it does not judge the material world evil and thus faces a less acute problem.

From "Christ, A Symbol of the Self," CW 9 ii, par. 75

Thanks to the doctrine of the *privatio boni*, wholeness seemed guaranteed in the figure of Christ. One must, however, take evil rather more substantially when one meets it on the plane of empirical psychology. There it is simply the opposite of good. In the ancient world the Gnostics, whose arguments were very much influenced by psychic experience, tackled the problem of evil on a broader basis than the Church Fathers. For instance, one of the things they taught was that Christ "cast off his shadow from himself."[1] If we give this view the weight it deserves, we can easily recognize the cut-off counterpart in the figure of Antichrist. The Antichrist develops in legend as a perverse imitator of Christ's life. He is a true ἀντίμιμον πνεῦμα, an imitating spirit of evil who follows in Christ's footsteps like a shadow following the body. This complementing of the bright but one-sided figure of the Redeemer—we even find traces of it in the New Testament—must be of especial significance. And indeed, considerable attention was paid to it quite early.

From "The Historical Significance of the Fish," CW 9 ii, par. 171

As Bousset has plausibly suggested, the duality of the apocalyptic Christ is the outcome of Jewish-Gnostic speculations whose echoes we hear in the traditions mentioned above. The intensive preoccupation of the Gnostics with the problem of evil stands out in startling contrast to the peremptory nullification of it by the Church fathers, and shows that this question had already become topical at the beginning of the third century. In this connection we may recall the view expressed by Valentinus,[1] that Christ was born "not without a kind of shadow" and that he afterwards "cast off the shadow from himself."[2] Valentinus lived sometime in the first half

---

[1] Irenaeus (*Adversus haereses*, II, 5, 1) records the Gnostic teaching that when Christ, as the demiurgic Logos, created his mother's being, he "cast her out of the Pleroma—that is, he cut her off from knowledge." For creation took place outside the pleroma, in the shadow and the void. According to Valentinus (*Adv. haer.*, I, 11, 1), Christ did not spring from the Aeons of the pleroma, but from the mother who was outside it. She bore him, he says, "not without a kind of shadow." But he, "being masculine," cast off the shadow from himself and returned to the Pleroma (καί τοῦτον [Χριστὸν] μὲν ἅτε ἄρρενα ὑπάρχοντα ἀποκόψαντα ἀφ᾽ ἑαυτοῦ τὴν σκιάν, ἀναδραμεῖν εἰς τὸ Πλήρωμα κτλ.), while his mother, "being left behind in the shadow, and deprived of spiritual substance," there gave birth to the real "Demiurge and Pantokrator of the lower world." But the shadow which lies over the world is, as we know from the Gospels, the *princeps huius mundi*, the devil. Cf. *The Writings of Irenaeus*, I, pp. 45f.

[1] He was, it seems, a cleric, who is said to have been a candidate for the episcopal see in Rome.

[2] Irenaeus, *Adv. haer.*, I, 11, 1 (Roberts/Rambaut trans., I, p. 46).

of the second century, and the Apocalypse was probably written about A.D. 90, under Domitian. Like other Gnostics, Valentinus carried the gospels a stage further in his thinking, and for this reason it does not seem to me impossible that he understood the "shadow" as the Yahwistic law under which Christ was born. The Apocalypse and other things in the New Testament could easily have prompted him to such a view, quite apart from the more or less contemporaneous ideas about the demiurge and the prime Ogdoad that consists of light and shadow.[3] It is not certain whether Origen's doubt concerning the ultimate fate of the devil was original;[4] at all events, it proves that the possibility of the devil's reunion with God was an object of discussion in very early times, and indeed had to be if Christian philosophy was not to end in dualism. One should not forget that the theory of the *privatio boni* does not dispose of the eternity of hell and damnation. God's humanity is also an expression of dualism, as the controversy of the Monophysites and Dyophysites in the early Church shows. Apart from the religious significance of the decision in favour of a complete union of both natures, I would mention in passing that the Monophysite dogma has a noteworthy psychological aspect: it tells us (in psychological parlance) that since Christ, as a man, corresponds to the ego, and, as God, to the self, he is at once both ego and self, part and whole. Empirically speaking, consciousness can never comprehend the whole, but it is probable that the whole is unconsciously present in the ego. This would be equivalent to the highest possible state of τελείωσις (completeness or perfection).

From "**A Psychological Approach to the Dogma of the Trinity,**" CW 11, pars. 249–50

But if the devil has the power to put a spoke in God's Creation, or even corrupt it, and God does nothing to stop this nefarious activity

---

[3] Doctrine of the Valentinian Secundus (ibid., I, p. 46).

[4] *De oratione*, 27: ". . . so that that supreme sinner and blasphemer against the Holy Ghost may be kept from sin through all this present age, and hereafter in the age to come from its beginning to its end be treated I know not how" (. . . ita ut summus ille peccator et in Spiritum sanctum blasphemus per totum hoc praesens saeculum a peccato detineatur, et post haec in futuro ab initio ad finem sit nescio quomodo tractandus), thus giving rise to the view that "even the devil will some day be saved." [Cf. alternative trans. by J. E. L. Oulton and H. Chadwick, p. 304.]

and leaves it all to man (who is notoriously stupid, unconscious, and easily led astray), then, despite all assurances to the contrary, the evil spirit must be a factor of quite incalculable potency. In this respect, anyhow, the dualism of the Gnostic systems makes sense, because they at least try to do justice to the real meaning of evil. They have also done us the supreme service of having gone very thoroughly into the question of where evil comes from. Biblical tradition leaves us very much in the dark on this point, and it is only too obvious why the old theologians were in no particular hurry to enlighten us. In a monotheistic religion everything that goes against God can only be traced back to God himself. This thought is objectionable, to say the least of it, and has therefore to be circumvented. That is the deeper reason why a highly influential personage like the devil cannot be accommodated properly in a trinitarian cosmos. It is difficult to make out in what relation he stands to the Trinity. As the adversary of Christ, he would have to take up an equivalent counterposition and be, like him, a "son of God."[1] But that would lead straight back to certain Gnostic views according to which the devil, as Satanaël,[2] is God's first son, Christ being the second.[3] A further logical inference would be the abolition of the Trinity formula and its replacement by a quaternity.

The idea of a quaternity of divine principles was violently attacked by the Church Fathers when an attempt was made to add a fourth—God's "essence"—to the Three Persons of the Trinity. This resistance to the quaternity is very odd, considering that the central Christian symbol, the Cross, is unmistakably a quaternity. The Cross, however, symbolizes God's suffering in his immediate encounter with the world.[4] The "prince of this world," the devil (John 12:31, 14:30), vanquishes the God-man at this point, although by so doing he is presumably preparing his own defeat and digging his own grave. According to an old view, Christ is the "bait on the hook" (the Cross), with which he catches "Leviathan" (the

[1] In her "Die Gestalt des Satans im Alten Testament" (*Symbolik des Geistes*, pp. 153ff.), Riwkah Schärf shows that Satan is in fact one of God's sons, at any rate in the Old Testament sense.

[2] The suffix *-el* means god, so Satanaël = Satan-God.

[3] Michael Psellus, "De Daemonibus," 1497, fol. NV^v, ed. M. Ficino. Cf. also Epiphanius, *Panarium*, Haer. XXX, in Migne, *P.G.*, vol. 41, cols. 406ff.

[4] Cf. Przywara's meditations on the Cross and its relation to God in *Deus Semper Major*, I. Also the early Christian interpretation of the Cross in the Acts of John, trans. by James, pp. 228ff.

devil).[5] It is therefore significant that the Cross, set up midway between heaven and hell as a symbol of Christ's struggle with the devil, corresponds to the quaternity.

From **Letters,** vol. 2, pp. 58–61

To Father Victor White

[ORIGINAL IN ENGLISH]

Dear Victor, 30 April 1952

The *privatio boni* seems to be a puzzle.[1] A few days ago I had an interesting interview with a Jesuit father from Munich (Lotz is his name). He is professor of dogmatics (?) or Christian philosophy. He was just in the middle of *Antwort auf Hiob* and under the immediate impact of my argument against the *privatio.* He admitted that it is a puzzle, but that the modern interpretation would explain "Evil" as a "disintegration" or a "decomposition" of "Good." If you hyposta-tize—as the Church does—the concept or idea of Good and give to it metaphysical substance (i.e., *bonum* = *esse* or having *esse*), then "decomposition" would be indeed a very suitable formula, also satisfactory from the psychological standpoint, as Good is always an effort and a composite achievement while Evil is easily sliding down or falling asunder. But if you take your simile of the good egg,[2] it would become a bad egg by decomposition. A bad egg is not characterized by a mere decrease of goodness however, since it produces qualities of its own that did not belong to the good egg. It develops among other things H_2S, which is a particularly unpleas-ant substance in its own right. It derives very definitely from the highly complex albumen of the good egg and thus forms a most obvious evidence for the thesis: Evil derives from Good.

Thus the formula of "decomposition" is rather satisfactory in so far as it acknowledges that Evil is as substantial as Good, because H_2S is as tangibly real as the albumen. In this interpretation Evil is

<hr/>

[5] See *Psychology and Alchemy,* fig. 28.

[1] Cf. White, 9 Apr. 52, to which he sent a short reply on 20 Apr., complaining of "the deadlock of assertion and counter-assertion" in spite of good will. "We move in different circles, and our minds have been formed in different philosophical climates."

[2] In his letter of 20 Apr. W. wrote: "The validity of any particular judgment of value is surely quite another question from the meaning of the terms [good and evil] employed. There is surely nothing religious or archetypal in my motivation, nor anything illogical or transcendental, when I call an egg 'bad' because it *lacks* what I think an egg ought to have."

far from being a μὴ ὄν. Pater Lotz therefore had my applause. But what about the *privatio boni*? Good, by definition, must be good throughout, even in its smallest particles. You cannot say that a small good is bad. If then a good thing disintegrates into minute fragments, each of them remains good and therefore eatable like a loaf of bread divided into small particles. But when the bread rots, it oxidizes and changes its original substance. There are no more nourishing carbohydrates, but acids, i.e., from a good substance has come a bad thing. The "decomposition" theory would lead to the ultimate conclusion that the Summum Bonum can disintegrate and produce H_2S, the characteristic smell of Hell. Good then would be corruptible, i.e., it would possess an inherent possibility of decay. This possibility of corruption means nothing less than a tendency inherent in the Good to decay and to change into Evil. That obviously confirms my heretical views. But I don't even go as far as Pater Lotz: I am quite satisfied with non-hypostatizing Good and Evil. I consider them not as substances but as a merely psychological judgment since I have no means of establishing them as metaphysical substances. I don't deny the possibility of a belief that they are substances and that Good prevails against Evil. I even take into consideration that there is a large consensus in that respect, for which there must be important reasons (as I have pointed out in *Aion*).[3] But if you try to make something logical or rationalistic out of that belief, you get into a remarkable mess, as the argument with Pater Lotz clearly shows.

You know, I am not only empirical but also practical. In practice you say nothing when you hold that in an evil deed is a small Good: there is big Evil and a little bit of Good. In practice you just can't deny the ὀυσία of Evil. On the metaphysical plane you are free to declare that what we call "substantially evil" is in metaphysical reality a small Good. But such a statement does not make much sense to me. You call God the Lord over Evil, but if the latter is μὴ ὄν, He is Lord over nothing, not even over the Good, because He is it Himself as the Summum Bonum that has created only good things which have however a marked tendency to go wrong. Nor does evil or corruption derive from man, since the serpent is prior to him, so πόθεν τὸ κακόν???[4]

The necessary answer is: Metaphysically there is no evil at all; it

---

[3] Cf. pars. 81ff., 100f.
[4] = whence evil?

is only in man's world and it stems from man. This statement however contradicts the fact that paradise was not made by man. He came last into it, nor did he make the serpent. If even God's most beautiful angel, Lucifer, has such a desire to get corrupt, his nature must show a considerable defect of moral qualities—like Yahweh, who insists jealously on morality and is himself unjust. No wonder that His creation has a yellow streak.

Does the doctrine of the Church admit Yahweh's moral defects? If so, Lucifer merely portrays his creator; if not, what about the 89th Psalm,[5] etc.? *Yahweh's immoral behaviour rests on biblical facts. A morally dubious creator cannot be expected to produce a perfectly good world,* not even perfectly good angels.

I know theologians always say: one should not overlook the Lord's greatness, majesty, and kindness and one shouldn't ask questions anyhow. I don't overlook God's fearful greatness, but I should consider myself a coward and immoral if I allowed myself to be deterred from asking questions.

On the practical level the *privatio boni* doctrine is morally dangerous, because it belittles and irrealizes Evil and thereby weakens the Good, because it deprives it of its necessary opposite: there is no white without black, no right without left, no above without below, no warm without cold, no truth without error, no light without darkness, etc. If Evil is an illusion, Good is necessarily illusory too. That is the reason why I hold that the *privatio boni* is illogical, irrational and even a nonsense. The moral opposites are an epistemological necessity and, when hypostatized, they produce an amoral Yahweh and a Lucifer and a Serpent and sinful Man and a suffering Creation.

I hope we can continue worrying this bone in the summer!

Cordially yours, C. G.

P.S. Unfortunately I have no copy of the letter to the Prot. theologian.[6] But I will send you an offprint of my answer to Buber,[7] who has called me a Gnostic. He does not understand psychic reality.

---

[5] In *Aion*, par. 169, Jung mentions a story told by Abraham ben Meier ibn Ezra (Jewish scholar and poet, 1092–1167) of "a great sage who was reputed to be unable to read the 89th Psalm because it saddened him too much." The story occurs in Ibn Ezra's Commentary on the Psalms.—Psalm 89 deals with Yahweh's lack of loyalty toward King David; to Jung this was a parallel to the tragedy of Job.

[6] Cf. White, Spring 52, n. 7.

[7] Cf. Neumann, 28 Feb. 52, n. 9.

Chapter 5. Gnosticism as Dealing with the Feminine

The ideal state in Jungian psychology involves the acceptance of sexual as well as moral opposites. Realization of the self requires the acceptance of not only one's dominant gender, which is represented by the shadow archetype, but also its opposite, which is represented by the anima archetype in the male and the animus archetype in the female. As the embodiment of perfection, the Gnostic godhead is appropriately androgynous. Likewise the division of human beings into distinct genders appropriately symbolizes their fall.

The Gnostic rejection of the body is not inconsistent with the espousal of androgyny, for androgyny in Gnosticism is an immaterial rather than a material state. Similarly, for Jung androgyny, like sexuality in general, is a psychological state. Indeed, Jung continually berates Freud not merely for overemphasizing sexuality but also for viewing it entirely physically. Still, Jung does not reduce—or elevate—sexuality to sheer immateriality. If he did, he would be eliminating the prime difference between his psychological ideal and its Gnostic counterpart: his acceptance of the body as part of the self.

From "**Rex and Regina**," CW 14, par. 526

In this connection it should not be forgotten that in antiquity certain influences, evidently deriving from the Gnostic doctrine of the hermaphroditic Primordial Man,[1] penetrated into Christianity and there gave rise to the view that Adam had been created an androgyne.[2] And since Adam was the prototype of Christ, and Eve,

---

[1] Cf. the androgynous statue in the form of a cross, in Bardesanes.

[2] As late as Boehme, Adam was described as a "male virgin." Cf. "Three Principles of the Divine Essence" (*Works*, I), X, 18, p. 68, and XVII, 82, p. 159. Such views had been attacked by Augustine.

sprung from his side, that of the Church, it is understandable that a picture of Christ should develop showing distinctly feminine features.[3] In religious art the Christ-image has retained this character to the present day.[4] Its veiled androgyny reflects the hermaphroditism of the lapis, which in this respect has more affinity with the view of the Gnostics.

From "**The Psychology of the Child Archetype**," CW 9 i, pars. 292–95

THE HERMAPHRODITISM OF THE CHILD

It is a remarkable fact that perhaps the majority of cosmogonic gods are of a bisexual nature. The hermaphrodite means nothing less than a union of the strongest and most striking opposites. In the first place this union refers back to a primitive state of mind, a twilight where differences and contrasts were either barely separated or completely merged. With increasing clarity of consciousness, however, the opposites draw more and more distinctly and irreconcilably apart. If, therefore, the hermaphrodite were only a product of primitive non-differentiation, we would have to expect that it would soon be eliminated with increasing civilization. This is by no means the case; on the contrary, man's imagination has been preoccupied with this idea over and over again on the high and even the highest levels of culture, as we can see from the late Greek and syncretic philosophy of Gnosticism. The hermaphroditic *rebis* has an important part to play in the natural philosophy of the Middle Ages. And in our own day we hear of Christ's androgyny in Catholic mysticism.[1]

We can no longer be dealing, then, with the continued existence of a primitive phantasm, or with an original contamination of opposites. Rather, as we can see from medieval writings,[2] the primordial idea has become a *symbol of the creative union of opposites*, a "uniting symbol" in the literal sense. In its functional significance

---

[3] Cf. the picture of his baptism in the Reichenau Codex Lat. Mon. 4453, reproduced in Goldschmidt, *German Illumination*, II, 27.

[4] How different is the picture of the "Holy Shroud" in Turin! Cf. Vignon, *The Shroud of Christ*.

[1] Koepgen, *Die Gnosis des Christentums*, pp. 315ff.

[2] For the *lapis* as mediator and medium, cf. *Tractatus aureus*, in Manget, *Bibliotheca chemica curiosa*, I, p. 408b, and *Artis auriferae* (1572), p. 641.

the symbol no longer points back, but forward to a goal not yet reached. Notwithstanding its monstrosity, the hermaphrodite has gradually turned into a subduer of conflicts and a bringer of healing, and it acquired this meaning in relatively early phases of civilization. This vital meaning explains why the image of the hermaphrodite did not fade out in primeval times but, on the contrary, was able to assert itself with increasing profundity of symbolic content for thousands of years. The fact that an idea so utterly archaic could rise to such exalted heights of meaning not only points to the vitality of archetypal ideas, it also demonstrates the rightness of the principle that the archetype, because of its power to unite opposites, mediates between the unconscious substratum and the conscious mind. It throws a bridge between present-day consciousness, always in danger of losing its roots, and the natural, unconscious, instinctive wholeness of primeval times. Through this mediation the uniqueness, peculiarity, and onesidedness of our present individual consciousness are linked up again with its natural, racial roots. Progress and development are ideals not lightly to be rejected, but they lose all meaning if man only arrives at his new state as a fragment of himself, having left his essential hinterland behind him in the shadow of the unconscious, in a state of primitivity or, indeed, barbarism. The conscious mind, split off from its origins, incapable of realizing the meaning of the new state, then relapses all too easily into a situation far worse than the one from which the innovation was intended to free it—*exempla sunt odiosa!* It was Friedrich Schiller who first had an inkling of this problem; but neither his contemporaries nor his successors were capable of drawing any conclusions. Instead, people incline more than ever to educate *children* and nothing more. I therefore suspect that the *furor paedogogicus* is a god-sent method of by-passing the central problem touched on by Schiller, namely the *education of the educator*. Children are educated by what the grown-up *is* and not by what he *says*. The popular faith in words is a veritable disease of the mind, for a superstition of this sort always leads farther and farther away from man's foundations and seduces people into a disastrous identification of the personality with whatever slogan may be in vogue. Meanwhile everything that has been overcome and left behind by so-called "progress" sinks deeper and deeper into the unconscious, from which there re-emerges in the end the primitive condition of *identity with the mass*. Instead of the expected progress, this condition now becomes reality.

As civilization develops, the bisexual primordial being turns into a symbol of the unity of personality, a symbol of the self, where the war of opposites finds peace. In this way the primordial being becomes the distant goal of man's self-development, having been from the very beginning a projection of his unconscious wholeness. Wholeness consists in the union of the conscious and the unconscious personality. Just as every individual derives from masculine and feminine genes, and the sex is determined by the predominance of the corresponding genes, so in the psyche it is only the conscious mind, in a man, that has the masculine sign, while the unconscious is by nature feminine. The reverse is true in the case of a woman. All I have done in my anima theory is to rediscover and reformulate this fact.[3] It had long been known.

The idea of the *coniunctio* of male and female, which became almost a technical term in Hermetic philosophy, appears in Gnosticism as the *mysterium iniquitatis*, probably not uninfluenced by the Old Testament "divine marriage" as performed, for instance, by Hosea.[4] Such things are hinted at not only by certain traditional customs,[5] but by the quotation from the Gospel according to the Egyptians in the second epistle of Clement: "When the two shall be one, the outside as the inside, and the male with the female neither male nor female."[6] Clement of Alexandria introduces this logion with the words: "When ye have trampled on the garment of shame (with thy feet) . . . ,"[7] which probably refers to the body; for Clement as well as Cassian (from whom the quotation was taken over), and the pseudo-Clement, too, interpreted the words in a spiritual sense, in contrast to the Gnostics, who would seem to have taken the *coniunctio* all too literally. They took care, however, through the practice of abortion and other restrictions, that the biological meaning of their acts did not swamp the religious significance of the rite. While, in Church mysticism, the primordial image of the *hieros gamos* was sublimated on a lofty plane and only

---

[3] *Psychological Types*, Def. 48; and "Relations between the Ego and the Unconscious," pars. 296ff.

[4] Hosea 1:2ff.

[5] Cf. Fendt, *Gnostische Mysterien*.

[6] James, *The Apocryphal New Testament*, p. 11.

[7] Clement, *Stromata*, III, 13, 92, 2.

occasionally—as for instance with Mechthild of Magdeburg[8]—approached the physical sphere in emotional intensity, for the rest of the world it remained very much alive and continued to be the object of especial psychic preoccupation. In this respect the symbolical drawings of Opicinus de Canistris[9] afford us an interesting glimpse of the way in which this primordial image was instrumental in uniting opposites, even in a pathological state. On the other hand, in the Hermetic philosophy that throve in the Middle Ages the *coniunctio* was performed wholly in the physical realm in the admittedly abstract theory of the *coniugium solis et lunae,* which despite this drawback gave the creative imagination much occasion for anthropomorphic flights.

[8] *The Flowing Light of the Godhead.*
[9] Salomon, *Opicinus de Canistris.*

Chapter 6. Gnosticism and Mainstream Christianity

While Jung certainly recognizes the existence of non-Christian varieties of Gnosticism, he regularly appeals to Christian Gnosticism as a standard by which to measure mainstream Christianity. Where, according to Jung, Gnosticism deals fully with both evil and the feminine, mainstream Christianity barely tends to either. While both varieties of Christianity tout the symbol of the Cross, only Gnosticism aspires to the state of wholeness represented by this quaternity symbol; mainstream Christianity confines itself to the partial state signified by the Trinity. In the first selection in this section Jung analyzes the psychological meaning of the Cross. In the second selection he contrasts Gnostic Christians to mainstream ones as embodiments of distinct psychological types: mainstream Christianity sacrifices thinking for sensation and feeling; Gnosticism prizes thinking over sensation and feeling. Although a mainstream Church Father, Origen is "almost a Christian Gnostic" because of his commitment to thinking over sensation and feeling—a commitment manifested most dramatically in his castration of himself.

From "**Transformation Symbolism in the Mass**," CW 11, pars. 433–40

The cross signifies order as opposed to the disorderly chaos of the formless multitude. It is, in fact, one of the prime symbols of order, as I have shown elsewhere. In the domain of psychological processes it functions as an organizing centre, and in states of psychic disorder[1] caused by an invasion of unconscious contents it appears as a mandala divided into four. No doubt this was a frequent

---

[1] Symbolized by the formless multitude.

phenomenon in early Christian times, and not only in Gnostic circles.[2] Gnostic introspection could hardly fail, therefore, to perceive the numinosity of this archetype and be duly impressed by it. For the Gnostics the cross had exactly the same function that the atman or Self has always had for the East. This realization is one of the central experiences of Gnosticism.

The definition of the cross or centre as διορισμός, the "boundary" of all things, is exceedingly original, for it suggests that the limits of the universe are not to be found in a nonexistent periphery but in its centre. There alone lies the possibility of transcending this world. All instability culminates in that which is unchanging and quiescent, and in the self all disharmonies are resolved in the "harmony of wisdom."

As the centre symbolizes the idea of totality and finality, it is quite appropriate that the text should suddenly start speaking of the dichotomy of the universe, polarized into right and left, brightness and darkness, heaven and the "nether root," the *omnium genetrix*. This is a clear reminder that everything is contained in the centre and that, as a result, the Lord (i.e., the cross) unites and composes all things and is therefore "nirdvanda," free from the opposites, in conformity with Eastern ideas and also with the psychology of this archetypal symbol. The Gnostic Christ-figure and the cross are counterparts of the typical mandalas spontaneously produced by the unconscious. They are *natural symbols* and they differ fundamentally from the dogmatic figure of Christ, in whom all trace of darkness is expressly lacking.

In this connection mention should be made of Peter's valedictory words, which he spoke during his martyrdom (he was crucified upside down, at his own request):

O name of the cross, hidden mystery! O grace ineffable that is pronounced in the name of the cross! O nature of man, that cannot be separated from God! O love unspeakable and indivisible, that cannot be shown forth by unclean lips! I grasp thee now, I that am at the end of my earthly course. I will declare thee as thou art, I will not keep silent the mystery of the cross which was once shut and hidden from my soul. You that hope in Christ, let not the cross be for you that which appears; for it is another

2 Cf. "speaking with tongues" and glossolalia.

thing, and different from that which appears, this suffering which is in accordance with Christ's. And now above all, because you that can hear are able to hear it of me, who am at the last and farewell hour of my life, hearken: separate your souls from everything that is of the senses, from everything that appears to be but in truth is not. Lock your eyes, close your ears, shun those happenings which are seen! Then you shall perceive that which was done to Christ, and the whole mystery of your salvation. . . .

Learn the mystery of all nature and the beginning of all things, as it was. For the first man, of whose race I bear the likeness, fell head downwards, and showed forth a manner of birth such as had not existed till then, for it was dead, having no motion. And being pulled downwards, and having also cast his origin upon the earth, he established the whole disposition of things; for, being hanged up in the manner appointed, he showed forth the things of the right as those of the left, and the things of the left as those of the right, and changed about all the marks of their nature, so that things that were not fair were perceived to be fair, and those that were in truth evil were perceived to be good. Wherefore the Lord says in a mystery: "Except ye make the things of the right as those of the left, and those of the left as those of the right, and those that are above as those below, and those that are behind as those that are before, ye shall not have knowledge of the kingdom."

This understanding have I brought you, and the figure in which you now see me hanging is the representation of that first man who came to birth.

In this passage, too, the symbolical interpretation of the cross is coupled with the problem of opposites, first in the unusual idea that the creation of the first man caused everything to be turned upside down, and then in the attempt to unite the opposites by identifying them with one another. A further point of significance is that Peter, crucified head downwards, is identical not only with the first created man, but with the cross:

For what else is Christ but the word, the sound of God? So the word is this upright beam on which I am crucified; and the sound is the beam which crosses it, the nature of man; but the nail which holds the centre of the crossbeam to the upright is man's conversion and repentance (μετάνοια).[3]

In the light of these passages it can hardly be said that the author of the Acts of John—presumably a Gnostic—has drawn the necessary conclusions from his premises or that their full implications have become clear to him. On the contrary, one gets the impression that the light has swallowed up everything dark. Just as the enlightening vision appears high above the actual scene of crucifixion, so, for John, the enlightened one stands high above the formless multitude. The text says: "Therefore care not for the many, and despise those that are outside the mystery!"[4] This overweening attitude arises from an inflation caused by the fact that the enlightened John has identified with his own light and confused his ego with the self. Therefore he feels superior to the darkness in him. He forgets that light only has a meaning when it illuminates something dark and that his enlightenment is no good to him unless it helps him to recognize his own darkness. If the powers of the left are as real as those of the right, then their union can only produce a third thing that shares the nature of both. Opposites unite in a new energy potential: the "third" that arises out of their union is a figure "free from the opposites," beyond all moral categories. This conclusion would have been too advanced for the Gnostics. Recognizing the danger of Gnostic irrealism, the Church, more practical in these matters, has always insisted on the concretism of the historical events despite the fact that the original New Testament texts predict the ultimate deification of man in a manner strangely reminiscent of the words of the serpent in the Garden of Eden: "Ye shall be as gods."[5] Nevertheless, there was some justification for postponing the elevation of man's status until after death, as this avoided the danger of Gnostic inflation.[6]

Had the Gnostic not identified with the self, he would have been bound to see how much darkness was in him—a realization that comes more naturally to modern man but causes him no less diffi-

[3] Based on James, pp. 334f.

[4] Ibid., p. 255.

[5] Genesis 3:5.

[6] The possibility of inflation was brought very close indeed by Christ's words: "Ye are gods" (John 10:34).

culties. Indeed, he is far more likely to assume that he himself is wholly of the devil than to believe that God could ever indulge in paradoxical statements. For all the ill consequences of his fatal inflation, the Gnostic did, however, gain an insight into religion, or into the psychology of religion, from which we can still learn a thing or two today. He looked deep into the background of Christianity and hence into its future developments. This he could do because his intimate connection with pagan Gnosis made him an "assimilator" that helped to integrate the Christian message into the spirit of the times.

The extraordinary number of synonyms piled on top of one another in an attempt to define the cross have their analogy in the Naassene and Peratic symbols of Hippolytus, all pointing to this one centre. It is the $\grave{\varepsilon}\nu$ $\tau\grave{o}$ $\pi\tilde{\alpha}\nu$ of alchemy, which is on the one hand the heart and governing principle of the macrocosm, and on the other hand its reflection in a point, in a microcosm such as man has always been thought to be. He is of the same essence as the universe, and his own mid-point is its centre. This inner experience, shared by Gnostics, alchemists, and mystics alike, has to do with the nature of the unconscious—one could even say that it *is* the experience of the unconscious; for the unconscious, though its objective existence and its influence on consciousness cannot be doubted, is in itself undifferentiable and therefore unknowable. Hypothetical germs of differentiation may be conjectured to exist in it, but their existence cannot be proved, because everything appears to be in a state of mutual contamination. The unconscious gives the impression of multiplicity and unity at once. However overwhelmed we may be by the vast quantity of things differentiated in space and time, we know from the world of the senses that the validity of its laws extends to immense distances. We therefore believe that it is one and the same universe throughout, in its smallest part as in its greatest. On the other hand the intellect always tries to discern differences, because it cannot discriminate without them. Consequently the unity of the cosmos remains, for it, a somewhat nebulous postulate which it doesn't rightly know what to do with. But as soon as introspection starts penetrating into the psychic background it comes up against the unconscious, which, unlike consciousness, shows only the barest traces of any definite contents, surprising the investigator at every turn with a confusing medley of relationships, parallels, contaminations, and identifications. Although he is forced, for epistemological reasons, to postulate an indefinite number of distinct and separate archetypes, yet he is constantly overcome by doubt as to how far they are really distinguishable from one another. They overlap to such a degree and have such a capacity for combination that all attempts to isolate them conceptually must appear hopeless. In addition the unconscious, in sharpest contrast to consciousness and its contents, has a tendency to personify itself in a uniform way, just as if it possessed only one shape or one voice. Because of this peculiarity, the unconscious conveys an experience of unity, to which are due all those qualities enumerated by the Gnostics and alchemists, and a lot more besides.

From "The Problem of Types in the History of Classical and Medieval Thought," CW 6, pars. 8–30

PSYCHOLOGY IN THE CLASSICAL AGE: THE GNOSTICS, TERTULLIAN, ORIGEN

So long as the historical world has existed there has always been psychology, but an objective psychology is only of recent growth. We could say of the science of former times that in proportion to the lack of objective psychology there is an increase in the rate of subjectivity. Hence, though the works of the ancients are full of psychology, only little of it can be described as objective psychology. This may be due in no small measure to the peculiar character of human relationships in classical and medieval times. The ancients had, so to speak, an almost entirely biological valuation of their fellow-men; this is everywhere apparent in their habits of life and in the legislation of antiquity. The medieval man, in so far as his value judgments found any expression at all, had on the contrary a metaphysical valuation of his fellows, and this had its source in the idea of the imperishable value of the human soul. This metaphysical valuation, which may be regarded as compensatory to the standpoint of antiquity, is just as unfavourable as the biological one so far as a *personal* valuation is concerned, which alone can form the basis of an objective psychology.

Although not a few people think that a psychology can be written *ex cathedra*, nowadays most of us are convinced that an objective psychology must be founded above all on observation and experience. This foundation would be ideal if only it were possible. The ideal and aim of science do not consist in giving the most exact possible description of the facts—science cannot compete as a recording instrument with the camera and the gramophone—but in establishing certain laws, which are merely abbreviated expressions for many diverse processes that are yet conceived to be somehow correlated. This aim goes beyond the purely empirical by means of the *concept*, which, though it may have general and proved validity, will always be a product of the subjective psychological constellation of the investigator. In the making of scientific theories and concepts many personal and accidental factors are involved. There is also a personal equation that is psychological and not merely psychophysical. We see colours but not wave-lengths. This well-known fact must nowhere be taken to heart more seriously than in psychology. The effect of the personal equation begins already in the act of observation. *One sees what one can best see oneself.* Thus, first and foremost, one sees the mote in one's brother's eye. No doubt the mote is there, but the beam sits in one's own eye—and may considerably hamper the act of seeing. I mistrust the principle of "pure observation" in so-called objective psychology unless one confines oneself to the eye-pieces of chronoscopes and tachistoscopes and suchlike "psychological" apparatus. With such methods one also guards against too embarrassing a yield of empirical psychological facts.

But the personal equation asserts itself even more in the presentation and communication of one's own observations, to say nothing of the interpretation and abstract exposition of the empirical material. Nowhere is the basic requirement so indispensable as in psychology that the observer should be adequate to his object, in the sense of being able to see not only subjectively but also objectively. The demand that he should see *only* objectively is quite out of the question, for it is impossible. We must be satisfied if he does not see *too* subjectively. That the subjective observation and interpretation accord with the objective facts proves the truth of the interpretation only in so far as the latter makes no pretence to be generally valid, but valid only for that area of the object which is being considered. To this extent it is just the beam in one's own eye that enables one to detect the mote in one's brother's eye. The beam in one's own eye, as we have said, does not prove that one's brother has no mote in his. But the impairment of one's own vision might easily give rise to a general theory that all motes are beams.

The recognition and taking to heart of the subjective determination of knowledge in general, and of psychological knowledge in particular, are basic conditions for the scientific and impartial evaluation of a psyche different from that of the observing subject. These conditions are fulfilled only when the observer is sufficiently informed about the nature and scope of his own personality. He can, however, be sufficiently informed only when he has in large measure freed himself from the levelling influence of collective opinions and thereby arrived at a clear conception of his own individuality.

The further we go back into history, the more we see personality disappearing beneath the wrappings of collectivity. And if we go right back to primitive psychology, we find absolutely no trace of the concept of an individual. Instead of individuality we find only collective relationship or what Lévy-Bruhl calls *participation mystique*. The collective attitude hinders the recognition and evaluation of a psychology different from the subject's, because the mind that is collectively oriented is quite incapable of thinking and feeling in any other way than by projection. What we understand by the concept "individual" is a relatively recent acquisition in the history of the human mind and human culture. It is no wonder, therefore, that the earlier all-powerful collective attitude prevented almost completely an objective psychological evaluation of individual psychological processes. It was owing to this very lack of psychological thinking that knowledge became "psychologized," i.e., filled with projected psychology. We find striking examples of this in man's first attempts at a philosophical explanation of the cosmos. The development of individuality, with the consequent psychological differentiation of man, goes hand in hand with the de-psychologizing work of objective science.

These reflections may explain why objective psychology has such a meagre source in the material handed down to us from antiquity. The differentiation of the four temperaments, which we took over from the ancients, hardly rates as a psychological typology since the temperaments are scarcely more than psychophysical colourings. But this lack of information does not mean that we can find no trace in classical literature of the effects of the psychological pairs of opposites we are discussing.

Gnostic philosophy established three types, corresponding perhaps to three of the basic psychological functions: thinking, feeling, and sensation. The *pneumatikoi* could be correlated with thinking, the *psychikoi* with feeling, and the *hylikoi* with sensation. The inferior rating of the *psychikoi* was in accord with the spirit of Gnosticism, which, unlike Christianity, insisted on the value of knowledge. The Christian principles of love and faith kept knowledge at a distance. In the Christian sphere the *pneumatikoi* would accordingly get the lower rating, since they were distinguished merely by the possession of Gnosis, i.e., knowledge.

Type differences should also be borne in mind when we consider the long and perilous struggle which the Church from its earliest beginnings waged against Gnosticism. Owing to the predominantly practical trend of early Christianity the intellectual hardly came into his own, except when he followed his fighting instincts by indulging in polemical apologetics. The rule of faith was too strict and allowed no freedom of movement. Moreover, it was poor in positive intellectual content. It boasted of few ideas, and though these were of immense practical value they were a definite obstacle to thought. The intellectual was much worse hit by the *sacrificium intellectus* than the feeling type. It is therefore understandable that the vastly superior intellectual content of Gnosis, which in the light of our present mental development has not lost but has considerably gained in value, must have made the greatest possible appeal to the intellectual within the Church. For him it held out in very truth all the temptations of this world. Docetism in particular caused grave trouble to the Church with its contention that Christ possessed only an apparent body and that his whole earthly existence and passion had been merely a semblance. In this contention the purely intellectual element predominates at the expense of human feeling.

Perhaps the struggle with Gnosis is most vividly presented to us in two figures who were of the utmost significance not only as Church Fathers but as personalities. These are Tertullian and Origen, who lived towards the end of the second century. Schultz says of them:

> One organism is able to take in nourishment and assimilate it almost completely into its own nature; another with equal persistence eliminates it with every sign of passionate resistance.

Thus Origen on one side, and Tertullian on the other, reacted in diametrically opposite ways to Gnosis. Their reaction is not only characteristic of the two personalities and their philosophical outlook; it is of fundamental significance with regard to the position of Gnosis in the spiritual life and religious currents of that age.[1]

Tertullian was born in Carthage somewhere about A.D. 160. He was a pagan, and he abandoned himself to the lascivious life of his city until about his thirty-fifth year, when he became a Christian. He was the author of numerous writings wherein his character, which is our especial interest, is unmistakably displayed. Most clearly of all we see his unparalleled noble-hearted zeal, his fire, his passionate temperament, and the profundity of his religious understanding. He was a fanatic, brilliantly one-sided in his defence of a recognized truth, possessed of a matchless fighting spirit, a merciless opponent who saw victory only in the total annihilation of his adversary, his language a flashing blade wielded with ferocious mastery. He was the creator of the Church Latin that lasted for more than a thousand years. It was he who coined the terminology of the early Church. "Once he had seized upon a point of view, he had to follow it through to its ultimate conclusion as though lashed by the legions of hell, even when right had long since ceased to be on his side and all reasonable order lay in shreds before him."[2] His impassioned thinking was so inexorable that again and again he alienated himself from the very thing for which he had given his heart's blood. Accordingly his ethical code was bitterly severe. Martyrdom he commanded to be sought and not shunned; he permitted no second marriage, and required the permanent veiling of persons of the female sex. Gnosis, which in reality is a passion for thinking and knowing, he attacked with unrelenting fanaticism, together with philosophy and science which differed from it so little. To him is ascribed the sublime confession: *Credo quia absurdum est* (I believe because it is absurd). This does not altogether accord with historical fact, for he merely said: "And the Son of God

---

[1] *Dokumente der Gnosis*, p. xxix.
[2] Ibid., p. xxv.

died, which is immediately credible because it is absurd. And buried he rose again, which is certain because it is impossible."[3]

Thanks to the acuteness of his mind, he saw through the poverty of philosophical and Gnostic knowledge, and contemptuously rejected it. He invoked against it the testimony of his own inner world, his own inner realities, which were one with his faith. In shaping and developing these realities he became the creator of those abstract conceptions which still underlie the Catholic system of today. The irrational inner reality had for him an essentially dynamic nature; it was his principle, his foundation in face of the world and of all collectively valid and rational science and philosophy. I quote his own words:

I summon a new witness, or rather a witness more known than any written monument, more debated than any system of life, more published abroad than any promulgation, greater than the whole of man, yea that which constitutes the whole of man. Approach then, O my soul, whether you be something divine and eternal, as many philosophers believe—the less then will you lie—or not wholly divine, because mortal, as Epicurus alone contends—the less then ought you to lie—whether you come from heaven or are born of earth, whether compounded of numbers or of atoms, whether you have your beginning with the body or are later joined to it; what matter indeed whence you come and how you make man to be what he is, a reasonable being, capable of perception and of knowledge. But I summon you not, O soul, as proclaiming wisdom, trained in the schools, conversant with libraries, fed and nourished in the academies and pillared halls of Athens. No, I would speak with you, O soul, as wondrous simple and unlearned, awkward and inexperienced, such as you are for those who possess nothing else but you, even as you come from the alleys, from the street-corners, and from the workshops. It is just your unknowingness that I need.[4]

The self-mutilation performed by Tertullian in the *sacrificium intellectus* led him to an unqualified recognition of the irrational

---

[3] "Et mortuus est dei filius, prorsus credibile est, quia ineptum est. Et sepultus resurrexit; certum est, quia impossibile est" (*De carne Christi*, 5). Cf. *Treatise on the Incarnation*, p. 19.
[4] *De Testimonio animae*, 1. Cf. *The Writings of Tertullian*, I, p. 132.

inner reality, the true rock of his faith. The necessity of the religious process which he sensed in himself he crystallized in the incomparable formula *anima naturaliter christiana* (the soul is by nature Christian). With the *sacrificium intellectus* philosophy and science, and hence also Gnosis, fell to the ground. In the further course of his life the qualities I have described became exacerbated. When the Church was driven to compromise more and more with the masses, he revolted against it and became a follower of the Phrygian prophet Montanus, an ecstatic, who stood for the principle of absolute denial of the world and complete spiritualization. In violent pamphlets he now began to assail the policy of Pope Calixtus I, and this together with his Montanism put him more or less outside the pale of the Church. According to a report of Augustine, he even quarrelled with Montanism later and founded a sect of his own.

Tertullian is a classic example of introverted thinking. His very considerable and keenly developed intellect was flanked by an unmistakable sensuality. The psychological process of development which we call specifically Christian led him to the sacrifice, the amputation, of the most valuable function—a mythical idea that is also found in the great and exemplary symbol of the sacrifice of the Son of God. His most valuable organ was the intellect and the clarity of knowledge it made possible. Through the *sacrificium intellectus* the way of purely intellectual development was closed to him; it forced him to recognize the irrational dynamism of his soul as the foundation of his being. The intellectuality of Gnosis, the specifically rational stamp it gave to the dynamic phenomena of the soul, must have been odious to him, for that was just the way he had to forsake in order to acknowledge the principle of feeling.

In Origen we may recognize the absolute opposite of Tertullian. He was born in Alexandria about A.D. 185. His father was a Christian martyr. He himself grew up in that quite unique mental atmosphere where the ideas of East and West mingled. With an intense yearning for knowledge he eagerly absorbed all that was worth knowing, and accepted everything, whether Christian, Jewish, Hellenistic, or Egyptian, that the teeming intellectual world of Alexandria offered him. The pagan philosopher Porphyry, a pupil of Plotinus, said of him: "His outward life was that of a Christian and against the law; but in his opinions about material things and the Deity he thought like a Greek, and introduced Greek ideas into foreign fables."[5]

His self-castration had taken place sometime before A.D. 211; his inner motives for this may be guessed, but historically they are not known to us. Personally he was of great influence, and had a winning speech. He was constantly surrounded by pupils and a whole host of amanuenses who gathered up the precious words that fell from the revered master's lips. As an author he was extraordinarily prolific and he developed into a great teacher. In Antioch he even delivered lectures on theology to the Emperor's mother Mammaea. In Caesarea he was the head of a school. His teaching activities were frequently interrupted by his extensive journeyings. He possessed an extraordinary erudition and had an astounding capacity for careful investigation. He hunted up old biblical manuscripts and earned special merit for his textual criticism. "He was a great scholar, indeed the only true scholar the early Church possessed," says Harnack. In complete contrast to Tertullian, Origen did not cut himself off from the influence of Gnosticism; on the contrary, he even channelled it, in attenuated form, into the bosom of the Church, or such at least was his aim. Indeed, judging by his thought and fundamental views, he was himself almost a Christian Gnostic. His position in regard to *faith* and *knowledge* is described by Harnack in the following psychologically significant words:

> The Bible is equally needful to both: the believers receive from it the facts and commandments they need, while the Gnostics decipher thoughts in it and gather from it the powers which guide them to the contemplation and love of God—whereby all material things, through spiritual interpretation (allegorical exegesis, hermeneutics), seem to be melted into a cosmos of ideas, until at last everything is surmounted and left behind as a stepping-stone, while only this remains: the blessed and abiding relationship of the God-created creaturely soul to God (*amor et visio*).[6]

His theology as distinguished from Tertullian's was essentially philosophical; it fitted neatly into the framework of Neo-platonic

---

[5] [Cf. Harnack, *A History of Dogma*, I, p. 357; Eusebius, *The Ecclesiastical History and the Martyrs of Palestine*, I, p. 192.]

[6] [Reference cannot be traced.—EDITORS.]

philosophy. In Origen the two worlds of Greek philosophy and Gnosis on the one hand, and Christian ideas on the other, interpenetrate in a peaceful and harmonious whole. But this daring, perspicacious tolerance and fair-mindedness led Origen, too, to the fate of condemnation by the Church. Actually the final condemnation took place only posthumously, after Origen as an old man had been tortured in the persecution of the Christians under Decius and had subsequently died from the effects of the torture. Pope Anastasius I pronounced the condemnation in 399, and in 543 his heretical teachings were anathematized at a synod convoked by Justinian, which judgment was upheld by later councils.

Origen is a classic example of the extraverted type. His basic orientation was towards the object; this showed itself in his scrupulous regard for objective facts and their conditions, as well as in the formulation of that supreme principle: *amor et visio Dei.* The Christian process of development encountered in Origen a type whose ultimate foundation was the relation to the object—a relation that has always symbolically expressed itself in sexuality and accounts for the fact that there are certain theories today which reduce all the essential psychic functions to sexuality too. Castration was therefore an adequate expression of the sacrifice of the most valuable function. It is entirely characteristic that Tertullian should perform the *sacrificium intellectus,* whereas Origen was led to the *sacrificium phalli,* because the Christian process demands a complete abolition of the sensual tie to the object; in other words, it demands the sacrifice of the hitherto most valued function, the dearest possession, the strongest instinct. Considered biologically, the sacrifice serves the interests of domestication, but psychologically it opens a door for new possibilities of spiritual development through the dissolution of old ties.

Tertullian sacrificed the intellect because it bound him most strongly to worldliness. He fought against Gnosis because for him it represented a deviation into intellectuality, which at the same time involved sensuality. In keeping with this fact we find that in reality Gnosticism also was divided into two schools: one school striving after a spirituality that exceeded all bounds, the other losing itself in an ethical anarchism, an absolute libertinism that shrank from no lewdness and no depravity however atrocious and perverse. A definite distinction was made between the Encratites, who practised continence, and the Antitactae or Antinomians, who were opposed to law and order, and who in obedience to certain doctrines sinned on principle and purposely gave themselves up to unbridled debauchery. To the latter school belong the Nicolaitans, Archontics, etc., and the aptly named Borborians. How closely the seeming contraries lay side by side is shown by the example of the Archontics, for this same sect was divided into an Encratite and an Antinomian school, both of which pursued their aims logically and consistently. If anyone wants to know what are the ethical consequences of intellectualism pushed to the limit and carried out on a grand scale, let him study the history of Gnostic morals. He will then fully understand the *sacrificium intellectus*. These people were also consistent in practice and carried their crazy ideas to absurd lengths in their actual lives.

Origen, by mutilating himself, sacrificed his sensual tie to the world. For him, evidently, the specific danger was not the intellect but feeling and sensation, which bound him to the object. Through castration he freed himself from the sensuality that was coupled with Gnosticism; he could then surrender without fear to the treasures of Gnostic thought, whereas Tertullian through his sacrifice of the intellect turned away from Gnosis but also reached a depth of religious feeling that we miss in Origen. "In one way he was superior to Origen," says Schultz, "because in his deepest soul he lived every one of his words; it was not reason that carried him away, like the other, but the heart. Yet in another respect Tertullian stands far behind him, inasmuch as he, the most passionate of all thinkers, was on the verge of rejecting knowledge altogether, for his battle against Gnosis was tantamount to a complete denial of human thought."[7]

We see here how, in the Christian process, the original type has actually become reversed: Tertullian, the acute thinker, becomes the man of feeling, while Origen becomes the scholar and loses himself in intellectuality. Logically, of course, it is quite easy to put it the other way round and say that Tertullian had always been the man of feeling and Origen the intellectual. Apart from the fact that the difference of type is not thereby done away with but exists as before, the reversal does not explain how it comes that Tertullian

[7] *Dokumente der Gnosis*, p. xxvii.

saw his most dangerous enemy in the intellect, and Origen in sexuality. One could say they were both deceived, adducing as evidence the fatal outcome of both lives by way of argument. If that were the case, one would have to assume that they both sacrificed the less important thing, and that both of them made a crooked bargain with fate. That is certainly a point of view whose validity should be recognized in principle. Are there not just such slyboots among primitives who approach their fetish with a black hen under the arm, saying; "See, here is thy sacrifice, a beautiful black pig." I am, however, of the opinion that the depreciatory method of explanation, notwithstanding the unmistakable relief which the ordinary mortal feels in dragging down something great, is not under all circumstances the correct one, even though it may appear to be very "biological." From what we can personally know of these two great figures in the realm of the spirit, we must say that their whole nature was so sincere that their conversion to Christianity was neither an underhand trick nor a fraud, but had both reality and truthfulness.

We shall not be digressing if we take this opportunity to try to grasp the psychological meaning of this rupture of the natural course of instinct, which is what the Christian process of sacrifice appears to be. From what has been said it follows that conversion signifies at the same time a transition to another attitude. This also makes it clear from what source the impelling motive for conversion comes, and how far Tertullian was right in conceiving the soul as *naturaliter Christiana*. The natural course of instinct, like everything in nature, follows the line of least resistance. One man is rather more gifted here, another there; or again, adaptation to the early environment of childhood may demand relatively more reserve and reflection or relatively more empathy and participation, according to the nature of the parents and the circumstances. In this way a certain preferential attitude is built up automatically, resulting in different types. Since every man, as a relatively stable being, possesses all the basic psychological functions, it would be a psychological necessity with a view to perfect adaptation that he should also employ them in equal measure. For there must be a reason why there are different modes of psychological adaptation: evidently one alone is not enough, since the object seems to be only partially comprehended when, for example, it is something that is merely thought or merely felt. A one-sided ("typical") attitude leaves a deficiency in the adaptive performance which accumulates during the course of life, and sooner or later this will produce a disturbance of adaptation that drives the subject toward some kind of compensation. But the compensation can be obtained only by means of an amputation (sacrifice) of the hitherto one-sided attitude. This results in a temporary accumulation of energy and an overflow into channels not used consciously before though lying ready unconsciously. The adaptive deficiency, which is the *causa efficiens* of the process of conversion, is subjectively felt as a vague sense of dissatisfaction. Such an atmosphere prevailed at the turning-point of our era. A quite astonishing need of redemption came over mankind, and brought about that unparalleled efflorescence of every sort of possible and impossible cult in ancient Rome. Nor was there any lack of advocates of "living life to the full," who operated with arguments based on the science of that day instead of with biological ones. They, too, could never be done with speculations as to why mankind was in such a bad way. Only, the causalism of that epoch, as compared with our science, was considerably less restricted; they could hark back far beyond childhood to cosmogony, and numerous systems were devised proving that what had happened in the remote abyss of time was the source of insufferable consequences for mankind.

The sacrifice that Tertullian and Origen carried out was drastic—too drastic for our taste—but it was in keeping with the spirit of the age, which was thoroughly concretistic. Because of this spirit the Gnostics took their visions as absolutely real, or at least as relating directly to reality, and for Tertullian the reality of his feeling was objectively valid. The Gnostics projected their subjective inner perception of the change of attitude into a cosmogonic system and believed in the reality of its psychological figures.

In my book *Wandlungen und Symbole der Libido*[8] I left the whole question open as to the origin of the peculiar course the libido took in the Christian process of development. I spoke of a splitting of libido into two halves, each directed against the other. The explanation of this is to be found in a one-sided psychological attitude so extreme that compensations from the unconscious became an

---

[8] [1911–12; first translated as *Psychology of the Unconscious* (1916); revised edition (1952) retitled *Symbols of Transformation*.]

urgent necessity. It is precisely the Gnostic movement in the early centuries of our era that most clearly demonstrates the breakthrough of unconscious contents at the moment of compensation. Christianity itself signified the collapse and sacrifice of the cultural values of antiquity, that is, of the classical attitude. At the present time it is hardly necessary to remark that it is a matter of indifference whether we speak of today or of that age two thousand years ago.

Chapter 7. Gnosticism and Alchemy

For Jung, Gnosticism and alchemy are linked both historically and thematically. Medieval alchemy is the continuation of ancient Gnosticism: the alchemical process of extracting precious metals from base ones carries on the Gnostic process of freeing divine sparks from matter. Both processes are outwardly physical or metaphysical ones which are actually psychological ones: they signify the development of the self. Yet Jung may in fact be overlooking a conspicuous difference between the Gnostic ideal and the alchemical one: see, in my introduction, the section on "The Difference Between Gnosticism and Alchemy." Even though Jung writes as if modern Gnosticism were a resumption of its ancient counterpart, surely for him only the perpetuation of ancient Gnosticism in medieval alchemy makes modern Gnosticism possible.

From "**Background to the Psychology of Christian Alchemical Symbolism,**" CW 9 ii, par. 267

"Mater Alchimia" could serve as the name of a whole epoch. Beginning, roughly, with Christianity, it gave birth in the sixteenth and seventeenth centuries to the age of science, only to perish, unrecognized and misunderstood, and sink from sight in the stream of the centuries as an age that had been outlived. But, just as every mother was once a daughter, so too was alchemy. It owes its real beginnings to the Gnostic systems, which Hippolytus rightly regarded as philosophic, and which, with the help of Greek philosophy and the mythologies of the Near and Middle East, together with Christian dogmatics and Jewish cabalism, made extremely interesting attempts, from the modern point of view, to synthetize a unitary vision of the world in which the physical and the mystical aspects played equal parts. Had this attempt succeeded, we would not be witnessing today the curious spectacle of two parallel world-views neither of which knows, or wishes to know, anything about the other. Hippolytus was in the enviable position of being able to see Christian doctrine side by side with its pagan sisters, and similar comparisons had also been attempted by Justin Martyr. To the honour of Christian thinking it must be said that up till the time of Kepler there was no lack of praiseworthy attempts to interpret and understand Nature, in the broadest sense, on the basis of Christian dogma.

From "**Religious Ideas in Alchemy**," CW 12, par. 453

EVIDENCE FOR THE RELIGIOUS INTERPRETATION OF THE LAPIS

Raymond Lully

It is not surprising that the *lapis*-Christ parallel came to the fore among the medieval Latin authors at a comparatively early date, since alchemical symbolism is steeped in ecclesiastical allegory. Although there is no doubt that the allegories of the Church Fathers enriched the language of alchemy, it remains in my opinion exceedingly doubtful just how far the *opus alchemicum*, in its various forms, can be regarded as a transmogrification of ecclesiastical rites (baptism, Mass) and dogmas (Christ's conception, birth, passion, death, and resurrection). Undeniably, borrowings were made over and over again from the Church, but when we come to the original basic ideas of alchemy we find elements that derive from pagan, and more particularly from Gnostic, sources. The roots of Gnosticism do not lie in Christianity at all—it is far truer to say that Christianity was assimilated through Gnosticism.[1] Apart from this we have a Chinese text,[2] dating from the middle of the second century, which displays fundamental similarities with Western alchemy. Whatever the connection between China and the West may have been, there is absolutely no doubt that parallel ideas exist outside the sphere of Christianity, in places where Christian influence is simply out of the question. A. E. Waite[3] has expressed

---

[1] Cf. for example Simon Magus, who belonged to the apostolic era and already possessed a richly developed system.

[2] Wei Po-yang, "An Ancient Chinese Treatise on Alchemy."

[3] *The Secret Tradition in Alchemy.*

the opinion that the first author to identify the stone with Christ was the Paracelsist, Heinrich Khunrath (1560–1605), whose *Amphitheatrum* appeared in 1598. In the writings of the somewhat later Jakob Böhme, who frequently uses alchemical terms, the stone has already become a metaphor for Christ (fig. 192). Waite's assumption is undoubtedly erroneous, for we have much earlier testimonies to the connection between Christ and the *lapis,* the oldest that I have so far been able to discover being contained in the *Codicillus* (Ch. IX) of Raymond Lully (1235–1315). Even if many of the treatises ascribed to him were written by his Spanish and Provençal disciples, that does not alter the approximate date of his main works, to which the *Codicillus* belongs. At any rate I know of no authoritative opinion that puts this treatise later than the fourteenth century. There it is said:

> And as Jesus Christ, of the house of David, took on human nature for the deliverance and redemption of mankind, who were in the bonds of sin on account of Adam's disobedience, so likewise in our art that which has been wrongfully defiled by one thing is absolved by its opposite; cleansed, and delivered from that stain.[4]

From "**Religious Ideas in Alchemy,**" CW 12, par. 461

Zosimos discloses practically the whole of the recondite and highly peculiar theology of alchemy, by drawing a parallel between the esoteric meaning of the *opus* and the Gnostic mystery of redemption. This is only one indication that the *lapis*-Christ parallel of the scholastic alchemists had a pagan Gnostic precursor and was by no means a mere speculation of the Middle Ages.

From "**Religious Ideas in Alchemy,**" CW 12, par. 513

Once more the Gnostic vision of Nous entangled in the embrace of Physis flashes forth in the work of this latecomer to alchemy. But

---

[4] "Et ut Jesus Christus de stirpe Davidica pro liberatione et dissolutione generis humani, peccato captivati, ex transgressione Adae, naturam assumpsit humanam, sic etiam in arte nostra quod per unum nequiter maculatur, per aliud suum contrarium a turpitudine illa absolvitur, lavatur et resolvitur."—*Bibl. chem.,* I, p. 884, 2.

the philosopher who once descended like a Hercules into the darkness of Acheron to fulfil a divine *opus* has become a laboratory worker with a taste for speculation; having lost sight of the lofty goal of Hermetic mysticism, he now labours to discover a tonic potion that will "keep body and soul together," as our grandfathers used to say of a good wine. This change of direction in alchemy was due to the all-powerful influence of Paracelsus, the father of modern medicine. Orthelius is already tending towards natural science, leaving mystical experience to the Church.

From "The Spirit Mercurius," CW 13, pars. 252–53

PART II

Introductory

The interested reader will want, as I do, to find out more about this spirit—especially what our forefathers believed and said about him. I will therefore try with the aid of text citations to draw a picture of this versatile and shimmering god as he appeared to the masters of the royal art. For this purpose we must consult the abstruse literature of alchemy, which has not yet been properly understood. Naturally, in later times, the history of alchemy was mainly of interest to the chemist. The fact that it recorded the discovery of many chemical substances and drugs could not, however, reconcile him to the pitiful meagreness, so it seemed to him, of its scientific content. He was not in the position of the older authors, such as Schmieder, who could look on the possibility of goldmaking with hopeful esteem and sympathy; instead he was irritated by the futility of the recipes and the fraudulence of alchemical speculation in general. To him alchemy was bound to seem a gigantic aberration that lasted for more than two thousand years. Had he only asked himself whether the chemistry of alchemy was authentic or not, that is, whether the alchemists were really chemists or merely spoke a chemical jargon, then the texts themselves would have suggested a line of observation other than the purely chemical. The scientific equipment of the chemist does not, however, fit him to pursue this other line, since it leads straight into the history of religion. Thus it was a philologist, Reitzenstein, whom we have to thank for preliminary researches of the greatest value in this field. It was he who recognized the mythological and Gnostic ideas embedded in alchemy, thereby opening up the whole subject from an angle which promises to be most fruitful. For alchemy, as the earliest Greek and Chinese texts show, originally formed part of Gnostic philosophical speculations which also included a detailed knowledge of the techniques of the goldsmith and ironsmith, the faker of precious stones, the druggist and apothecary. In East and West alike, alchemy contains as its core the Gnostic doctrine of the Anthropos and by its very nature has the character of a peculiar doctrine of redemption. This fact necessarily escaped the chemist, although it is expressed clearly enough in the Greek and Latin texts as well as in the Chinese of about the same period.

To begin with, of course, it is almost impossible for our scientifically trained minds to feel their way back into that primitive state of *participation mystique* in which subject and object are identical. Here the findings of modern psychology stood me in very good stead. Practical experience shows us again and again that any prolonged preoccupation with an unknown object acts as an almost irresistible bait for the unconscious to project itself into the unknown nature of the object and to accept the resultant perception, and the interpretation deduced from it, as objective. This phenomenon, a daily occurrence in practical psychology and more especially in psychotherapy, is without doubt a vestige of primitivity. On the primitive level, the whole of life is governed by animistic assumptions, that is, by projections of subjective contents into objective situations. For example, Karl von den Steinen says that the Bororos think of themselves as red cockatoos, although they readily admit that they have no feathers.[1] On this level, the alchemists' assumption that a certain substance possesses secret powers, or that there is a *prima materia* somewhere which works miracles, is self-evident. This is, however, not a fact that can be understood or even thought of in chemical terms, it is a psychological phenomenon. Psychology, therefore, can make an important contribution towards elucidating the alchemists' mentality. What to the chemist seem to be the absurd fantasies of alchemy can be recognized by the

[1] Von den Steinen, *Unter den Naturvölkern Zentral-Brasiliens*, pp. 352f., 512.

psychologist without too much difficulty as psychic material con-
taminated with chemical substances. This material stems from the
collective unconscious and is therefore identical with fantasy products that can still be found today among both sick and healthy
people who have never heard of alchemy. On account of the primitive character of its projections, alchemy, so barren a field for the
chemist, is for the psychologist a veritable gold-mine of materials
which throw an exceedingly valuable light on the structure of the
unconscious.

From "**Psychology and Religion**," CW 11, pars. 158–61

It is a remarkable fact that this symbol is a natural and spontaneous occurrence and that it is always an essentially unconscious
product, as our dream shows. If we want to know what happens
when the idea of God is no longer projected as an autonomous
entity, this is the answer of the unconscious psyche. The unconscious produces the idea of a deified or divine man who is imprisoned, concealed, protected, usually depersonalized, and represented by an abstract symbol. The symbols often contain allusions
to the medieval conception of the microcosm, as was the case with
my patient's world clock, for instance. Many of the processes that
lead to the mandala, and the mandala itself, seem to be direct
confirmations of medieval speculation. It looks as if the patients
had read those old treatises on the philosophers' stone, the divine
water, the *rotundum*, the squaring of the circle, the four colours,
etc. And yet they have never been anywhere near alchemical philosophy and its abstruse symbolism.

It is difficult to evaluate such facts properly. They could be
explained as a sort of regression to archaic ways of thinking, if one's
chief consideration was their obvious and impressive parallelism
with medieval symbolism. But whenever such regressions occur,
the result is always inferior adaptation and a corresponding lack of
efficiency. This is by no means typical of the psychological development depicted here. On the contrary, neurotic and dissociated conditions improve considerably and the whole personality undergoes
a change for the better. For this reason I do not think the process in
question should be explained as regression, which would amount

to saying that it was a morbid condition. I am rather inclined to understand the apparently retrograde connections of mandala psychology[1] as the continuation of a process of spiritual development which began in the early Middle Ages, and perhaps even further back, in early Christian times. There is documentary evidence that the essential symbols of Christianity were already in existence in the first century. I am thinking of the Greek treatise entitled: "Comarius, the Archpriest, teaches Cleopatra the Divine Art."[2] The text is of Egyptian origin and bears no trace of Christian influence. There are also the mystical texts of Pseudo-Democritus and Zosimos.[3] Jewish and Christian influences are noticeable in the last-named author, though the main symbolism is Neo-platonist and is closely connected with the philosophy of the *Corpus Hermeticum*.[4]

The fact that the symbolism of the mandala can be traced back through its near relatives to pagan sources casts a peculiar light upon these apparently modern psychological phenomena. They seem to continue a Gnostic trend of thought without being supported by direct tradition. If I am right in supposing that every religion is a spontaneous expression of a certain predominant psychological condition, then Christianity was the formulation of a condition that predominated at the beginning of our era and lasted for several centuries. But a particular psychological condition which predominates for a certain length of time does not exclude the existence of other psychological conditions at other times, and these are equally capable of religious expression. Christianity had at one time to fight for its life against Gnosticism, which corresponded to another psychological condition. Gnosticism was stamped out completely and its remnants are so badly mangled that special study is needed to get any insight at all into its inner meaning. But if the historical roots of our symbols extend beyond the Middle Ages they are certainly to be found in Gnosticism. It would

---

[1] Koepgen (see above, p. 59n.), rightly speaks of the "circular thinking" of the Gnostics. This is only another term for totality or "all-round" thinking, since, symbolically, roundness is the same as wholeness.

[2] Berthelot, *Alch. grecs*, IV, xx. According to F. Sherwood Taylor, in "A Survey of Greek Alchemy," pp. 109ff., this is probably the oldest Greek text of the 1st century. Cf. also Jensen, *Die älteste Alchemie*.

[3] Berthelot, III, i*ff*.

[4] Scott, *Hermetica*.

not seem to me illogical if a psychological condition, previously suppressed, should reassert itself when the main ideas of the suppressive condition begin to lose their influence. In spite of the suppression of the Gnostic heresy, it continued to flourish throughout the Middle Ages under the disguise of alchemy. It is a well-known fact that alchemy consisted of two parts which complement one another—on the one hand chemical research proper and on the other the "theoria" or "philosophia."[5] As is clear from the writings of Pseudo-Democritus in the first century, entitled τὰ φυσικὰ καὶ τὰ μυστικά,[6] the two aspects already belonged together at the beginning of our era. The same holds true of the Leiden papyri and the writings of Zosimos in the third century. The religious or philosophical views of ancient alchemy were clearly Gnostic. The later views seem to cluster round the following central idea: The *anima mundi*, the demiurge or divine spirit that incubated the chaotic waters of the beginning, remained in matter in a potential state, and the initial chaotic condition persisted with it.[7] Thus the phi-

---

[5] *Psychology and Alchemy*, pars. 401ff.

[6] Berthelot, *Alch. grecs*, II, *if*.

[7] Very early among the Greek alchemists we encounter the idea of the "stone that has a spirit" (Berthelot, *Alch. grecs*, III, vi). The "stone" is the *prima materia*, called *hyle* or chaos or *massa confusa*. This alchemical terminology was based on Plato's *Timaeus*. Joannes C. Steeb (*Coelum sephiroticum Hebraeorum*, 1679) says: "Neither earth, nor air, nor fire, nor water, nor those things which are made of these things nor those things of which these are made, should be called the *prima materia*, which must be the receptacle and the mother of that which is made and that which can be beheld, but a certain species which cannot be beheld and is formless and sustains all things" (p. 26). The same author calls the *prima materia* "the primeval chaotic earth, Hyle, Chaos, the abyss, the mother of things. . . . That first chaotic matter . . . was watered by the streams of heaven, and adorned by God with numberless Ideas of the species." He explains how the spirit of God descended into matter and what became of him there (p. 33): "The spirit of God fertilized the upper waters with a peculiar fostering warmth and made them as it were milky. . . . The fostering warmth of the Holy Spirit brought about, therefore, in the waters that are above the heavens [*aquis supracoelestibus;* cf. Genesis 1:7], a virtue subtly penetrating and nourishing all things, which, combining with light, generated in the mineral kingdom of the lower regions the mercurial serpent [this could refer just as well to the caduceus of Aesculapius, since the serpent is also the origin of the *medicina catholica*, the panacea], in the vegetable kingdom the blessed greenness [chlorophyll], in the animal kingdom a formative virtue, so that the supracelestial spirit of the waters united in marriage with light may justly be called the soul of the world." "The lower waters are darksome, and absorb the outflowings of light in their capacious depths" (p. 38). This doctrine is based on nothing less than the Gnostic legend of the Nous descending from the higher spheres and being caught in the embrace of Physis. The Mercurius of the alchemists is winged ("volatile"). Abu'l-Qāsim Muhammad (*Kitāb al'ilm al muktasab*, etc., ed. Holmyard), speaks of "Hermes, the volatile" (p. 37), and in many other places he is called a "spiritus." Moreover, he was understood to be a Hermes *psychopompos*, showing the way to Paradise (Michael Maier, *Symbola*, p. 592). This is very much the role of a redeemer, which was

losophers, or the "sons of wisdom" as they called themselves, took their *prima materia* to be a part of the original chaos pregnant with spirit. By "spirit" they understood a semimaterial pneuma, a sort of "subtle body," which they also called "volatile" and identified chemically with oxides and other dissoluble compounds. They called this spirit Mercurius, which was chemically quicksilver—though "Mercurius noster" was no ordinary Hg!—and philosophically Hermes, the god of revelation, who, as Hermes Trismegistus, was the arch-authority on alchemy.[8] Their aim was to extract the original divine spirit out of the chaos, and this extract was called the *quinta essentia, aqua permanens,* ὕδωϱ θεῖον, βαφή or *tinctura.* A famous alchemist, Johannes de Rupescissa (d. 1375),[9] calls the quintessence "le ciel humain," the human sky or heaven. For him it

---

attributed to the Nous in "*Ἑϱμοῦ πϱὸς Τάτ.*" (Scott, *Hermetica,* I, pp. 149ff.). For the Pythagoreans the soul was entirely devoured by matter, except for its reasoning part. (Zeller, *Die Philosophie der Griechen,* III, II, p. 158.)

In the old "Commentariolum in Tabulam smaragdinam" (*Ars chemica*), Hortulanus speaks of the "massa confusa" or the "chaos confusum" from which the world was created and from which also the mysterious *lapis* is generated. The *lapis* was identified with Christ from the beginning of the 14th century (Petrus Bonus, *Pretiosa margarita,* 1546). Orthelius (*Theatr. chem.,* VI, p. 431) says: "Our Saviour Jesus Christ . . . partakes of two natures. . . . So likewise is that earthly saviour made up of two parts, the heavenly and the earthly." In the same way the Mercurius imprisoned in matter was identified with the Holy Ghost. Johannes Grasseus ("Arca arcani," *Theatr. chem.,* VI, p. 314) quotes: "The gift of the Holy Spirit, that is the lead of the philosophers which they call the lead of the air, wherein is a resplendent white dove which is called the salt of the metals, in which consists the magistery of the work."

Concerning the extraction and transformation of the Chaos, Christopher of Paris ("Elucidarius artis transmutatoriae," *Theatr. chem.,* VI, p. 228) writes: "In this Chaos the said precious substance and nature truly exists potentially, in a single confused mass of the elements. Human reason ought therefore to apply itself to bringing our heaven into actuality." "Our heaven" refers to the microcosm and is also called the "quintessence." It is "incorruptible" and "immaculate." Johannes de Rupescissa (*La Vertu et la Propriété de la Quinte Essence,* 1581) calls it "le ciel humain." It is clear that the philosophers projected the vision of the golden and blue circle onto their *aurum philosophicum* (which was named the "rotundum"; see Maier, *De circulo,* 1616, p. 15) and onto the blue quintessence. The terms chaos and *massa confusa* were in general use, according to the testimony of Bernardus Sylvestris, a contemporary of William of Champeaux (1070–1121). His work, *De mundi universitate libri duo,* had a widespread influence. He speaks of the "confusion of the primary matter, that is, Hyle" (p. 5, li. 18), the "congealed mass, formless chaos, refractory matter, the face of being, a discolored mass discordant with itself" (p. 7, li, 18–19), "a mass of confusion" (p. 56, XI, li. 10). Bernardus also mentions the *descensus spiritus* as follows: "When Jove comes down into the lap of his bride, all the world is moved and would urge the soil to bring forth" (p. 51, li. 21–22). Another variant is the idea of the King submerged or concealed in the sea (Maier, *Symbola,* p. 380; "Visio Arislei," *Art. aurif.,* I, pp. 146ff.). [Cf. *Psychology and Alchemy,* pars. 434ff.]

[8] For instance, the genius of the planet Mercury reveals the mysteries to Pseudo-Democritus. (Berthelot, *Alch. grecs,* I, Introduction, p. 236.)

[9] J. de Rupescissa, *La Vertu,* p. 19.

was a blue liquid and incorruptible like the sky. He says that the quintessence is of the colour of the sky "and our sun has adorned it, as the sun adorns the sky." The sun is an allegory of gold. He says: "This sun is true gold." He continues: "These two things joined together influence in us . . . the condition of the Heaven of heavens, and of the heavenly Sun." His idea is, obviously, that the quintessence, the blue sky with the golden sun in it, evokes corresponding images of the heaven and the heavenly sun in ourselves. It is a picture of a blue and golden microcosm,[10] and I take it to be a direct parallel to Guillaume's celestial vision. The colours are, however, reversed; with Rupescissa the disc is golden and the sky blue. My patient, therefore, having a similar arrangement, seems to lean more towards the alchemical side.

The miraculous liquid, the divine water, called sky or heaven, probably refers to the supra-celestial waters of Genesis 1:7. In its functional aspect it was thought to be a sort of baptismal water which, like the holy water of the Church, possesses a creative and transformative quality.[11] The Catholic Church still performs the rite of the *benedictio fontis* on Holy Saturday before Easter.[12] The

[10] Djabir, in *La Livre de la Miséricorde*, says that the philosophers' stone is equal to a microcosm. (Berthelot, *La Chimie au moyen âge*, III, p. 179.)

[11] It is difficult not to assume that the alchemists were influenced by the allegorical style of patristic literature. They even claimed some of the Fathers as representatives of the Royal Art, for instance Albertus Magnus, Thomas Aquinas, Alanus de Insulis. A text like the "Aurora consurgens" is full of allegorical interpretations of the scriptures. It has even been ascribed to Thomas Aquinas. Nevertheless, water was in fact used as an allegory of the Holy Spirit: "Water is the living grace of the Holy Spirit" (Rupert, Abbott of Deutz, in Migne, *P.L.*, vol. 169, col. 353). "Flowing water is the Holy Spirit" (Bruno, Bishop of Würzburg, in Migne, *P.L.*, vol. 142, col. 293). "Water is the infusion of the Holy Spirit" (Garnerius of St. Victor, in Migne, *P.L.*, vol. 193, col. 279). Water is also an allegory of Christ's humanity (Gaudentius, in Migne, *P.L.*, vol. 20, col. 983). Very often water appears as dew (*ros Gedeonis*), and dew, likewise, is an allegory of Christ: "Dew is seen in the fire" (Romanus, *De theophania*, in Pitra, *Analecta sacra*, I, p. 21). "Now has Gideon's dew flowed on earth" (Romanus, *De nativitate*, ibid., p. 237). The alchemists thought that their *aqua permanens* was endued with a virtue which they called "flos" (flower). It had the power of changing body into spirit and giving it an incorruptible quality (*Turba phil.*, ed. Ruska, p. 197). The water was also called "acetum" (acid), "whereby God finished his work, whereby also bodies take on spirit and are made spiritual" (*Turba*, p. 126). Another name for it is "spiritus sanguis" (blood spirit, *Turba*, p. 129). The *Turba* is an early Latin treatise of the 12th century, translated from an originally Arabic compilation dating back to the 9th and 10th centuries. Its contents, however, stem from Hellenistic sources. The Christian allusion in "spiritualis sanguis" might be due to Byzantine influence. *Aqua permanens* is quicksilver, *argentum vivum* (Hg). "Our living silver is our clearest water" (*Rosarium phil.*, in *Art. aurif.*, II, p. 213). The *aqua* is also called fire (ibid., p. 218). The body, or substance, is transformed by water and fire, a complete parallel to the Christian idea of baptism and spiritual transformation.

[12] Missale Romanum. The rite is old and was known as the "lesser (or greater) blessing of salt and water" from about the 8th century.

rite consists in a repetition of the *descensus spiritus sancti in aquam*. The ordinary water thereby acquires the divine quality of transforming and giving spiritual rebirth to man. This is exactly the alchemical idea of the divine water, and there would be no difficulty whatever in deriving the *aqua permanens* of alchemy from the rite of the *benedictio fontis* were it not that the former is of pagan origin and certainly the older of the two. We find the miraculous water mentioned in the first treatises of Greek alchemy, which belong to the first century.[13] Moreover the descent of the spirit into Physis is a Gnostic legend that greatly influenced Mani. And it was possibly through Manichean influences that it became one of the main ideas of Latin alchemy. The aim of the philosophers was to transform imperfect matter chemically into gold, the panacea, or the *elixir vitae*, but philosophically or mystically into the divine hermaphrodite, the second Adam,[14] the glorified, incorruptible body of resurrection,[15] or the *lumen luminum*,[16] the illumination of the human mind, or *sapientia*. As I have shown, together with Richard Wilhelm, Chinese alchemy produced the same idea, that the goal of the *opus magnum* is the creation of the "diamond body."[17]

[13] In "Isis the Prophetess to her Son Horus" (Berthelot, *Alch. grecs*, I, xiii), an angel brings Isis a small vessel filled with transparent water, the arcanum. This is an obvious parallel to the krater of Hermes (*Corpus Hermeticum*, I) and of Zosimos (Berthelot, III, li, 8), which was filled with *nous*. In the φυσικὰ καὶ μυστικά of Pseudo-Democritus (Berthelot, II, i, 63), the divine water is said to effect a transformation by bringing the "hidden nature" to the surface. And in the treatise of Comarius we find the miraculous waters that produce a new springtime (Berthelot, Traductions, p. 281).

[14] Gnosius (in *Hermetis Trismegisti Tractatus vere Aureus, cum Scholiis Dominici Gnosii*, 1610, pp. 44 and 101) speaks of "Hermaphroditus noster Adamicus" when treating of the quaternity in the circle. The centre is the "mediator making peace between enemies," obviously a uniting symbol (cf. *Psychological Types*, ch. V, sec. 3, and Def. 51). [Further developed in *Aion*, pp. 194ff.—EDITORS.] The hermaphrodite is born of the "self-impregnating dragon" (*Art. aurif.*, I, p. 303), who is none other than Mercurius, the *anima mundi*. (Maier, *Symbola*, p. 43; Berthelot, I, 87.) The uroboros is an hermaphroditic symbol. The hermaphrodite is also called the Rebis ("made of two"), frequently depicted in the form of an apotheosis (for instance in the *Rosarium*, in *Art. aurif.*, II, pp. 291 and 359; Reusner, *Pandora*, 1588, p. 253).

[15] *Aurora Consurgens* (ed. von Franz, p. 129) says, quoting Senior: "There is One thing that never dieth, for it continueth by perpetual increase, when the body shall be glorified in the final resurrection of the dead. . . . Then saith the second Adam to the first and to his sons: Come ye blessed of my Father," etc.

[16] Alphidius (12th cent.?): "Of them is born the modern light (*lux moderna*), to which no light is like in all the world." (*Rosarium*, in *Art. aurif.*, II, p. 248; "Tractatus aureus," *Ars chem.*)

[17] Jung and Wilhelm, *The Secret of the Golden Flower* (1962), p. 69.

Chapter 8. Modern Gnosticism

In the following selections Jung parallels the psychological state of "moderns"—what I call "contemporaries"—with that of ancient Gnostics. Contemporaries confront the same "spiritual problem" as ancient Gnostics: the demise of traditional ways of experiencing the unconscious and consequently the need to forge new ways of doing so. While Jung refers to "modern Gnosticism," he likely means the modern— contemporary—counterpart to ancient Gnosticism rather than the contemporary version of it. The central difference between contemporaries and Gnostics is that contemporaries largely experience the unconscious nonprojectively rather than, like Gnostics, projectively. They experience the unconscious psychologically rather than metaphysically, nonreligiously rather than religiously, within themselves rather through god. Where Gnostics encounter god within themselves, contemporaries encounter themselves as god. Still, Jung at once characterizes as Gnostic contemporary metaphysical movements like Theosophy and characterizes the Gnostics as psychologists. The difference between Gnostics and contemporaries is, then, less sharp than it might seem. See, in my introduction, the section on "Gnostics and Contemporaries."

From "**The Spiritual Problem of Modern Man**," CW 10, pars. 161–71

We cannot suppose that the unconscious or hinterland of man's mind has developed this aspect only in recent times. Probably it was always there, in every culture. And although every culture had its destructive opponent, a Herostratus who burned down its temples, no culture before ours was ever forced to take these psychic undercurrents in deadly earnest. The psyche was merely part of a metaphysical system of some sort. But the conscious, modern man can no longer refrain from acknowledging the might of the psyche, despite the most strenuous and dogged efforts at self-defence. This distinguishes our time from all others. We can no longer deny that the dark stirrings of the unconscious are active powers, that psychic forces exist which, for the present at least, cannot be fitted into our rational world order. We have even elevated them into a science—one more proof of how seriously we take them. Previous centuries could throw them aside unnoticed; for us they are a shirt of Nessus which we cannot strip off.

The revolution in our conscious outlook, brought about by the catastrophic results of the World War, shows itself in our inner life by the shattering of our faith in ourselves and our own worth. We used to regard foreigners as political and moral reprobates, but the modern man is forced to recognize that he is politically and morally just like anyone else. Whereas formerly I believed it was my bounden duty to call others to order, I must now admit that I need calling to order myself, and that I would do better to set my own house to rights first. I admit this the more readily because I realize only too well that my faith in the rational organization of the world—that old dream of the millennium when peace and harmony reign—has grown pale. Modern man's scepticism in this respect has chilled his enthusiasm for politics and world-reform; more than that, it is the worst possible basis for a smooth flow of psychic energies into the outer world, just as doubt concerning the morality of a friend is bound to prejudice the relationship and hamper its development. Through his scepticism modern man is thrown back on himself; his energies flow towards their source, and the collision washes to the surface those psychic contents which are at all times there, but lie hidden in the silt so long as the stream flows smoothly in its course. How totally different did the world appear to medieval man! For him the earth was eternally fixed and at rest in the centre of the universe, circled by a sun that solicitously bestowed its warmth. Men were all children of God under the loving care of the Most High, who prepared them for eternal blessedness; and all knew exactly what they should do and how they should conduct themselves in order to rise from a corruptible world to an incorruptible and joyous existence. Such a life no longer seems real to us, even in our dreams. Science has long ago torn this lovely veil to shreds. That age lies as far behind as childhood, when one's own father was unquestionably the handsomest and strongest man on earth.

Modern man has lost all the metaphysical certainties of his medieval brother, and set up in their place the ideals of material security, general welfare and humanitarianism. But anyone who has still managed to preserve these ideals unshaken must have been injected with a more than ordinary dose of optimism. Even security has gone by the board, for modern man has begun to see that every step forward in material "progress" steadily increases the threat of a still more stupendous catastrophe. The imagination shrinks in terror from such a picture. What are we to think when the great cities today are perfecting defence measures against gas attacks, and even practise them in dress rehearsals? It can only mean that these attacks have already been planned and provided for, again on the principle "in time of peace prepare for war." Let man but accumulate sufficient engines of destruction and the devil within him will soon be unable to resist putting them to their fated use. It is well known that fire-arms go off of themselves if only enough of them are together.

An intimation of the terrible law that governs blind contingency, which Heraclitus called the rule of *enantiodromia* (a running towards the opposite), now steals upon modern man through the byways of his mind, chilling him with fear and paralysing his faith in the lasting effectiveness of social and political measures in the face of these monstrous forces. If he turns away from the terrifying prospect of a blind world in which building and destroying successively tip the scales, and then gazes into the recesses of his own mind, he will discover a chaos and a darkness there which everyone would gladly ignore. Science has destroyed even this last refuge; what was once a sheltering haven has become a cesspool.

And yet it is almost a relief to come upon so much evil in the depths of our own psyche. Here at least, we think, is the root of all the evil in mankind. Even though we are shocked and disillusioned at first, we still feel, just because these things are part of our psyche, that we have them more or less in hand and can correct them or at any rate effectively suppress them. We like to assume that, if we succeeded in this, we should at least have rooted out some fraction of the evil in the world. Given a widespread knowledge of the unconscious, everyone could see when a statesman was being led

astray by his own bad motives. The very newspapers would pull
him up: "Please have yourself analysed; you are suffering from a
repressed father-complex."

I have purposely chosen this grotesque example to show to what
absurdities we are led by the illusion that because something is
psychic it is under our control. It is, however, true that much of the
evil in the world comes from the fact that man in general is hope-
lessly unconscious, as it is also true that with increasing insight we
can combat this evil at its source in ourselves, in the same way that
science enables us to deal effectively with injuries inflicted from
without.

The rapid and worldwide growth of a psychological interest over
the last two decades shows unmistakably that modern man is turning his attention from outward material things to his own inner
processes. Expressionism in art prophetically anticipated this subjective development, for all art intuitively apprehends coming
changes in the collective unconsciousness.

The psychological interest of the present time is an indication
that modern man expects something from the psyche which the
outer world has not given him: doubtless something which our
religion ought to contain, but no longer does contain, at least for
modern man. For him the various forms of religion no longer
appear to come from within, from the psyche; they seem more like
items from the inventory of the outside world. No spirit not of this
world vouchsafes him inner revelation; instead, he tries on a variety
of religions and beliefs as if they were Sunday attire, only to lay
them aside again like worn-out clothes.

Yet he is somehow fascinated by the almost pathological manifestations from the hinterland of the psyche, difficult though it is
to explain how something which all previous ages have rejected
should suddenly become interesting. That there is a general interest in these matters cannot be denied, however much it offends
against good taste. I am not thinking merely of the interest taken in
psychology as a science, or of the still narrower interest in the
psychoanalysis of Freud, but of the widespread and ever-growing
interest in all sorts of psychic phenomena, including spiritualism,
astrology, Theosophy, parapsychology, and so forth. The world has
seen nothing like it since the end of the seventeenth century. We
can compare it only to the flowering of Gnostic thought in the first

and second centuries after Christ. The spiritual currents of our time have, in fact, a deep affinity with Gnosticism. There is even an "Église gnostique de la France," and I know of two schools in Germany which openly declare themselves Gnostic. The most impressive movement numerically is undoubtedly Theosophy, together with its continental sister, Anthroposophy; these are pure Gnosticism in Hindu dress. Compared with them the interest in scientific psychology is negligible. What is striking about these Gnostic systems is that they are based exclusively on the manifestations of the unconscious, and that their moral teachings penetrate into the dark side of life, as is clearly shown by the refurbished European version of *Kundalini-yoga*. The same is true of parapsychology, as everyone acquainted with this subject will agree.

The passionate interest in these movements undoubtedly arises from psychic energy which can no longer be invested in obsolete religious forms. For this reason such movements have a genuinely religious character, even when they pretend to be scientific. It changes nothing when Rudolf Steiner calls his Anthroposophy "spiritual science," or when Mrs. Eddy invents a "Christian Science." These attempts at concealment merely show that religion has grown suspect—almost as suspect as politics and world-reform.

I do not believe that I am going too far when I say that modern man, in contrast to his nineteenth-century brother, turns to the psyche with very great expectations, and does so without reference to any traditional creed but rather with a view to Gnostic experience. The fact that all the movements I have mentioned give themselves a scientific veneer is not just a grotesque caricature or a masquerade, but a positive sign that they are actually pursuing "science," i.e., *knowledge,* instead of *faith,* which is the essence of the Western forms of religion. Modern man abhors faith and the religions based upon it. He holds them valid only so far as their knowledge-content seems to accord with his own experience of the psychic background. He wants to *know*—to experience for himself.

From "**Richard Wilhelm: In Memoriam**," CW 15, par. 91

Human instinct knows that all great truth is simple. The man whose instincts are atrophied therefore supposes that it is found in cheap simplifications and platitudes; or, as a result of his disappointment, he falls into the opposite error of thinking that it must be as obscure and complicated as possible. Today we have a Gnostic movement in the anonymous masses which is the exact psychological counterpart of the Gnostic movement nineteen hundred years ago. Then, as today, solitary wanderers like Apollonius of Tyana spun the spiritual threads from Europe to Asia, perhaps to remotest India. Viewing him in this historical perspective, I see Wilhelm as one of those great Gnostic intermediaries who brought the Hellenic spirit into contact with the cultural heritage of the East and thereby caused a new world to rise out of the ruins of the Roman Empire.

From "On the Psychology of the Unconscious," CW 7, par. 118

We mentioned earlier that the unconscious contains, as it were, two layers: the personal and the collective. The personal layer ends at the earliest memories of infancy, but the collective layer comprises the pre-infantile period, that is, the residues of ancestral life. Whereas the memory-images of the personal unconscious are, as it were, filled out, because they are images personally experienced by the individual, the archetypes of the collective unconscious are not filled out because they are forms not personally experienced. When, on the other hand, psychic energy regresses, going beyond even the period of early infancy, and breaks into the legacy of ancestral life, the mythological images are awakened: these are the archetypes.[1] An interior spiritual world whose existence we never suspected opens out and displays contents which seem to stand in sharpest contrast to all our former ideas. These images are so intense that it is quite understandable why millions of cultivated persons should be taken in by theosophy and anthroposophy. This

[1] The reader will note the admixture here of a new element in the idea of the archetypes, not previously mentioned. This admixture is not a piece of unintentional obscurantism, but a deliberate extension of the archetype by means of the *karmic* factor, which is so very important in Indian philosophy. The *karma* aspect is essential to a deeper understanding of the nature of an archetype. Without entering here into a closer description of this factor, I would like at least to mention its existence. I have been severely attacked by critics for my idea of archetypes. I admit at once that it is a controversial idea and more than a little perplexing. But I have always wondered what sort of idea my critics would have used to characterize the empirical material in question.

happens simply because such modern gnostic systems meet the need for expressing and formulating the wordless occurrences going on within ourselves *better* than any of the existing forms of Christianity, not excepting Catholicism. The latter is certainly able to express, far more comprehensively than Protestantism, the facts in question through its dogma and ritual symbolism. But neither in the past nor in the present has even Catholicism attained anything like the richness of the old pagan symbolism, which is why this symbolism persisted far into Christianity and then gradually went underground, forming currents that, from the early Middle Ages to modern times, have never quite lost their vitality. To a large extent they vanished from the surface; but, changing their form, they come back again to compensate the one-sidedness of our conscious mind with its modern orientation.[2] Our consciousness is so saturated with Christianity, so utterly moulded by it, that the unconscious counter-position can discover no foothold there, for the simple reason that it seems too much the antithesis of our ruling ideas. The more one-sidedly, rigidly, and absolutely the one position is held, the more aggressive, hostile, and incompatible will the other become, so that at first sight there would seem to be little prospect of reconciling the two. But once the conscious mind admits at least the *relative* validity of all human opinion, then the opposition loses something of its irreconcilable character. In the meantime the conflict casts round for appropriate expression in, for instance, the oriental religions—Buddhism, Hinduism, Taoism. The syncretism of theosophy goes a long way towards meeting this need, and that explains its numerous successes.

[2] Cf. "Paracelsus as a Spiritual Phenomenon" and *Psychology and Alchemy*.

Chapter 9. Jung as a Psychologist Rather Than a Metaphysician

As enthusiastically as Jung pairs his brand of psychology with ancient Gnosticism, he resolutely denies that he himself is a Gnostic. It is not any particular Gnostic tenets that he spurns. It is the characterization of himself as a metaphysician rather than a natural scientist. For Jung, Gnosticism is metaphysics and psychology is natural science. That distinction underscores the difference between ancient Gnostics and any contemporary incarnations. See, in my introduction, the section on "Jung as Gnostic."

"Religion and Psychology: A Reply to Martin Buber,"[1] CW 18, pars. 1499–1513

Some while ago the readers of your magazine were given the opportunity to read a posthumous article by Count Keyserling,[2] in which I was characterized as "unspiritual." Now, in your last issue, I find an article by Martin Buber[3] which is likewise concerned with my classification. I am indebted to his pronouncements at least in so far as they raise me out of the condition of unspirituality, in which

---

[1] [Written 22 Feb. 1952 as a letter to the editor, published as "Religion und Psychologie" in *Merkur* (Stuttgart), VI:5 (May 1952), 467–73, and reprinted as "Antwort an Martin Buber" in *Gesam. Werke*, XI, Anhang. The present translation was published in *Spring*, 1973.]

[2] [Hermann Keyserling (1880–1946), "Begegnungen mit der Psychoanalyse," *Merkur*, IV:11 (Nov. 1950), 1151–68.]

[3] ["Religion und modernes Denken," *Merkur* VI:2 (Feb. 1952). Trans., "Religion and Modern Thinking," together with Buber's reply to Jung (in the same issue with Jung's reply, *Merkur*, VI:5), in *Eclipse of God* (1953).]

Count Keyserling saw fit to present me to the German public, into the sphere of spirituality, even though it be the spirituality of early Christian Gnosticism, which has always been looked at askance by theologians. Funnily enough this opinion of Buber's coincides with another utterance from an authoritative theological source accusing me of agnosticism—the exact opposite of Gnosticism.

Now when opinions about the same subject differ so widely, there is in my view ground for the suspicion that none of them is correct, and that there has been a misunderstanding. Why is so much attention devoted to the question of whether I am a Gnostic or an agnostic? Why is it not simply stated that I am a psychiatrist whose prime concern is to record and interpret his empirical material? I try to investigate facts and make them more generally comprehensible. My critics have no right to slur over this in order to attack individual statements taken out of context.

To support his diagnosis Buber even resorts to a sin of my youth, committed nearly forty years ago, which consists in my once having perpetrated a poem.[4] In this poem I expressed a number of psychological *aperçus* in "Gnostic" style, because I was then studying the Gnostics with enthusiasm. My enthusiasm arose from the discovery that they were apparently the first thinkers to concern themselves (after their fashion) with the contents of the collective unconscious. I had the poem printed under a pseudonym and gave a few copies to friends, little dreaming that it would one day bear witness against me as a heretic.

I would like to point out to my critic that I have in my time been regarded not only as a Gnostic and its opposite, but also as a theist and an atheist, a mystic and a materialist. In this concert of contending opinions I do not wish to lay too much stress on what I consider myself to be, but will quote a judgment from a leading article in the *British Medical Journal* (9 February 1952), a source that would seem to be above suspicion. "Facts first and theories later is the keynote of Jung's work. He is an empiricist first and last." This view meets with my approval.

Anyone who does not know my work will certainly ask himself how it is that so many contrary opinions can be held about one and

---

[4] [*VII Sermones ad Mortuos*, by Basilides of Alexandria (n.d. [1916]), privately printed. English trans. by H. G. Baynes, privately printed 1925; reprinted in the 2nd edn. of *Memories, Dreams, Reflections*, appendix.]

the same subject. The answer to this is that they are all thought up by "metaphysicians," that is, by people who for one reason or another think they know about unknowable things in the Beyond. I have never ventured to declare that such things do *not* exist; but neither have I ventured to suppose that any statement of mine could in any way touch them or even represent them correctly. I very much doubt whether our conception of a thing is identical with the nature of the thing itself, and this for very obvious scientific reasons.

But since views and opinions about metaphysical or religious subjects play a very great role in empirical psychology,[5] I am obliged for practical reasons to work with concepts corresponding to them. In so doing I am aware that I am dealing with anthropomorphic ideas and not with actual gods and angels, although, thanks to their specific energy, such (archetypal) images behave so autonomously that one could describe them metaphorically as "psychic daimonia." The fact that they are autonomous should be taken very seriously; first, from the theoretical standpoint, because it explains the dissociability of the psyche as well as actual dissociation, and second, from the practical one, because it forms the basis for a dialectical discussion between the ego and the unconscious, which is one of the mainstays of the psychotherapeutic method. Anyone who has any knowledge of the structure of a neurosis will be aware that the pathogenic conflict arises from the counterposition of the unconscious relative to consciousness. The so-called "forces of the unconscious" are not intellectual concepts that can be arbitrarily manipulated, but dangerous antagonists which can, among other things, work frightful devastation in the economy of the personality. They are everything one could wish for or fear in a psychic "Thou." The layman naturally thinks he is the victim of some obscure organic disease; but the theologian, who suspects it is the devil's work, is appreciably nearer to the psychological truth.

I am afraid that Buber, having no psychiatric experience, fails to understand what I mean by the "reality of the psyche" and by the dialectical process of individuation. The fact is that the ego is confronted with psychic powers which from ancient times have borne sacred names, and because of these they have always been

[5] Cf. G. Schmaltz, *Östliche Weisheit und westliche Psychotherapie* (1951).

identified with metaphysical beings. Analysis of the unconscious has long since demonstrated the existence of these powers in the form of archetypal images which, be it noted, *are not identical with the corresponding intellectual concepts*. One can, of course, believe that the concepts of the conscious mind are, through the inspiration of the Holy Ghost, direct and correct representations of their metaphysical referent. But this conviction is possible only for one who already possesses the gift of faith. Unfortunately I cannot boast of this possession, for which reason I do not imagine that when I say something about an archangel I have thereby confirmed that a metaphysical fact. I have merely expressed an opinion about something that can be experienced, that is, about one of the very palpable "powers of the unconscious". These powers are numinous "types"—unconscious contents, processes, and dynamisms—and such types are, if one may so express it, immanent-transcendent. Since my sole means of cognition is experience I may not overstep its boundaries, and cannot therefore pretend to myself that my description coincides with the portrait of a real metaphysical archangel. What I have described is a psychic factor only, but one which exerts a considerable influence on the conscious mind. Thanks to its autonomy, it forms the counterposition to the subjective ego because it is a piece of the *objective psyche*. It can therefore be designated as a "Thou." For me its reality is amply attested by the truly diabolical deeds of our time: the six million murdered Jews, the uncounted victims of the slave labour camps in Russia, as well as the invention of the atom bomb, to name but a few examples of the darker side. But I have also seen the other side which can be expressed by the words beauty, goodness, wisdom, grace. These experiences of the depths and heights of human nature justify the metaphorical use of the term "daimon."

It should not be overlooked that what I am concerned with are psychic phenomena which can be proved empirically to be the bases of metaphysical concepts, and that when, for example, I speak of "God" I am unable to refer to anything beyond these demonstrable psychic models which, we have to admit, have shown themselves to be devastatingly real. To anyone who finds their reality incredible I would recommend a reflective tour through a lunatic asylum.

The "reality of the psyche" is my working hypothesis, and my principal activity consists in collecting factual material to describe and explain it. I have set up neither a system nor a general theory, but have merely formulated auxiliary concepts to serve me as tools, as is customary in every branch of science. If Buber misunderstands my empiricism as Gnosticism, it is up to him to prove that the facts I describe are nothing but inventions. If he should succeed in proving this with empirical material, then indeed I am a Gnostic. But in that case he will find himself in the uncomfortable position of having to dismiss all religious experiences as self-deception. Meanwhile I am of the opinion that Buber's judgment has been led astray. This seems especially evident in his apparent inability to understand how an "autonomous psychic content" like the God-image can burst upon the ego, and that such a confrontation is a living experience. It is certainly not the task of an empirical science to establish how far such a psychic content is dependent on and determined by the existence of a metaphysical deity. That is the concern of theology, revelation, and faith. My critic does not seem to realize that when he himself talks about God, his statements are dependent firstly on his conscious and then on his unconscious assumptions. Of *which* metaphysical deity he is speaking I do not know. If he is an orthodox Jew he is speaking of a God to whom the incarnation in the year 1 has not yet been revealed. If he is a Christian, then his deity knows about the incarnation of which Yahweh still shows no sign. I do not doubt his conviction that he stands in a living relationship to a divine Thou, but now as before I am of the opinion that this relationship is primarily to an autonomous psychic content which is defined in one way by him and in another by the Pope. Consequently I do not permit myself the least judgment as to whether and to what extent it has pleased a metaphysical deity to reveal himself to the devout Jew as he was before the incarnation, to the Church Fathers as the Trinity, to the Protestants as the one and only Saviour without co-redemptrix, and to the present Pope as a Saviour with co-redemptrix. Nor should one doubt that the devotees of other faiths, including Islam, Buddhism, Hinduism, and so on, have the same living relationship to "God," or to Nirvana and Tao, as Buber has to the God-concept peculiar to himself.

It is remarkable that he takes exception to my statement that God cannot exist apart from man and regards it as a transcendental assertion. Yet I say expressly that everything asserted about "God" is a human statement, in other words a psychological one. For surely the image we have or make for ourselves of God is never detached from man? Can Buber show me where, apart from man, God has made an image of himself? How can such a thing be substantiated and by whom? Here, just for once, and as an exception, I shall indulge in transcendental speculation and even in "poetry": God has indeed made an inconceivably sublime and mysteriously contradictory image of himself, without the help of man, and implanted it in man's unconscious as an archetype, an ἀϱχέτυπον φῶς, archetypal light: not in order that theologians of all times and places should be at one another's throats, but in order that the unpresumptuous man might glimpse an image, in the stillness of his soul, that is akin to him and is wrought of his own psychic substance. This image contains everything he will ever imagine concerning his gods or concerning the ground of his psyche.

This archetype, whose existence is attested not only by ethnology but by the psychic experience of individuals, satisfies me completely. It is so humanly close and yet so strange and "other"; also, like all archetypes, it possesses the utmost determinative power with which it is absolutely necessary that we come to terms. The dialectical relationship to the autonomous contents of the collective unconscious is therefore, as I have said, an essential part of therapy.

Buber is mistaken in thinking that I start with a "fundamentally Gnostic viewpoint" and then proceed to "elaborate" metaphysical assertions. One should not misconstrue the findings of empiricism as philosophical premises, for they are not obtained by deduction but from clinical and factual material. I would recommend him to read some autobiographies of the mentally ill, such as John Custance's *Wisdom, Madness and Folly* (1951), or D. P. Schreber's *Memoirs of My Nervous Illness* (first published 1903), which certainly do not proceed from Gnostic hypotheses any more than I do; or he might try an analysis of mythological material, such as the excellent work of Dr. Erich Neumann, his neighbour in Tel Aviv: *Amor and Psyche* (1952). My contention that the products of the unconscious are analogous and related to certain metaphysical ideas is founded on my professional experience. In this connection I would point out that I know quite a number of influential theologians, Catholics as well as Protestants, who have no difficulty in grasping my empirical standpoint. I therefore see no reason why I should take my method of exposition to be quite so misleading as Buber would have us believe.

There is one misunderstanding which I would like to mention here because it comes up so often. This is the curious assumption that when a projection is withdrawn nothing more of the object remains. When I correct my mistaken opinion of a man I have not negated him and caused him to vanish; on the contrary, I see him more nearly as he is, and this can only benefit the relationship. So if I hold the view that all statements about God have their origin in the psyche and must therefore be distinguished from God as a metaphysical being, this is neither to deny God nor to put man in God's place. I frankly confess that it goes against the grain with me to think that the metaphysical God himself is speaking through everyone who quotes the Bible or ventilates his religious opinions. Faith is certainly a splendid thing if one has it, and knowledge by faith is perhaps more perfect than anything we can produce with our laboured and wheezing empiricism. The edifice of Christian dogma, for instance, undoubtedly stands on a much higher level than the somewhat wild "philosophoumena" of the Gnostics. Dogmas are spiritual structures of supreme beauty, and they possess a wonderful meaning which I have sought to fathom in my fashion. Compared with them our scientific endeavors to devise models of the objective psyche are unsightly in the extreme. They are bound to earth and reality, full of contradictions, incomplete, logically and aesthetically unsatisfying. The empirical concepts of science and particularly of medical psychology do not proceed from neat and seemly principles of thought, but are the outcome of our daily labours in the sloughs of ordinary human existence and human pain. They are essentially irrational, and the philosopher who criticizes them as though they were philosophical concepts tilts against windmills and gets into the greatest difficulties, as Buber does with the concept of the self. Empirical concepts are names for existing complexes of facts. Considering the fearful paradoxicality of human existence, it is quite understandable that the unconscious contains an equally paradoxical God-image which will not square at all with the beauty, sublimity, and purity of the dogmatic concept of God. The God of Job and of the 89th Psalm is clearly a bit closer to reality, and his behaviour does not fit in badly with the God-image in the unconscious. Of course this image, with its Anthropos symbolism, lends support to the idea of the incarnation. I do not feel responsible for the fact that the history of dogma has made some progress since the days of the Old Testament. This is not to preach a new religion, for to do that I would have to follow the old-established custom of appealing to a divine revelation. I am essentially a physician, whose business is with the sickness of man and his times, and with remedies that are as real as the suffering. Not only Buber, but every theologian who baulks at my odious psychology is at liberty to heal my patients with the word of God. I would welcome this experiment with open arms. But since the ecclesiastical cure of souls does not always produce the desired results, we doctors must do what we can, and at present we have no better standby than that modest "gnosis" which the empirical method gives us. Or have any of my critics better advice to offer?

As a doctor one finds oneself in an awkward position, because unfortunately one can accomplish nothing with that little word "ought." We cannot demand of our patients a faith which they reject because they do not understand it, or which does not suit them even though we may hold it ourselves. We have to rely on the curative powers inherent in the patient's own nature, regardless of whether the ideas that emerge agree with any known creed or philosophy. My empirical material seems to include a bit of everything—it is an assortment of primitive, Western, and Oriental ideas. There is scarcely any myth whose echoes are not heard, nor any heresy that has not contributed an occasional oddity. The deeper, collective layers of the human psyche must surely be of a like nature. Intellectuals and rationalists, happy in their established beliefs, will no doubt be horrified by this and will accuse me of reckless eclecticism, as though I had somehow invented the facts of man's nature and mental history and had compounded out of them a repulsive theosophical brew. Those who possess faith or prefer to talk like philosophers do not, of course, need to wrestle with the facts, but a doctor is not at liberty to dodge the grim realities of human nature.

It is inevitable that the adherents of traditional religious systems should find my formulations hard to understand. A Gnostic would not be at all pleased with me, but would reproach me for having no cosmogony and for the cluelessness of my gnosis in regard to the happenings in the Pleroma. A Buddhist would complain that I was deluded by Maya, and a Taoist that I was too complicated. As for an orthodox Christian, he can hardly do otherwise than deplore the nonchalance and lack of respect with which I navigate through the empyrean of dogmatic ideas. I must, however, once more beg my unmerciful critics to remember that I start from *facts* for which I seek an interpretation.

From "**Jung and Religious Belief**," CW 18, pars. 1642–47

The designation of my "system" as "Gnostic" is an invention of my theological critics. Moreover I have no "system." I am not a philosopher, merely an empiricist. The Gnostics have the merit of having raised the problem of πόθεν τὸ κακόν; [whence evil?]. Valentinus as well as Basilides are in my view great theologians, who tried to cope with the problems raised by the inevitable influx of the collective unconscious, a fact clearly portrayed by the "gnostic" gospel of St. John and by St. Paul, not to mention the Book of Revelation, and even by Christ himself (unjust steward and Codex Bezae to Luke 6:4). In the style of their time they hypostatized their ideas as metaphysical entities. Psychology does not hypostatize, but considers such ideas as psychological statements about, or models of, essential unconscious factors inaccessible to immediate experience. This is about as far as scientific understanding can go. In our days there are plenty of people who are unable to believe a statement they cannot understand, and they appreciate the help psychology can give them by showing them that human behaviour is deeply influenced by numinous archetypes. That gives them some understanding of why and how the religious factor plays an important role. It also gives them ways and means of recognizing the operation of religious ideas in their own psyche.

I must confess that I myself could find access to religion only through the psychological understanding of inner experiences, whereas traditional religious interpretations left me high and dry. It was only psychology that helped me to overcome the fatal impressions of my youth that everything untrue, even immoral, in our ordinary empirical world *must* be believed to be the eternal truth in religion. Above all, the killing of a human victim to placate the senseless wrath of a God who had created imperfect beings unable to fulfil his expectations poisoned my whole religion. Nobody knew an answer. "With God all things are possible." Just so! As the perpetrator of incredible things he is himself incredible, and yet I was supposed to believe what every fibre of my body refused to admit! There are a great many questions which I could elucidate only by psychological understanding. I loved the Gnostics in spite of everything, because they recognized the necessity of some further *raisonnement*, entirely absent in the Christian cosmos. They were at least human and therefore understandable. But I have no γνῶσις τοῦ θεοῦ. I know the reality of religious experience and of psychological models which permit a limited understanding. I have Gnosis so far as I have immediate experience, and my models are greatly helped by the *représentations collectives* of all religions. But I cannot see why one creed should possess the unique and perfect truth. Each creed claims this prerogative, hence the general disagreement! This is not very helpful. Something must be wrong. I think it is the immodesty of the claim to god-almightiness of the believers, which compensates their inner doubt. Instead of basing themselves upon immediate experience they believe in words for want of something better. The *sacrificium intellectus* is a sweet drug for man's all-embracing spiritual laziness and inertia.

I owe you quite a number of apologies for the fact that my layman's mental attitude must be excruciatingly irritating to your point of view. But you know, as a psychologist I am not concerned with theology directly, but rather with the incompetent general public and its erroneous and faulty convictions, which are however just as real to it as their competent views are to the theologians. I am continually asked "theological" questions by my patients, and when I say that I am only a doctor and they should ask the theologian, then the regular answer is, "Oh, yes, we have done so," or "we do not ask a priest because we get an answer we already know, which explains nothing."

Well this is the reason why I have to try for better or worse to help my patients to some kind of understanding at least. It gives them a certain satisfaction as it has done to me, although it is admittedly inadequate. But to them it sounds as if somebody were speaking their language and understanding their questions which they take very seriously indeed. Once, for instance, it was a very important question to me to discover how far modern Protestantism considers that the God of the Old Testament is identical with the God of the New Testament. I asked two university professors. They did not answer my letter. The third (also a professor) said he didn't know. The fourth said, "Oh, that is quite easy. Yahweh is a somewhat more archaic conception contrasted with the more differentiated view of the New Testament." I said to him, "That is exactly the kind of psychologism you accuse me of." My question must have been singularly inadequate or foolish. But I do not know why. I am speaking for the layman's psychology. The layman is a reality and his questions do exist. My "Answer to Job" voices the questions of thousands, but the theologians don't answer, contenting themselves with dark allusions to my layman's ignorance of Hebrew, higher criticism, Old Testament exegesis, etc., but there is not a single answer. A Jesuit professor of theology asked me rather indignantly how I could suggest that the Incarnation has remained incomplete. I said, "The human being is born under the *macula peccati*. Neither Christ nor his mother suffers from original sin. They are therefore not human, but superhuman, a sort of God." What did he answer? Nothing.

Why is that so? My layman's reasoning is certainly imperfect, and my theological knowledge regrettably meagre, but not as bad as all that, at least I hope not. But I do know something about the psychology of man now and in the past, and as a psychologist I raise the questions I have been asked a hundred times by my patients and other laymen. Theology would certainly not suffer by paying attention. I know you are too busy to do it. I am all the more anxious to prevent avoidable mistakes and I shall feel deeply obliged to you if you take the trouble of showing me where I am wrong.

Gnosis is characterized by the hypostatizing of psychological apperceptions, i.e., by the integration of archetypal contents beyond the revealed "truth" of the Gospels. Hippolytus still considered classical Greek philosophy along with Gnostic philosophies as perfectly possible views. Christian Gnosis to him was merely the best and superior to all of them. The people who call me a Gnostic cannot understand that I am a psychologist, describing modes of psychic behaviour precisely like a biologist studying the instinctual activities of insects. He does not *believe* in the tenets of the bee's philosophy. When I show the parallels between dreams and Gnostic fantasies I *believe* in neither. They are just facts one does not need to believe or to hypostatize. An alienist is not necessarily crazy because he describes and analyses the delusions of lunatics, nor is a scholar studying the *Tripitaka* necessarily a Buddhist.

From "**Foreword to White's** *God and the Unconscious*," CW 11, pars. 460–62

Psychology, like every empirical science, cannot get along without auxiliary concepts, hypotheses, and models. But the theologian as well as the philosopher is apt to make the mistake of taking them for metaphysical postulates. The atom of which the physicist speaks is not an *hypostasis*, it is a *model*. Similarly, my concept of the archetype or of psychic energy is only an auxiliary idea which can be exchanged at any time for a better formula. From a philosophical standpoint my empirical concepts would be logical monsters, and as a philosopher I should cut a very sorry figure. Looked at theologically, my concept of the anima, for instance, is pure Gnosticism; hence I am often classed among the Gnostics. On top of that, the individuation process develops a symbolism whose nearest affinities are to be found in folklore, in Gnostic, alchemical, and suchlike "mystical" conceptions, not to mention shamanism. When material of this kind is adduced for comparison, the exposition fairly swarms with "exotic" and "far-fetched" proofs, and anyone who merely skims through a book instead of reading it can easily succumb to the illusion that he is confronted with a Gnostic system. In reality, however, individuation is an expression of that biological process—simple or complicated as the case may be—by which every living thing becomes what it was destined to become from the beginning. This process naturally expresses itself in man as much psychically as somatically. On the psychic side it produces those well-known quaternity symbols, for instance, whose parallels are found in mental asylums as well as in Gnosticism and other exoticisms, and—last but not least—in Christian allegory. Hence it is by no means a case of mystical speculations, but of clinical observations and their interpretation through comparison with analogous phenomena in other fields. It is not the daring fantasy of the anatomist that can be held responsible when he discovers the nearest analogies to the human skeleton in certain African anthropoids of which the layman has never heard.

It is certainly remarkable that my critics, with few exceptions, ignore the fact that, as a doctor and scientist, I proceed from facts which everyone is at liberty to verify. Instead, they criticize me as if I were a philosopher, or a Gnostic with pretensions to supernatural knowledge. As a philosopher and speculating heretic I am, of course, easy prey. That is probably the reason why people prefer to ignore the facts I have discovered, or to deny them without scruple. But it is the facts that are of prime importance to me and not a provisional terminology or attempts at theoretical reflections. The fact that archetypes exist is not spirited away by saying that there are no inborn ideas. I have never maintained that the archetype *an sich* is an idea, but have expressly pointed out that I regard it as a form without definite content.

In view of these manifold misunderstandings, I set a particularly high value on the real understanding shown by the author, whose *point de départ* is diametrically opposed to that of natural science. He has successfully undertaken to feel his way into the empiricist's manner of thinking as far as possible, and if he has not always entirely succeeded in his attempt, I am the last person to blame him, for I am convinced that I am unwittingly guilty of many an offence against the theological way of thinking. Discrepancies of this kind can only be settled by lengthy discussions, but they have their good side: not only do two apparently incompatible mental spheres come into contact, they also animate and fertilize one another. This calls for a great deal of good will on either side, and here I can give the author unstinted praise. He has taken the part of the opposite standpoint very fairly, and—what is especially valuable to me—has at the same time illustrated the theological standpoint in a highly instructive way. The medical psychotherapist cannot in the long run afford to overlook the religious systems of healing—if one may so describe certain aspects of religion—any more than the theologian, if he has the cure of souls at heart, can afford to ignore the experience of medical psychology.

From **Letters,** vol. 2, pp. 53–55

*To H. Haberlandt**

Dear Colleague,   23 April 1952
  Very many thanks for kindly sending me your review of *Aion*.[1] It
stands out from all the others because it is obvious that its author
has really read the book, which is something I am grateful for. I
therefore venture to ask you to let me know in what sense you use
the term "Gnosis." You can hardly mean γνῶσις = knowledge in
general, but more specifically the Christian γνῶσις θεοῦ or even
that of Gnosticism. In both the latter cases it has to do with *metaphysical* assertions or postulates, i.e., it is assumed that γνῶσις
actually consists in the knowledge of a metaphysical object. Now I
state expressly and repeatedly in my writings that psychology can
do no more than concern itself with assertions and anthropomorphic images. The possible metaphysical significance of these assertions is completely outside the bounds of empirical psychology as a
science. When I say "God" I mean an anthropomorphic (archetypal) God-image and do not imagine I have said anything about
God. I have neither denied nor affirmed him, unlike the Christian
or Gnostic γνῶσις which thinks it has said or has to say something
about a metaphysical God.
  The difficulty which gives rise to misunderstandings is that archetypes are "real." That is to say, effects can be empirically established whose cause is described hypothetically as *archetype*, just as
in physics effects can be established whose cause is assumed to be
the *atom* (which is merely a model). Nobody has ever seen an
archetype, and nobody has ever seen an atom either. But the former
is known to produce numinous effects and the latter explosions.
When I say "atom" I am talking of the model made of it; when I say
"archetype" I am talking of ideas corresponding to it, but never of
the thing-in-itself, which in both cases is a transcendental mystery.[2] It would never occur to a physicist that he has bagged the bird
with his atomic model (for instance Niels Bohr's planetary sys-

---

* A professor in Vienna.
[1] Published in *Wissenschaft und Weltbild* (Vienna), IV (1952).
[2] Cf. Devatmananda, 9 Feb. 37, n.1.

tem).[3] He is fully aware that he is handling a variable schema or model which merely points to unknowable facts.

This is scientific gnosis, such as I also pursue. Only it is news to me that such knowledge is accounted "metaphysical." You see, for me the psyche is something real *because it works*,[4] as can be established empirically. One must therefore assume that the effective archetypal ideas, including our model of the archetype, rest on something actual even though unknowable, just as the model of the atom rests on certain unknowable qualities of matter. But science cannot possibly establish that, or to what extent, this unknowable substrate is in both cases God. This can be decided only by dogmatics or faith, as for instance in Islamic philosophy (Al-Ghazzali), which explained gravitation as the will of Allah. This is Gnosticism with its characteristic overstepping of epistemological barriers. The Church's proofs of God likewise come under this heading, all of which beg the question if looked at logically.

By contrast I pursue a scientific psychology which could be called a comparative anatomy of the psyche. I postulate the psyche as something real. But this hypothesis can hardly be called "gnostic" any more than the atomic theory can.

So my question is: Wherein consists my "gnosis" in your view, or what do *you* understand by "gnosis"?

Excuse me for bothering you with such a long letter. But I wonder how it comes that so many people think I am a gnostic while equally many others accuse me of being an agnostic. I would like to know whether I am making a fundamental mistake somewhere that occasions such misunderstandings. I would be sincerely grateful to you if you could lighten my darkness. With collegial regards,

Yours very sincerely, C. G. JUNG

---

[3] (1885–1962), Danish physicist, head of the Copenhagen Institute for Theoretical Physics; received the Nobel Prize for Physics in 1922. He elaborated the model of the atom as a miniature solar system first put forward by the English physicist Ernest Rutherford (1871–1937) on the basis of the spectrum of hydrogen.

[4] The German play on words, "wirklich" (real) and "wirkt" (works), cannot be rendered satisfactorily in English. "Actual because it acts" is a lame duck. [Tr.]

From **Letters,** vol. 2, pp. 64–65

*To Fritz Buri**

Dear Professor Buri,   5 May 1952

Since you were kind enough to send me your review,[1] I am taking the liberty of going more closely into a few points in it.

As you know, I apply my method not only to my patients but also to all historical and contemporary products of the mind. With regard to Yahweh's "cure" it should be noted that anything that happens in our consciousness has a retroactive effect on the unconscious archetype. Submission to the archetype that appears as an unjust God must bring about a change in this "God." And this, as subsequent history proves, is what actually happened. Yahweh's injustice and amorality were known to the Jews and were a source of disquiet and distress. (Cf. the drastic passages cited in *Aion*, pp. 93ff.)[2] The transformation of the God of the Old Testament into the God of the New is not my invention but was known long ago in the Middle Ages.[3]

I am in truth concerned with the "depths of the human psyche," as I expressly point out. But I cannot make statements about a metaphysical God, nor do I imagine that with the term "God" I have "posited" anything metaphysical. I speak always and exclusively only of the anthropomorphic God-image. The verbal inspiration of the Bible seems to me an implausible and unprovable hypothesis. I do not by any means dispute the existence of a metaphysical God, but I allow myself to put human statements under the microscope. Had I criticized the *chronique scandaleuse* of Olympus this would have caused an uproar 2500 years ago. Today nobody would bat an eyelid.

I do not pretend to know anything tenable or provable about a metaphysical God. I therefore don't quite understand how you can smell "gnostic" arrogance in this attitude. In strictest contrast to Gnosticism *and* theology, I confine myself to the psychology of anthropomorphic ideas and have never maintained that I possess the slightest trace of metaphysical knowledge. Just as the physicist regards the atom as a model, I regard archetypal ideas as sketches

---

* Basel. Cf. Buri, 10 Dec. 45 (in vol. 1).
[1] Cf. Billeter, 3 May 52, n. 1.
[2] Pars. 106ff.
[3] Cf. *Psychology and Alchemy*, CW 12, pars. 522f.

for the purpose of visualizing the unknown background. One would hardly call a physicist a Gnostic because of his atomic models. Nor should one want to know better than God, who himself *regrets* his actions and thereby plainly says what *he himself* thinks of them.

Anyway I am very grateful to you for having expounded my shocking thought-processes so objectively—a rare experience for me!

Yours sincerely, C. G. JUNG

From **Letters,** vol. 2, p. 147

To Erich Neumann

Dear Neumann,   30 January 1954

Best thanks for your friendly letter. I was just writing to Hull, who is to insert a passage on your work in the English edition of *Symbole der Wandlung.*[1]

The transition to the New Year has not passed without difficulties: liver and intestine revolted against the too oily hotel cooking in Locarno, though this had its good side in that my holiday was $1^1/_2$ weeks longer than expected.

I have already penetrated a good way into your "Kulturentwicklung"[2] and shall be able to read further as soon as the mountain of letters that have accumulated during my absence is cleared away.

I would abandon the term "Gnostic" without compunction were it not a swearword in the mouths of theologians. They accuse me of the very same fault they commit themselves: presumptuous disregard of epistemological barriers. When a theologian says "God," then God has to be, and be just as the magician wants, without the latter feeling in any way impelled to make clear to himself and his public exactly which concept he is using. He fraudulently offers his

---

[1] Cf. *Symbols of Transformation,* CW 5, par. 3, where Jung refers to N.'s "massive contribution towards solving the countless difficult problems that crop up everywhere in this hitherto little explored territory [of historical and ethnological parallels]."

[2] *Kulturentwicklung und Religion* (1953), containing N.'s 1948–50 Eranos lectures.

(limited) God-concept to the naïve listener as a special revelation. What sort of God is Buber talking about, for instance? Yahweh? With or without *privatio boni?* And if Yahweh, where does he say that this God is certainly not the God of the Christians? This under-hand way of doing holy business I fling in the teeth of theologians of all colours. I do not maintain that my "gnostic" images are a faith-ful reflection of their transcendental background, binding on ev-eryone, or that this is conjured up by my naming it. It is evident that Buber has a bad conscience, as he publishes only *his* letters[3] and does not represent me fairly, since I am a mere Gnostic, though he hasn't the faintest idea of what the Gnostic was moved by. Meanwhile with best regards and wishes,

Yours sincerely, C. G. JUNG

From **Letters**, vol. 2, pp. 244–45

To Pater Raymond Hostie*

Dear Pater,   25 April 1955

Unfortunately I am unable to thank you for sending me your book.[1] As you know through Father Bruno,[2] you criticize me as though I were a philosopher. But you know very well that I am an empiricist whose concepts have—as such—no content, since they are mere *nomina* that can be changed as convention requires. I have given you every opportunity in the past to discuss obscurities. You never came out with your criticism.

I have no doctrine and no philosophical system, but have pre-sented new *facts* which you studiously ignore. It is as though one were to criticize the labels on the drawers of a collection of minerals without looking at their contents. It is not so much your fault that you do not appear to understand how it is that the psychic facts designated by my concepts possess an autonomy of their own. This is an empirical fact which is not understood by most people any-

[3] Cf. Neumann, 28 Feb. 52, n. 9.
* S. J., Louvain. This letter is published without omissions at the specific request of H.
[1] *Du Mythe à la réligion* (1955; tr., *Religion and the Psychology of Jung*, 1957).
[2] Jung expressed his criticism of the book in a letter of 22 Dec. 54 to Father Bruno de Jésus-Marie (not in this selection). A long letter to Bruno is in CW 18, pars. 1518ff. Cf. below, 20 Nov. 56.

way, because they have never gone through the same experiences—
quite understandably, since they take no notice of my method. *Si
parva licet componere magnis,* the situation is the same as with
Galileo, who discovered the hitherto unknown moons of Jupiter by
means of a telescope. But no one wanted to look through it. So
Jupiter had no moons. Mandala symbols, for instance, are seen not
only in Zurich but also in Rio de Janeiro and San Francisco—
naturally only by psychiatrists who get their patients to draw.
These are the facts that count, not the names. You overlook the
facts and then think that the name is the fact, and thus you reach
the nonsensical conclusion that I hypostatize ideas and am therefore a "Gnostic." *It is your theological standpoint that is a gnosis, not
my empiricism,* of which you obviously haven't the faintest inkling.

I must also express the conjecture that I may be doing injustice to
you personally by taking your criticism as a perversion of the facts.
You are, after all, the member of an Order whose principle is: *Quod
oculis nostris apparet album, nigrum illa esse definierit, debemus itidem,
quod nigrum sit, pronuntiare.*[3] Hence in any discussion there is no
personal opponent with whom one could come to an
understanding.

Yours truly, C. G. JUNG

From **Letters,** vol. 2, pp. 570–73

*To Robert C. Smith**   [ORIGINAL IN ENGLISH]

Dear Mr. Smith,   29 June 1960

Buber and I[1] start from an entirely different basis: I make no
transcendental statements. I am essentially empirical, as I have

---

[3] "We have to pronounce as black what appears to our eyes white if she [the Church] calls
it black." Ignatius of Loyola, *Exercitia Spiritualia,* in the 13th of the "Rules for the Unity
of the Church."

* Then in Villanova, Pennsylvania. Now assistant professor of philosophy and religion,
Trenton State College (New Jersey). At the time of writing S. was preparing as a thesis "A
Critical Analysis of Religious and Philosophical Issues between Buber and Jung." Cf.
Neumann, 28 Feb. 52, n. 9.

[1] In his letter S. had reported a conversation with Buber in which the latter had accused
Jung of being a "monologist," having reduced God to an object, and maintaining that
Jung's statement that without man no God would be possible was an ontological denial of
God.

stated more than once. I am dealing with psychic phenomena and not with metaphysical assertions. Within the frame of psychic events I find the fact of the belief in God. It *says:* "God is." This is the fact I am concerned with. I am not concerned with the truth or untruth of God's existence. *I am concerned with the statement only,* and I am interested in its structure and behaviour. It is an emotionally "toned" complex like the father- or mother-complex or the Oedipus complex. It is obvious that if man does not exist, no such statement can exist either, nor can anybody prove that the statement "God" exists in a non-human sphere.

What Buber misunderstands as Gnosticism is *psychiatric observation,* of which he obviously knows nothing. It is certainly not my invention. Buber has been led astray by a poem in Gnostic style I made 44 years ago for a friend's birthday celebration[2] (a private print!), a poetic paraphrase of the psychology of the unconscious.

"Every pioneer is a monologist" until other people have tried out his method and confirmed his results. Would you call all the great minds which were not popular among their contemporaries, monologists, even that "voice of one crying in the wilderness"?

Buber, having no practical experience in depth psychology, does not know of the *autonomy of complexes,* a most easily observable fact however. Thus God, as an autonomous complex,[3] is a *subject* confronting me. One must be really blind if one cannot get that from my books. Likewise the *self* is a redoubtable reality, as everybody learns who has tried or was compelled to do something about it. Yet I define the Self as a *borderline concept.* This must be a puzzler for people like Buber, who are unacquainted with the empiricist's epistemology.

Why cannot Buber get into his head that I deal with psychic facts and not with metaphysical assertions? Buber is a theologian and has far more information about God's true existence and other of His qualities than I could ever dream of acquiring. My ambitions are not soaring to theological heights. I am merely concerned with the practical and theoretical problem of how-do-complexes-behave? F.i. how does a mother-complex behave in a child and in an adult? How does the God-complex behave in different individuals and societies? How does the self-complex compare with the *Lapis Phi-*

[2] *Septem Sermones ad Mortuos.* Cf. Maeder, 19 Jan. 17, n. 1.
[3] Cf. White, 5 Oct. 45, n. 2.

losophorum in Hermetic philosophy and with the Christ-figure in patristic allegories, with Al Chadir in Islamic tradition, with Tifereth in the Kabbalah, with Mithras, Attis, Odin, Krishna, and so on?

As you see, I am concerned with *images*, human phenomena, of which only the ignorant can assume that they are within our control or that they can be reduced to mere "objects." Every psychiatrist and psychotherapist can tell you to what an enormous degree man is delivered over to the terrific power of a complex which has assumed superiority over his mind. (*Vide* compulsion neurosis, schizophrenia, drugs, political and private nonsense, etc.) Mental possessions are just as good as ghosts, demons, and gods.

It is the task of the psychologist to investigate these matters. The theologian certainly has not done it yet. I am afraid it is sheer prejudice against science which hinders theologians from understanding my empirical standpoint. Seen from this standpoint the "experience of God" is *nolens volens* the psychic fact that I find myself confronted with, a factor in myself (more or less represented also by external circumstances) which proves to me to be of insurmountable power. F.i. a most rational professor of philosophy is entirely possessed by the fear of cancer which he knows does not exist. Try to liberate such an unfortunate fellow from his predicament and you will get an idea of "psychic autonomy."

I am sorry if X. bothers about the question of the basis upon which "religion rests." This is a metaphysical question the solution of which I do not know. I am concerned with *phenomenal religion*, with its observable facts, to which I try to add a few psychological observations about basic events in the collective unconscious, the existence of which I can prove. Beyond this I know nothing and I have never made any assertions about it.

How does Buber know of something he cannot "experience psychologically"? How is such a thing possible at all? If not in the psyche, then where else? You see, it is always the same matter: *the complete misunderstanding of the psychological argument:* "God" within the frame of psychology is an *autonomous complex, a dynamic image, and that is all psychology is ever able to state.* It cannot know more about God. It cannot prove or disprove God's actual existence, but it does know how fallible images in the human mind are.

If Niels Bohr compares the model of atomic structure with a

planetary system, he knows it is merely a model of a transcendent and unknown reality, and if I talk of the God-image I do not deny a transcendental reality. I merely insist on the psychic reality of the God-complex or the God-image, as Niels Bohr proposes the analogy of a planetary system. He would not be as dumb as to believe that his model is an exact and true replica of the atom. No empiricist in his senses would believe his models to be the eternal truth itself. He knows too well how many changes any kind of reality undergoes in becoming a conscious representation.

All my ideas are names, models, and hypotheses for a better understanding of observable facts. I never dreamt that intelligent people could misunderstand them as theological statements, i.e., hypostases. I was obviously too naïve in this regard and that is the reason why I was sometimes not careful enough to repeat time and again: "But what I mean is only the psychic image of a *noumenon*"[4] (Kant's thing-in-itself, which is not a negation as you know).

My empirical standpoint is so disappointingly simple that it needs only an average intelligence and a bit of common sense to understand it, but it needs an uncommon amount of prejudice or even ill-will to misunderstand it, as it seems to me. I am sorry if I bore you with my commonplaces. But you asked for it. You can find them in most of my books, beginning with the year 1912,[5] almost half a century ago and not yet noticed by authorities like Buber. I have spent a lifetime of work on psychological and psychopathological investigations. Buber criticizes me in a field in which he is incompetent and which he does not even understand.

Sincerely yours, C. G. JUNG

---

[4] "An object of purely intellectual intuition, devoid of all phenomenal attributes" (*Shorter Oxford Dict.*). The term was introduced by Kant to distinguish between "noumenon" and "phenomenon" as "an immediate object of perception."
[5] Date of publication of *Wandlungen und Symbole der Libido* (orig. version of *Symbols of Transformation*).

From **Letters**, vol. 2, pp. 583–84

To Robert C. Smith
                              [ORIGINAL IN ENGLISH]
Dear Mr. Smith,   16 August 1960
    Why can't you understand that the therapeutic performance is a
vital process,[1] which I call the "process of individuation"? It takes
place objectively and it is this experience which helps the patient
and not the more or less competent or foolish interpretation of the
analyst.
    The best the analyst can do is not to disturb the natural evolution
of this process. My so-called views about it are only poor means of
representing the very mysterious process of transformation in the
form of words, which serve no other purpose than to describe its
nature.
    The process consists in becoming whole or integrated, and that
is never produced by words or interpretations but wholly by the
nature of Psyche itself. When I say "Psyche" I mean something
unknown, to which I give the name "Psyche." There is a difference
between hypothesis and hypostasis. My hypothesis is that all psychic products referring to religious views are comparable on the
basis of a fundamental similarity of the human mind. This is a
scientific hypothesis. The Gnostic, which Buber accuses me of
being, makes no hypothesis, but a hypostasis in making metaphysical statements.
    When I try to establish a fundamental similarity of individual
psychic products and alchemistic or otherwise Gnostic noumena, I
carefully avoid making a hypostasis, remaining well within the
boundaries of the scientific hypothesis.
    The fact that I try to make you see my standpoint could show to
you that I don't mind the criticism. I only want to defend myself
against wrong premises. If I could not stand criticism I would have
been dead long ago, since I have had nothing but criticism for 60
years. Moreover I cannot understand what my alleged incapacity to
stand criticism has to do with the reproach that I am a Gnostic. You
simply add to the arbitrary assumption that I am a Gnostic the

---

[1] In reply to Jung's letter of 29 June 60, S. said "there are many times when a therapist's
theory affects the conceptions of his patients," and posed the question whether faith or
knowledge was the more effective healing agent.

blame of moral inferiority, and you don't realize that one could make the same subjective reproach against you.

I have accused nobody and if I am attacked I have the right to defend myself in explaining my point of view. There is no need at all to blame me under those circumstances for being intolerant.

Sincerely yours, C. G. JUNG

Part 2. Jung's Own Gnostic Myth

Chapter 10. "Seven Sermons to the Dead"

The most dramatic manifestation of Jung's preoccupation with Gnosticism is his own Gnostic myth, the "Seven Sermons to the Dead." Composed in 1916, the myth was originally published privately and circulated only to friends. At Jung's request it was excluded from the Collected Works. Both the German text and H. G. Baynes' English translation were first published privately in the early 1920s. Not until 1962 was either published publicly—as an appendix to the German and English editions of Jung's Memories, Dreams, Reflections. *Even then, the original American edition of* Memories, Dreams, Reflections *did not contain the Seven Sermons. On the history of the publication of the Seven Sermons see Stephan A. Hoeller,* The Gnostic Jung and the Seven Sermons to the Dead *(Wheaton, Ill.: Theosophical Publishing House, 1982), xxiii–xxiv, 8–9, 219–20. Hoeller also provides his own translation and analysis of the myth. On the origin, contents, and meaning of the work see, in my introduction, the section on "Jung's Own Gnostic Myth."*

"Septem Sermones ad Mortuos" (1916)

THE SEVEN SERMONS TO THE DEAD WRITTEN BY
BASILIDES IN ALEXANDRIA, THE CITY WHERE THE EAST
TOUCHETH THE WEST

Sermo I

The dead came back from Jerusalem, where they found not what they sought. They prayed me let them in and besought my word, and thus I began my teaching.

Harken: I begin with nothingness. Nothingness is the same as fullness. In infinity full is no better than empty. Nothingness is

both empty and full. As well might ye say anything else of nothingness, as for instance, white is it, or black, or again, it is not, or it is.
A thing that is infinite and eternal hath no qualities, since it hath all
qualities.

This nothingness or fullness we name the PLEROMA. Therein
both thinking and being cease, since the eternal and infinite possess
no qualities. In it no being is, for he then would be distinct from the
pleroma, and would possess qualities which would distinguish him
as something distinct from the pleroma.

In the pleroma there is nothing and everything. It is quite fruit-
less to think about the pleroma, for this would mean self-
dissolution.

CREATURA is not in the pleroma, but in itself. The pleroma is
both beginning and end of created beings. It pervadeth them, as
the light of the sun everywhere pervadeth the air. Although the
pleroma pervadeth altogether, yet hath created being no share
thereof, just as a wholly transparent body becometh neither light
nor dark through the light which pervadeth it. We are, however,
the pleroma itself, for we are a part of the eternal and infinite. But
we have no share thereof, as we are from the pleroma infinitely
removed; not spiritually or temporally, but essentially, since we are
distinguished from the pleroma in our essence as creatura, which is
confined within time and space.

Yet because we are parts of the pleroma, the pleroma is also in us.
Even in the smallest point is the pleroma endless, eternal, and
entire, since small and great are qualities which are contained in it.
It is that nothingness which is everywhere whole and continuous.
Only figuratively, therefore, do I speak of created being as a part of
the pleroma. Because, actually, the pleroma is nowhere divided,
since it is nothingness. We are also the whole pleroma, because,
figuratively, the pleroma is the smallest point (assumed only, not
existing) in us and the boundless firmament about us. But wherefore, then, do we speak of the pleroma at all, since it is thus everything and nothing?

I speak of it to make a beginning somewhere, and also to free you
from the delusion that somewhere, either without or within, there
standeth something fixed, or in some way established, from the
beginning. Every so-called fixed and certain thing is only relative.
That alone is fixed and certain which is subject to change.

What is changeable, however, is creatura. Therefore is it the one thing which is fixed and certain; because it hath qualities: it is even quality itself.

The question ariseth: How did creatura originate? Created beings came to pass, not creatura; since created being is the very quality of the pleroma, as much as non-creation which is the eternal death. In all times and places is creation, in all times and places is death. The pleroma hath all, distinctiveness and non-distinctiveness.

Distinctiveness is creatura. It is distinct. Distinctiveness is its essence, and therefore it distinguisheth. Therefore man discriminateth because his nature is distinctiveness. Wherefore also he distinguished qualities of the pleroma which are not. He distinguisheth them out of his own nature. Therefore must he speak of qualities of the pleroma which are not.

What use, say ye, to speak of it? Saidst thou not thyself, there is no profit in thinking upon the pleroma?

That said I unto you, to free you from the delusion that we are able to think about the pleroma. When we distinguish qualities of the pleroma, we are speaking from the ground of our own distinctiveness and concerning our own distinctiveness. But we have said nothing concerning the pleroma. Concerning our own distinctiveness, however, it is needful to speak, whereby we may distinguish ourselves enough. Our very nature is distinctiveness. If we are not true to this nature we do not distinguish ourselves enough. Therefore must we make distinctions of qualities.

What is the harm, ye ask, in not distinguishing oneself? If we do not distinguish, we get beyond our own nature, away from creatura. We fall into indistinctiveness, which is the other quality of the pleroma. We fall into the pleroma itself and cease to be creatures. We are given over to dissolution in the nothingness. This is the death of the creature. Therefore we die in such measure as we do not distinguish. Hence the natural striving of the creature goeth towards distinctiveness, fighteth against primeval, perilous sameness. This is called the PRINCIPIUM INDIVIDUATIONIS. This principle is the essence of the creature. From this you can see why indistinctiveness and non-distinction are a great danger for the creature.

We must, therefore, distinguish the qualities of the pleroma. The qualities are PAIRS OF OPPOSITES, such as—

The Effective and the Ineffective.
Fullness and Emptiness.

Living and Dead.
Difference and Sameness.
Light and Darkness.
The Hot and the Cold.
Force and Matter.
Time and Space.
Good and Evil.
Beauty and Ugliness.
The One and the Many. etc.

The pairs of opposites are qualities of the pleroma which are not, because each balanceth each. As we are the pleroma itself, we also have all these qualities in us. Because the very ground of our nature is distinctiveness, therefore we have these qualities in the name and sign of distinctiveness, which meaneth—

1. These qualities are distinct and separate in us one from the other; therefore they are not balanced and void, but are effective. Thus are we the victims of the pairs of opposites. The pleroma is rent in us.

2. The qualities belong to the pleroma, and only in the name and sign of distinctiveness can and must we possess or live them. We must distinguish ourselves from qualities. In the pleroma they are balanced and void; in us not. Being distinguished from them delivereth us.

When we strive after the good or the beautiful, we thereby forget our own nature, which is distinctiveness, and we are delivered over to the qualities of the pleroma, which are pairs of opposites. We labor to attain to the good and the beautiful, yet at the same time we also lay hold of the evil and the ugly, since in the pleroma these are one with the good and the beautiful. When, however, we remain true to our own nature, which is distinctiveness, we distinguish ourselves from the good and the beautiful, and, therefore, at the same time, from the evil and the ugly. And thus we fall not into the pleroma, namely, into nothingness and dissolution.

Thou sayest, ye object, that difference and sameness are also qualities of the pleroma. How would it be, then, if we strive after difference? Are we, in so doing, not true to our own nature? And must we none the less be given over to sameness when we strive after difference?

Ye must not forget that the pleroma hath no qualities. We create them through thinking. If, therefore, ye strive after difference or sameness, or any qualities whatsoever, ye pursue thoughts which flow to you out of the pleroma; thoughts, namely, concerning non-existing qualities of the pleroma. Inasmuch as ye run after these thoughts, ye fall again into the pleroma, and reach difference and sameness at the same time. Not your thinking, but your being, is distinctiveness. Therefore not after difference, as ye think it, must ye strive; but after YOUR OWN BEING. At bottom, therefore, there is only one striving, namely, the striving after your own being. If ye had this striving ye would not need to know anything about the pleroma and its qualities, and yet would ye come to your right goal by virtue of your own being. Since, however, thought estrangeth from being, that knowledge must I teach you wherewith ye may be able to hold your thought in leash.

Sermo II

In the night the dead stood along the wall and cried:
We would have knowledge of god. Where is god? Is god dead?
God is not dead. Now, as ever, he liveth. God is creatura, for he is something definite, and therefore distinct from the pleroma. God is quality of the pleroma, and everything which I said of creatura also is true concerning him.

He is distinguished, however, from created beings through this, that he is more indefinite and indeterminable than they. He is less distinct than created beings, since the ground of his being is effective fullness. Only in so far as he is definite and distinct is he creatura, and in like measure is he the manifestation of the effective fullness of the pleroma.

Everything which we do not distinguish falleth into the pleroma and is made void by its opposite. If, therefore, we do not distinguish god, effective fullness is for us extinguished.

Moreover god is the pleroma itself, as likewise each smallest point in the created and uncreated is the pleroma itself.

Effective void is the nature of the devil. God and devil are the first manifestations of nothingness, which we call the pleroma. It is indifferent whether the pleroma is or is not, since in everything it is balanced and void. Not so creatura. In so far as god and devil are creatura they do not extinguish each other, but stand one against the other as effective opposites. We need no proof of their existence.

It is enough that we must always be speaking of them. Even if both were not, creatura, of its own essential distinctiveness, would forever distinguish them anew out of the pleroma.

Everything that discrimination taketh out of the pleroma is a pair of opposites. To god, therefore, always belongeth the devil.

This inseparability is as close and, as your own life hath made you see, as indissoluble as the pleroma itself. Thus it is that both stand very close to the pleroma, in which all opposites are extinguished and joined.

God and devil are distinguished by the qualities fullness and emptiness, generation and destruction. EFFECTIVENESS is common to both. Effectiveness joineth them. Effectiveness, therefore, standeth above both; is a god above god, since in its effect it uniteth fullness and emptiness.

This is a god whom ye knew not, for mankind forgot it. We name it by its name ABRAXAS. It is more indefinite still than god and devil.

That god may be distinguished from it, we name god HELIOS or Sun. Abraxas is effect. Nothing standeth opposed to it but the ineffective; hence its effective nature freely unfoldeth itself. The ineffective is not, therefore resisteth not. Abraxas standeth above the sun and above the devil. It is improbable probability, unreal reality. Had the pleroma a being, Abraxas would be its manifestation. It is the effective itself, not any particular effect, but effect in general.

It is unreal reality, because it hath no definite effect.

It is also creatura, because it is distinct from the pleroma.

The sun hath a definite effect, and so hath the devil. Wherefore do they appear to us more effective than indefinite Abraxas.

It is force, duration, change.

The dead now raised a great tumult, for they were Christians.

Sermo III

Like mists arising from a marsh, the dead came near and cried: Speak further unto us concerning the supreme god.

Hard to know is the deity of Abraxas. Its power is the greatest, because man perceiveth it not. From the sun he draweth the *summum bonum;* from the devil the *infimum malum;* but from Abraxas LIFE, altogether indefinite, the mother of good and evil.

Smaller and weaker life seemeth to be than the *summum bonum;* wherefore is it also hard to conceive that Abraxas transcendeth even the sun in power, who is himself the radiant source of all the force of life.

Abraxas is the sun, and at the same time the eternally sucking gorge of the void, the belittling and dismembering devil.

The power of Abraxas is twofold; but ye see it not, because for your eyes the warring opposites of this power are extinguished.

What the god-sun speaketh is life.

What the devil speaketh is death.

But Abraxas speaketh that hallowed and accursed word which is life and death at the same time.

Abraxas begetteth truth and lying, good and evil, light and darkness, in the same word and in the same act. Wherefore is Abraxas terrible.

It is splendid as the lion in the instant he striketh down his victim. It is beautiful as a day of spring. It is the great Pan himself and also the small one. It is Priapos.

It is the monster of the under-world, a thousand-armed polyp, coiled knot of winged serpents, frenzy.

It is the hermaphrodite of the earliest beginning.

It is the lord of the toads and frogs, which live in the water and go up on the land, whose chorus ascendeth at noon and at midnight.

It is abundance that seeketh union with emptiness.

It is holy begetting.

It is love and love's murder.

It is the saint and his betrayer.

It is the brightest light of day and the darkest night of madness.

To look upon it, is blindness.

To know it, is sickness.

To worship it, is death.

To fear it, is wisdom.

To resist it not, is redemption.

God dwelleth behind the sun, the devil behind the night. What god bringeth forth out of the light the devil sucketh into the night. But Abraxas is the world, its becoming and its passing. Upon every gift that cometh from the god-sun the devil layeth his curse.

Everything that ye entreat from the god-sun begetteth a deed of the devil.

Everything that ye create with the god-sun giveth effective power to the devil.

That is terrible Abraxas.

It is the mightiest creature, and in it the creature is afraid of itself.

It is the manifest opposition of creatura to the pleroma and its nothingness.

It is the son's horror of the mother.

It is the mother's love for the son.

It is the delight of the earth and the cruelty of the heavens.

Before its countenance man becometh like stone.

Before it there is no question and no reply.

It is the life of creatura.

It is the operation of distinctiveness.

It is the love of man.

It is the speech of man.

It is the appearance and the shadow of man.

It is illusory reality.

Now the dead howled and raged, for they were unperfected.

Sermo IV

The dead filled the place murmuring and said:

Tell us of gods and devils, accursed one!

The god-sun is the highest good; the devil is the opposite. Thus have ye two gods. But there are many high and good things and many great evils. Among these are two god-devils; the one is the BURNING ONE, the other the GROWING ONE.

The burning one is EROS, who hath the form of flame. Flame giveth light because it consumeth.

The growing one is the TREE OF LIFE. It buddeth, as in growing it heapeth up living stuff.

Eros flameth up and dieth. But the tree of life groweth with slow and constant increase through unmeasured time.

Good and evil are united in the flame.

Good and evil are united in the increase of the tree. In their divinity stand life and love opposed.

Innumerable as the host of the stars is the number of gods and devils.

Each star is a god, and each space that a star filleth is a devil. But the empty-fullness of the whole is the pleroma.

The operation of the whole is Abraxas, to whom only the ineffective standeth opposed.

Four is the number of the principal gods, as four is the number of the world's measurements.

One is the beginning, the god-sun.

Two is Eros; for he bindeth twain together and outspreadeth himself in brightness.

Three is the Tree of Life, for it filleth space with bodily forms.

Four is the devil, for he openeth all that is closed. All that is formed of bodily nature doth he dissolve; he is the destroyer in whom everything is brought to nothing.

For me, to whom knowledge hath been given of the multiplicity and diversity of the gods, it is well. But woe unto you, who replace these incompatible many by a single god. For in so doing ye beget the torment which is bred from not understanding, and ye mutilate the creature whose nature and aim is distinctiveness. How can ye be true to your own nature when ye try to change the many into one? What ye do unto the gods is done likewise unto you. Ye all become equal and thus is your nature maimed.

Equality shall prevail not for god, but only for the sake of man. For the gods are many, whilst men are few. The gods are mighty and can endure their manifoldness. For like the stars they abide in solitude, parted one from the other by immense distances. But men are weak and cannot endure their manifold nature. Therefore they dwell together and need communion, that they may bear their separateness. For redemption's sake I teach you the rejected truth, for the sake of which I was rejected.

The multiplicity of the gods correspondeth to the multiplicity of man.

Numberless gods await the human state. Numberless gods have been men. Man shareth in the nature of the gods. He cometh from the gods and goeth unto god.

Thus, just as it serveth not to reflect upon the pleroma, it availeth not to worship the multiplicity of the gods. Least of all availeth it to worship the first god, the effective abundance and the *summum bonum*. By our prayer we can add to it nothing, and from it nothing take; because the effective void swalloweth all.

The bright gods form the celestial world. It is manifold and infinitely spreading and increasing. The god-sun is the supreme lord of that world.

The dark gods form the earth-world. They are simple and infinitely diminishing and declining. The devil is the earth-world's lowest lord, the moon-spirit, satellite of the earth, smaller, colder, and more dead than the earth.

There is no difference between the might of the celestial gods and those of the earth. The celestial gods magnify, the earth-gods diminish. Measureless is the movement of both.

Sermo V

The dead mocked and cried: Teach us, fool, of the church and holy communion.

The world of the gods is made manifest in spirituality and in sexuality. The celestial ones appear in spirituality, the earthly in sexuality.

Spirituality conceiveth and embraceth. It is womanlike and therefore we call it MATER COELESTIS, the celestial mother. Sexuality engendereth and createth. It is manlike, and therefore we call it PHALLOS, the earthly father.

The sexuality of man is more of the earth, the sexuality of woman is more of the spirit.

The spirituality of man is more of heaven, it goeth to the greater.

The spirituality of woman is more of the earth, it goeth to the smaller.

Lying and devilish is the spirituality of the man which goeth to the smaller.

Lying and devilish is the spirituality of the woman which goeth to the greater.

Each must go to its own place.

Man and woman become devils one to the other when they divide not their spiritual ways, for the nature of creatura is distinctiveness.

The sexuality of man hath an earthward course, the sexuality of woman a spiritual. Man and woman become devils one to the other if they distinguish not their sexuality.

Man shall know of the smaller, woman the greater.

Man shall distinguish himself both from spirituality and from sexuality. He shall call spirituality Mother, and set her between heaven and earth. He shall call sexuality Phallos, and set him between himself and earth. For the Mother and the Phallos are superhuman daemons which reveal the world of the gods. They are for us more effective than the gods, because they are closely akin to our own nature. Should ye not distinguish yourselves from sexuality and from spirituality, and not regard them as of a nature both above you and beyond, then are ye delivered over to them as qualities of the pleroma. Spirituality and sexuality are not your qualities, not things which ye possess and contain. But they possess and contain you; for they are powerful daemons, manifestations of the gods, and are, therefore, things which reach beyond you, existing in themselves. No man hath a spirituality unto himself, or a sexuality unto himself. But he standeth under the law of spirituality and of sexuality.

No man, therefore, escapeth these daemons. Ye shall look upon them as daemons, and as a common task and danger, a common burden which life hath laid upon you. Thus is life for you also a common task and danger, as are the gods, and first of all terrible Abraxas.

Man is weak, therefore is communion indispensable. If your communion be not under the sign of the Mother, then is it under the sign of the Phallos. No communion is suffering and sickness. Communion in everything is dismemberment and dissolution.

Distinctiveness leadeth to singleness. Singleness is opposed to communion. But because of man's weakness over against the gods and daemons and their invincible law is communion needful. Therefore shall there be as much communion as is needful, not for man's sake, but because of the gods. The gods force you to communion. As much as they force you, so much is communion needed, more is evil.

In communion let every man submit to others, that communion be maintained; for ye need it.

In singleness the one man shall be superior to the others, that every man may come to himself and avoid slavery.

In communion there shall be continence.

In singleness there shall be prodigality.

Communion is depth.

Singleness is height.

Right measure in communion purifieth and preserveth.
Right measure in singleness purifieth and increaseth.
Communion giveth us warmth, singleness giveth us light.

Sermo VI

The daemon of sexuality approacheth our soul as a serpent. It is half human and appeareth as thought-desire.

The daemon of spirituality descendeth into our soul as the white bird. It is half human and appeareth as desire-thought.

The serpent is an earthy soul, half daemonic, a spirit, and akin to the spirits of the dead. Thus too, like these, she swarmeth around in the things of earth, making us either to fear them or pricking us with intemperate desires. The serpent hath a nature like unto woman. She seeketh ever the company of the dead who are held by the spell of the earth, they who found not the way beyond that leadeth to singleness. The serpent is a whore. She wantoneth with the devil and with evil spirits; a mischievous tyrant and tormentor, ever seducing to evilest company. The white bird is a half-celestial soul of man. He bideth with the Mother, from time to time descending. The bird hath a nature like unto man, and is effective thought. He is chaste and solitary, a messenger of the Mother. He flieth high above earth. He commandeth singleness. He bringeth knowledge from the distant ones who went before and are perfected. He beareth our word above to the Mother. She intercedeth, she warneth, but against the gods she hath no power. She is a vessel of the sun. The serpent goeth below and with her cunning she lameth the phallic daemon, or else goadeth him on. She yieldeth up the too crafty thoughts of the earthy one, those thoughts which creep through every hole and cleave to all things with desirousness. The serpent, doubtless, willeth it not, yet she must be of use to us. She fleeth our grasp, thus showing us the way, which with our human wits we could not find.

With disdainful glance the dead spake: Cease this talk of gods and daemons and souls. At bottom this hath long been known to us.

Sermo VII

Yet when night was come the dead again approached with lamentable mien and said: There is yet one matter we forgot to mention. Teach us about man.

Man is a gateway, through which from the outer world of gods, daemons, and souls ye pass into the inner world; out of the greater into the smaller world. Small and transitory is man. Already is he behind you, and once again ye find yourselves in endless space, in the smaller or innermost infinity. At immeasurable distance standeth one single Star in the zenith.

This is the one god of this one man. This is his world, his pleroma, his divinity.

In this world is man Abraxas, the creator and the destroyer of his own world.

This Star is the god and the goal of man.

This is his one guiding god. In him goeth man to his rest. Toward him goeth the long journey of the soul after death. In him shineth forth as light all that man bringeth back from the greater world. To this one god man shall pray.

Prayer increaseth the light of the Star. It casteth a bridge over death. It prepareth life for the smaller world and assuageth the hopeless desires of the greater.

When the greater world waxeth cold, burneth the Star.

Between man and his one god there standeth nothing, so long as man can turn away his eyes from the flaming spectacle of Abraxas.

Man here, god there.

Weakness and nothingness here, there eternally creative power.

Here nothing but darkness and chilling moisture.

There wholly sun.

Whereupon the dead were silent and ascended like the smoke above the herdsman's fire, who through the night kept watch over his flock.

ANAGRAMMA:

NAHTRIHECCUNDE
GAHINNEVERAHTUNIN
ZEHGESSURKLACH
ZUNNUS.

Part 3. Other Authorities on Jungian Psychology and Gnosticism

Chapter 11. Victor White, "Some Notes on Gnosticism"

On February 20, 1948, Father Victor White spoke on Gnosticism to the Analytical Psychology Club of New York. A summary of the talk by Margarita Pennington Luttichau was published in the Club's Bulletin (10 [March 1948], 6–8). The talk was also given to the Guild of Pastoral Psychology in London on December 10, 1948. It was published as "Some Notes on Gnosticism" in both the Guild's Lecture Series (Lecture 59 [April 1949]) and Spring ([1949] 40–56). Retitled "Gnosis, Gnosticism and Faith," the essay was republished almost unaltered as chapter 11 of White's God and the Unconscious (London: Collins, 1952; reprint: Cleveland: Meridian Books, 1961; reprint: Dallas: Spring Publications, 1982). The following version is reprinted from Spring. White combines a keen Jungian analysis of the psychological state of the Gnostic, or "Gnosticist," with a staunch Catholic assessment of that state. His Jungian analysis of the Gnostic state departs strikingly from Jung's own. Where for Jung the Gnostic ideal symbolizes individuation, for White it betokens psychosis. On White and Jung see, in my introduction, the section on "Victor White."

"Some Notes on Gnosticism" (1949)

It was the numerous references to gnosis and gnostics in the writings of C. G. Jung that first gave me any idea that there might be more to it than a bygone form of nonsensical, fanatical superstition—of no interest to myself or to any modern man. One passage in particular aroused my interest:

> [Modern Man] is somehow fascinated by the almost pathological manifestations of the unconscious mind. We must admit the

fact, however difficult it is for us to understand that something which previous ages have discarded should suddenly command our attention. That there is a general interest in these matters is a truth which cannot be denied, their offence to good taste notwithstanding. I am not thinking merely of the interest in the psycho-analysis of Freud, but of the widespread interest in all sorts of psychic phenomena as manifested in the growth of spiritualism, astrology, theosophy, and so forth. . . . We can compare it only to the flowering of Gnostic thought in the first and second centuries after Christ. The spiritual currents of the present have, in fact, a deep affinity with Gnosticism. There is even a Gnostic church in France to-day, and I know of two schools in Germany which openly declare themselves Gnostic. The modern movement which is numerically most impressive is undoubtedly Theosophy, together with its continental sister, Anthroposophy; these are pure Gnosticism in a Hindu dress. Compared with these movements the interest in scientific psychology is negligible. What is striking about Gnostic systems is that they are based exclusively upon the manifestations of the unconscious, and that their moral teachings do not baulk at the shadow-side of life. Even in the form of its European revival, the Hindu *Kundalini-Yoga* shows this clearly. And as every person informed on the subject of occultism will testify, the statement holds true in this field as well.

The passionate interest in these movements arises undoubtedly from psychic energy which can no longer be invested in obsolete forms of religion. . . .

I do not believe that I am going too far when I say that modern man, in contrast to his nineteenth-century brother, turns his attention to the psyche with very great expectations; and that he does so without reference to any traditional creed, but rather in the Gnostic sense of religious experience. We should be wrong in seeing mere caricature or masquerade when the movements already mentioned try to give themselves scientific airs; their doing so is rather an indication that they are actually pursuing "science" or knowledge instead of the *faith* which is the essence of Western religions. The modern man abhors dogmatic postulates taken on faith and the religions based upon them. He holds them valid only in so far as their knowledge-content seems to accord with his own experience of the deeps of psychic life.[1]

Readers of Jung's books know how frequent are his references to the gnostics, and how often he compares our present situation with that which confronted them some two thousand years ago. It is worth while to inquire more closely, and perhaps more critically, into gnosis and gnosticism, and to ask what is to be understood by this contrast between the "faith which is the essence of Western religions" and psychic experience and knowledge. An obstinate adherent of an "obsolete" creed may be expected to have a somewhat different angle on the subject from that of Dr. Jung, but one which may not perhaps be without some psychological and cultural importance.

The subject concerns us, I would suggest, not only for the reasons indicated by Dr. Jung, but also because Jungian psychology in its later developments is itself often suspected of something very like gnosticism. "The Zürich school of Jung," pronounces Hans Prinzhorn, "no longer has psychotherapeutic actuality: it represents a philosophy which, for appreciation, requires esoteric association with the Master."[2] More recently and more moderately, Dr. Karl Stern has qualified his approval of much of Jung's work with the misgiving that it "frequently leads to some sort of noncommittal mysticism, a mysticism without discipline, so that in the end there remains a museum of religious experiences, with Christian, Hindu, Buddhist, etc., collector's items."[3] Similar qualms have been expressed by Dr. E. B. Strauss in his noteworthy presidential address to the Medical Section of the British Psychological Society.[4] This is not the place to examine these charges and misgivings, but they do indicate that gnosticism is by no means an issue with which we have nothing to do. However difficult the task, it may be profitable to inquire into the gnosticism of the past, and the controversies to which it gave rise, in order to see if they have

[1] *Modern Man in Search of a Soul*, pp. 238, 239.
[2] *Psychotherapy, its Nature, its Assumptions, its Limitations*, p. 24.
[3] "Religion and Psychiatry," *The Commonweal*, N.Y., Oct. 22, 1948.
[4] "Quo Vadimus?" *British Journal of Medical Psychology*. Vol. XXI. No. 1. pp. 1–11. Since this paper was written the charge of gnosticism has been laid against Jung by Martin Buber in *Merkur*, February 1952, prompting a vigorous rejoinder from Jung and a further comment from Buber in the May, 1952, number of the same review.

anything to teach us who are confronted with similar problems today.

First of all, we must understand that there never was such a thing
as gnosticism in the sense of a single sect, or a single coherent body
of belief or practice. In *Psychological Types* and elsewhere, Dr. Jung
follows common usage in speaking of "*The* Gnosis." This must not
mislead us into supposing that there was only one gnosis: in fact
there were almost as many gnoses as there were people who called
themselves gnostics or who have been called gnostics by later historians. It should be added that these historians are by no means
always agreed as to who should and who should not be called
gnostics. Nevertheless there is general agreement to label as gnosticism the characteristics of a luxuriant outcrop of variegated doctrines, sects and practices which were particularly in evidence in
the first two or three centuries of the Christian era, many of which
in greater or less degree claimed to be themselves in some way
Christian. But our task of getting a clear-cut picture is still further
complicated by the fact that these sects themselves are clearly the
inheritors of ideas, myths and practices which ante-date Christianity by several centuries; that (with modifications) kindred
ideas, myths and practices survived by many more centuries those
sects which historians are agreed to label as gnostic; and further by
the fact that the claim to gnosis, and even to be gnostic, was by no
means confined to adherents of those sects. There were few more
severe critics of what we would now call gnosticism than the pagan
philosopher Plotinus or the Christian Father Clement of Alexandria. Yet each claimed *gnosis;* and the latter, in his *Stromata*,
presents as the truly gnostic precisely the mature, wise, contempla-
tive, Catholic.

We must recall that the word "gnosis" is simply a Greek word
which means knowledge: it is akin to the Sanscrit *jnana*, to the
Latin *cognoscere*, to the English *I know*. A gnostic, then, is a Knowing One: one who knows, or claims to know, things unknown
(= unconscious) to the generality of men. But that much might be
said of any of the great Greek thinkers and scientists: of Socrates,
Plato or Aristotle, none of whom would we think of as gnostics.
Indeed, the *gnosis* which we find in gnosticism stands in striking
contrast to that sort of "knowledge" which had been sought by
classical Greek philosophy and science: nay further, the success of

gnosticism would seem to be largely due to the intellectual bank-
ruptcy and scepticism—the distrust both of the senses and of the
reason—which had been produced by the later phases of Greek
intellectualist thought. In his extensive study of the Hermetic literature and its sources, my Dominican colleague Professor Festugière has traced that development.[5] To the Golden Age of Greek
inquiry and speculation succeeded that amorphous movement
which we call Hellenism; to its search for clarity succeeded a search
for mystery and a love of mystification; to its confidence in reason, a
distrust of, if not a contempt for, reason, and a hankering for some
sort of revelation; to its optimistic view of an ordered cosmos, a
profound sense of the chaos and misery of the material world; to the
classical cult of the human body, a contempt for the body and for all
bodily manifestations; to the philosopher's attempt to overcome
and transmute phantasy and myth into exact logical concepts and
scientific thought, a reversion to myth, or rather the importation
and adaptation of foreign myths and the formation of new myths.
The philosophers themselves had perhaps contributed much to
their own undoing. Already, in that "Golden Age" itself, sceptics
were undermining their basic postulates, and the wandering so-
phists were making it their business to arouse distrust for the
senses and for reason among the populace. The charge of "atheism" brought against Socrates was not altogether misplaced. Rational thought demanded the existence of God indeed; but the
inferentially established God of Aristotle precisely discredited the
gods of the myths and cults, and at the same time failed utterly to
fulfil the psychological and social functions which they had met.
The established religions themselves—the cult of the gods of
Olympus, begotten in a much more primitive and less individu-
alised culture—had become increasingly an exteriorised and per-
functory performance, a social ritual which seemed to intensify
rather than to satisfy the individual's sense of loneliness, frustra-
tion and guilt, to increase his conflicts and need for personal liberation. We must leave to scholars to discuss the origin of the new cults
and practices which came to try to fill the vacuum and which,
transplanted to Greek soil, became what they know under the
general heading of Hellenist "mysteries." It must suffice us here, in

[5] A. J. Festugière, O.P. *La Révélation d'Hermés Trismégiste*, Vol. 1. (Collection "Etudes
Bibliques," Paris 1944).

our own psychological terms, to see in this movement a great reaction of introversion. The psychological law of compensation teaches us that the hypertrophy of one set of functions and attitudes, and the consequent atrophy of their opposites, call forth the compulsive domination of those opposites. Thwarted in its centrifugal flow into an external world which it is unable to assimilate and integrate, the *libido* of necessity is forced to flow back, centripetally, to the interior world of the collective unconscious. We may, I suggest, be still more specific. If it may be fairly said that the heyday of Greek thought and science was characterised in the main by an unprecedented differentiation of extroverted thinking and sensation, the revenge of introverted feeling and intuition is exactly what we should expect. And this is—speaking generally—exactly what we find. Already in the early pagan Hellenistic writings, "to the word gnosis there always adheres the suggestion of a knowledge obtained supernaturally [i.e., by way of unconscious sources] . . . an immediate vision as contrasted with a wisdom that comes by seeking."[6] On the other hand, some of the later "Christian" gnostics—the Naassenes, for instance—quite explicitly claimed to continue and adapt the pagan Hellenistic mysteries, as we learn from Hippolytus. All forms of gnosticism display affinities with the Hellenist myths and mysteries, not only in the supreme value they attribute to immediate interior vision and enlightenment, but also in the very content and pattern of many of their visions as they have been recorded for us.

But at this point it becomes necessary to introduce a distinction between *Gnosis* and a *Gnostic* on the one hand, and *Gnosticism* and what we may call a *Gnosticist* on the other. By the latter I would understand one who, in addition to being a gnostic, makes an "ism" of his gnosis. The distinction is of importance, if only because it is a profound mistake to suppose that, in rejecting gnosticism, the main body of the Christian Church thereby rejected gnosis or could find no room for the gnostic. It neither did—nor could. The revelation which the Church herself accepted, and which gave her her very *raison d'être*, was itself in its origins a gnosis.[7] Clement of Alexandria, we have already remarked,

---

[6] E. F. Scott, *Hastings' Encyc. of Religion and Ethics*, s.v. "Gnosticism."
[7] See *supra*, VII, "Revelation and the Unconscious," *passim*.

claimed to be a gnostic, yet was a determined opponent of gnosticism. St. Paul, we may recall, accounted gnosis among one of the most precious of the gifts of the Spirit to the Christian Church, and yet could warn Timothy against the "godless chatter" and contradictions of what is "*falsely* called *gnosis*" (I Tim. 6. 20). Elsewhere St. Paul passes the remark, of whose truth every analyst is aware, that gnosis "puffeth up." We hear Jung's own language in the Latin Vulgate translation of that text: "*scientia inflat*"—gnosis *inflates*.

In this remark we have, I would suggest, a key which will open to us the distinguishing psychological feature of all gnosticism as opposed to mere gnosis. It is customary, and certainly valid, to distinguish gnosticism by certain common characteristics of belief, certain common patterns and features of the myths, certain common practices, which will be found in greater or less degree among all or most of these gnosticist sects. First and foremost among these, though perhaps more often assumed than openly declared, is the primary, the supreme, value attributed to gnosis itself. Most authorities will agree with Professor Legge to define gnosticism as "the belief that man's place in the next world is determined by the knowledge of it that he acquires in this."[8] At least tacitly underlying all truly gnosticist writings, is the assumption of the possibility of liberation, not by faith, love or deeds, but primarily, even solely, by knowledge—knowledge of that kind of introverted intuition which we have seen gnosis to be, and understanding "intuition" with Jung as "perception by way of the unconscious."

Closely allied to this, and its necessary consequence, is a twofold dualism. A dualism in the first place of *mankind:* there are those who do know the saving mysteries, and those who do not: there are the favoured initiates, and the rest. Gnosticism is essentially esoteric and sectarian and (in the Greek sense) aristocratic. A dualism in the second place, of *reality:* there is the domain of Spirit, the field of the gnostic's own inward-turned vision, which he expressly calls the Pleroma, the Totality, the All; and over against this the world of Matter, which lies outside the Pleroma, and which is Chaos, hostile, inherently evil. Such are the presuppositions of every gnosticist mythos: it will seek to account for the origin of the "external

---

[8] Quoted by F. C. Burkitt, *Church and Gnosis*.

world," not in terms of a creation, in which a "good" God sees that what he has called into being is "good," and "very good," but in terms of a "Fall" from the Pleroma. And indeed we have symbols on gnosticist gems and charms in which the material world is pictured as altogether *outside* the mandala. Its mythos and its praxis alike will be concerned to impart a gnosis whereby the soul may be liberated, not in and through, but *from* the "external world" of matter.

It is not, I think, difficult for the psychologist to see in these very doctrines the expression, we may say, a rationalisation, of a familiar psychological condition: indeed the symptoms of that tricky phase of inflated introversion which is a commonplace in most deep analyses, and which indeed is often stabilised in certain paranoiac psychoses. In analysis it is a critical juncture, for it is at once the moment of intensest inward vision, but also the moment of greatest danger when the very fascination of the power of that vision threatens to swallow consciousness and to alienate it from its environment. Dr. Jung has written of this condition in the essay I have already quoted: "These claims of . . . psychic life are so pressing compared to similar claims in the past, that we may be tempted to see in this a sign of decadence. Yet it may also signify a rejuvenation, for as Hölderlin says:

> *Wo Gefahr ist*
> *Wächst das Rettende auch.*
> *(Danger itself*
> *Fosters the rescuing power)."*

Elsewhere Jung has frequently explained the mechanism of this type of inflation, with its dangers and its opportunities. Ego is identified with the newly activated function of inward vision, intoxicated, overwhelmed by it; and the more perhaps the previous habitual attitude has been extroverted, the greater will be the risk of identification with the new-found, hitherto unconscious, power: with the Saviour-Hero dream-figure who often emerges at this stage to quell the inner forces of evil which had hitherto held the soul captive in its neurosis. The subject is now indeed a gnostic, a Knowing One: one who sees that "Inner World of Man" which is hidden from Tom, Dick and Harry: nay (and here lies the danger) may fancy himself its lord and master in the very fact of consciously assimilating it; and in seeking to master and possess it he is in danger of becoming increasingly mastered and possessed *by* it.

As we read some of the records and accounts of any ancient gnosticist, we can hardly fail—I think—to recognise traces of these selfsame symptoms. His "enlightenment," his mastery of the collective, archetypal world has mastered him completely, he is fascinated, overwhelmed, carried away by it. His sectarianism and his esotericism—his conviction that he and his like alone *know*, and that in this knowledge lies salvation—are the inevitable corollary of the identification of Ego with the inward vision. So, too, is his equation of the external material world with evil: his fear and hatred of the body and all its works, which constantly betray themselves in gnosticist tenets. The doctrine of the evil of matter is plainly, I think, a rationalisation of the one-sided, introverted attitude. We have heard Dr. Jung say that the gnostic teachings "do not baulk at the shadow-side of life." That is profoundly true if we understand it to mean that the gnosticists were intrepid explorers of that side of life which is shadow to the "average sensual man" of to-day. Their writings show them to have been quite at home with the dark and noxious powers of the unconscious: the Serpent, for instance, was the principal cult-object of the Ophite gnostics, and all of them were on more or less familiar terms with demoniacal figures. But this is not to say that they had no "shadow" of their own. What is light to the "average sensual man" had become the dark of the gnosticist. The external world was clean outside his *Pleroma*, *his* All: hostile to it and irreconcilable with it. Absorbed in his lightsome world of phantasy, the world of fact was *his* shadow. For the gnosticist, it would seem, there was but one misfortune, and that was involvement in this material world. There was but one sin—any further involvement in this material world. There was but one repentance required, and that was to turn from the false light of the eyes to the true light of interior illumination. We shall not be surprised to find among some of the gnosticists other symptoms of inflation—if not of alienation. A private terminology, for instance, the use of foreign, preferably Oriental, languages which they plainly did not understand (one gnostic supposed that *"Eloi, Eloi lamma sabacthani?"*—"My God, my God, why hast thou forsaken me?"—was an esoteric Hebrew name for the Divinity). Neologism, also, a love for long, weird, invented words and names, high-sounding but seemingly meaningless: a thing which every alienist knows as a favourite means of asserting one's superiority. We find also in their writings bloated, grandiloquent language, of which Dr. Jung has written in his diagnosis of Adolf Hitler.[9] We shall be wise to take with a pinch of salt the assertions of the unfriendly critics of gnosticism of its own time. But neither can we be altogether surprised to be told by Irenaeus that, notwithstanding the gnosticists' contempt for the body and especially for sex (we might say because of it), they had a reputation for erotomanic licentiousness. And his remark that it was chiefly among the wealthier, leisured classes that gnosticism flourished, is again very much what we might expect.

I must insist that these are all generalities. It is doubtless possible to adduce many exceptions from the literature of gnosticism: I can only indicate general trends. I must trust that I shall not be misunderstood in drawing attention to the affinities between certain symptoms of gnosticism and those of inflation and even of certain psychoses. Neither the personal sincerity of these visionaries, nor yet the genuineness or the profundity of their vision is in question. An experienced psychologist knows better than to despise even lunatic ravings: he knows that in them he may find an insight into the interior life of the psyche seldom given to the so-called sane and "normal." The very concentration of the gnostic's *libido* in the activation of the interior images may make of his loss our profit. And many of the gnostics were certainly no lunatics. In the earlier part of an anonymous gnostic work called the *Pistis Sophia* we may witness, besides many of the more unhealthy features I have mentioned, a courageous process of confrontation with the archetypal mages which can arouse nothing but amazed and reverent admiration.

But it is time to leave these generalities *about* gnosticism, and to take a look at one or two of the gnostic myths themselves. One of the best known of the gnostic sects was that of Valentinus. The Valentinian *mythos*, as recorded by St. Irenaeus, opens as follows:

In invisible and ineffable heights the perfect Aeon called Bythos (Abyss) was pre-existent. Incomprehensible and invisible,

[9] C. G. Jung, *Aufsätze zur Zeitgeschichte*, pp. 73 ff.

eternal and unbegotten. He was throughout endless ages in se-
renity and quiescence. And with Him was Sigé (Silence). And
Bythos conceived the idea to send forth from Himself the Origin
of all and committed this Emanation, as if it were a seed, to the
womb of Sigé. She then, having received this seed and becoming
pregnant, gave birth to Nous (Mind). This Nous was both similar and equal to Him who had produced Him, and He alone was
capable of comprehending the greatness of the Father. Along
with Him, Aletheia (Truth) emanated.

And Nous, perceiving for what purpose He had been produced, also Himself sent forth Logos (Reason) and Zoë (Life);
He is the father of all those who come after him, and the origin
and formative principle of the whole Pleroma. By the intercourse
of Logos and Zoë were brought forth Anthropos (Man) and
Ekklesia (Church, Community). Each of these pairs is masculo-
feminine.

These Aeons, having produced to the glory of the Father, and
wishing to glorify Him on their own account, set forth more
Emanations in couples. Anthropos and Ekklesia sent forth *ten*
other Aeons, whose names are the following: Bythos (Deep) and
Mixis (Mixture); Ageratos (Undecaying, Permanence) and
Henosis (One-ness); Autophyes (Self-producing) and Hedone
(Pleasure); Akinetos (Immutable) and Synkrasis (Blending);
Monogenes (Only-Begotten) and Makaria (Bliss).

Anthropos also, together with Ekklesia, produced *twelve*
more Aeons: Parakletos (Strengthener or Comforter) and Pistis
(Faith); Patrikos (? Paternal Ancestry) and Elpis (Hope);
Metrikos (? Maternal Ancestry) and Agape (Charity); Aeinous
(?) and Synesis (Judgment or Conscience); Ekklesiastikos (?)
and Makariotes (Blissful); Theletos (masc. proper name from
Thelo = I will) and Sophia (fem. Wisdom).[10]

Here we have one of those preliminary accounts of the emanation
of a variety of figures from an unknown and unbegotten source, in
which gnostic myths abound and with which they commonly begin. These are, in all probability, the "endless genealogies" of
which we read in St. Paul's First Epistle to Timothy (I, 4). It cannot
be said that this example is particularly colourful or inspirational,

[10] Iranaeus, *Adversus Haereses*, I. i. 1 and 2, adapted from translation by G. Quispel, "The
Original Doctrine of Valentine," *Vigiliae Christianae*, Vol. I 1.

but in fairness it should be recognised that Irenaeus is giving us only a condensed summary of a probably much more detailed and interesting story. We ourselves hardly expect inspiration from the condensed potted myths of a classical dictionary. But this example has the advantage of being comparatively simple and intelligible. An unnamable Abyss, its Silence (unconsciousness?): the emergence from both of a transcendent co-equal consciousness or *Nous*, and its feminine consort *Aletheia* or Truth. The two pairs of opposites, male and female, in their turn producing a Dekad—five more pairs of opposites, and a Dodekad—six more pairs: it is almost *too* systematic and intelligible. The names, too, are fairly intelligible Greek words; they are almost personified abstractions. Such a myth as this, it seems to me, is hardly a myth at all, it is more like allegorised philosophy. We are very far indeed from the freedom and the innocence, the pure free phantasy uncontaminated by the pale cast of thought, of the primitive pre-philosophical and pre-scientific myth. We are a long way even from that world of the Old Testament or of Homer of which, in her book *On the Iliad*, Rachel Bespaloff writes: "The ambiguous universe of demoniac forces is just receding from view; the world of rational symbols has not yet been constituted. Magic no longer possesses anything but ineffectual rites to impose on recalcitrant nature, and philosophy has still to invent its own incantations for bringing beautiful abstractions to life. At this possibly privileged moment, in the lyric preaching of the prophets of Israel and in the epic of Homer, a particular mode of thought is evolved which cannot be expressed . . . in conceptual form. . . . The religion of *Fatum* and the worship of the Living God both involve a refusal to turn man's relation to the Divine into a technique or a mystical formula."[11]

But here, in the gnosticist myth, we commonly have the very opposite of all this. The world of systematic, rational symbols has been and gone—nay, rather, has been repressed; but being repressed still exercises its sway, producing a hybrid which is neither pure imagination nor yet clear, methodical, differentiated thought. Its abstractions have been transmuted back into figures of the imagination: no longer are they the seed, but rather the fruit, of intellectual concepts. Moreover, the characteristic gnosticist attitude to transcendent powers is precisely magical as opposed to

[11] R. Bespaloff, *On the Iliad*, p. 112 (New York, Bollingen Books).

religion—in Frazer's familiar sense of both these terms—and the elaboration of a technique and a mystical formula to govern man's relation to the Divine describes exactly the gnosticist's aim. We are not surprised to learn that gnosticist *praxis* came to be concerned increasingly with a vast apparatus of charms and amulets and magical pass-words. And so far from the gnosticist "mode of thought" being "inexpressible in conceptual form," the sample we have seen is almost too readily reducible to scientific concepts. The very word "Aeon" tells us at once that we have to do with these timeless, spaceless entities which are known to us as archetypal figures of the collective unconscious (as are the "Eternals" of William Blake). In the word "Emanation" (another word used by Blake) we must at once recognise our own word "Projection." "The masculine-feminine pair of opposites" is language very familiar to analytical psychologists.

Truly, not all the gnosticist myths of emanations are quite so simple, so rational, so schematic. At the beginning of the *Pistis Sophia* we are introduced to a far more numerous and complicated *dramatis personae*. There we find, not just a handful of Aeons distributed in sets of neatly paired males and females, but a populous Pleroma including the Treasury of the Light, the Head of the Universe, five Marks, five Helpers, three Triple Powers, twenty-four Aeons, twenty-four Invisibles, twenty-four Places, twenty-four Mysteries, three Amens, seven "other Amens," seven Voices, and an unspecified number of Unbegottens, Self-Begottens with their Begottens, Pairs and Unpaireds, Authentics, Lords, Rulers, Archangels, Angels, Dekans, Ministers, Houses, Spheres, Guardians, as well as the "Child of the Child" which is "the Place of the Twin Saviour." Here certainly we feel somewhat nearer the authentic dreamland of uncontrolled phantasy: the names, too, of these Beings are altogether less rational and more fanciful. In yet other gnosticist myths they often fail to yield any intelligible meaning whatever—though Gematria, the interpretation of names according to the numerical value of their letters, may sometimes produce significant results where dictionaries have failed.[12] But still, one has the impression of being nearer the realm of sophisticated allegory than pure myth.

But far more interesting than these "endless genealogies," which

[12] See Lee and Bond: *Materials for the Study of the Apostolic Gnosis.*

give us little more than the *dramatis personae* of the subsequent stories—the preliminary differentiations of the *libido* involved in the drama of the inner conflicts—are the subsequent stories of the "Fall" from the Pleroma, and of the redemption of the lost and afflicted soul. In the Valentinian version "the very latest and youngest of all the Aeons, Sophia-Acamoth [feminine Wisdom] suffers passion and desire apart from her consort"—who is Theletos, masculine controlled and controlling Will. She was, we are told, "led astray by disordered love, which was actually *hubris*, because she did not [as could Nous alone] comprehend the all-perfect Father"—the Abyss. "Her passion was a desire to know the Father, for she craved to grasp His greatness. Unable to realise her hope, because she aimed at the impossible, she fell into extreme agonies because of the unfathomable depth of the Father's unsearchable nature and her love for Him. Always yearning for Him, she would have been annihilated in His sweetness and dissolved into His infinite being, had she not been restricted by that power, Horos [the Limit, Finiteness], who exiled her from the Pleroma."[13] Then, the story goes on, she finds herself imprisoned, tortured and subjected to the tyranny of the other Aeons in the material chaos, which is, we are told (and the psychological insight is breathtaking), the product of her own disordered emotions.

We may, in Freudian terms, read this story as a transparent account of the formation of an Electra complex—the impossible, forbidden passion for the Father; thus understood, the *Horos* or Limit plays the repressive function of the Freudian incest-prohibiting Censor. Or we may, penetrating more deeply, see the Freudian myth itself as a shadow of the more metaphysical yearnings of the finite for the infinite, as doubtless did Valentinus himself. The story continues:

Left without, alone, Sophia was subject to every sort of emotion: *sorrow* she suffered because she did not obtain understanding; *fear* lest life should leave her as light had already done; moreover she was in *despair*. The root of all this suffering was lack of inward vision (*agnosis*). Thus being bereft of the Logos who had been invisibly present within her, she strained herself to

---

[13] Irenaeus (Quispel) *op. cit.* I. ii. 1.

discover that light which had forsaken her, but she could not achieve her purpose because she was prevented by the Limit (*Horos*). . . . This was the origin and essence of Matter, from which this world was made: from her *longing* for the bliss of the Ideal World, the soul of the whole universe derived its origin; earth arose from her *despair;* water from the agitation caused by her *sorrow;* air from the materialisation of her *fear;* while fire, causing death and destruction, was inherent in all these elements, as lack of insight (*agnosis*) lay concealed in the other three passions. . . .

When she had been expelled into the empty space devoid of insight (*gnosis*) which she had herself created by her trespass, she brought forth Jesus in remembrance of the higher world, but with a kind of shadow.[14]

Even in the condensed form of the critical Irenaeus, the story cannot be denied pathos and poignancy. We shall not, I suggest, be far wrong in equating this part of the story—the *hubris* and repression of Sophia, her persecution and agony—with the reductive phase of the analytical process. But then, we are told: "When she had passed through every state of suffering, she raised herself timidly and supplicated the light which had forsaken her, that is Jesus." There follows the story of her salvation by Jesus, her reintegration into the Pleroma.

In the *Pistis Sophia* (which, if not the work of a Valentinian sect, has many affinities with the Valentinian gnosis) we are told at much greater length the story of her Fall and of her rescue by Jesus. But before taking another glance at this perplexing text—one of the very few actual gnosticist texts that have been preserved for us—I want to say something about the struggle which took place between the main body of orthodox Christians and gnosticism. I do so the more readily because I believe that no more than is gnosticism itself are the issues of that conflict dead in the human psyche of to-day. I have already suggested that every analysant is in some measure a gnostic (I do not say a gnosticist): a Knowing One who has experienced some interior vision of the archetypal, collective psyche—or at least (like the other fringe of the old gnostic's followers) is proba-

[14] Irenaeus (Quispel) *loc. cit.* I. iv. and I. xi.

bly involved in a transference on someone who has. And whether we profess orthodox Christianity or not, we are all in more or less conscious degree inheritors also of its distinctive values and attitudes.

Whether we share their beliefs or not, let us put ourselves in the position of those early Christians who accepted the Gospels and the Apostolic writings. Already, as Professor Buber, writing as a Jew, has said, there was a fundamental opposition between the Old Testament revelation and the fundamental assumptions and attitudes of the gnosticist.[15]

For the Christian, endeavouring to be faithful to the Gospel witness, this opposition was immeasurably increased. We cannot read the Christian Fathers of the early centuries, especially Irenaeus and Tertullian and Hippolytus, without seeing that they saw in gnosticism a very serious menace which threatened the original purity and simplicity of the Gospel message, and the tradition received from the first disciples. The gnosticists were probably not very numerous, but they were wealthy and influential. We know that Valentinus himself aspired to the chief bishopric of Christendom—the See of Rome. The case against gnosticism reduced itself to a few very simple heads which seemed to cut clean across what was believed to be the very essence of the Christian revelation. They may be briefly summarised.

In the first place there was the very sectarianism and exclusivism of the gnostic. Each gnosticist sect was a chosen, superior, favoured people, alone in possession of the saving knowledge. This cut clean across the Christian conviction that Christ's life and teaching and death and rising had been for all men, a manifestation that "God wills all men to be saved, and come to the knowledge of the truth"; that there was consequently no more a particular Chosen People, but a universal, what they already called a Catholic, Church. The poor had had the Gospel preached to them, the saving message was to be proclaimed from the housetops. "Here," the Epistle to the Colossians had said (3. 11), "there cannot be Greek nor Jew, circumcised nor uncircumcised, barbarian nor Scythian, slave nor free man, but Christ is All and in all."

Yes; not only *for* all, but All and in all. The Christian faith, they

[15] See *Mamre* by Martin Buber, pp. 11 ff., also pp. 109, 142 (Melbourne University Press, 1942).

believed, was "*kath holon*"—Catholic, in accord with the whole—
not only because it was for *all* men, but because it was for the *whole*
man, and no mere part of him. In the Valentinian gnosis (and this
feature is common to gnosticism) not only was liberation not for
everybody, it was not for the *whole* of each. It was only *for* the
Pneuma—(the spirit, which the Valentinians expressly identified
with the imagination) *from* the body and *from* the psyche. The
Christian revelation of the Incarnation and the Resurrection of the
flesh was a message of salvation of the whole man, in and through
the flesh. One and all the Christian gnosticists were docetists: the
Christ-Saviour only *appeared* to be a man, to be born of Mary, to
suffer and to die. Matter was evil, the whole world of exterior
sensation was repudiated in the supposed interests of its opposite,
interior intuition. Christ, if not one substance with the Absolute,
the Abyss, the All-Father, was certainly some divine Spirit, an
Aeon from the Pleroma; but for that very reason he must "abhor
the Virgin's womb," the evil word of generation, and at most could
pass through it, himself uncontaminated, as "water through a
pipe"—as Valentinus himself put it. This transcendent Entity
might somehow have operated every now and again through the
man Jesus; but *become* a Man, really suffer and die in fact and
history, in the sphere of sensation as well as of intuition—that was
unthinkable. The apostolic witness, on the contrary, was to the
effect that Jesus was himself the Logos, not an inferior Aeon but
the *Nous* co-equal with the All-Father, and that he was made flesh
and dwelt among us in time and space—the world of fact and
sensation. The hidden mystery of existence was manifested precisely in space and time and history, and within the field of the
external senses. "That which was from the Beginning, whom we
have *heard*, whom we have *looked* upon, and *touched* with our
hands—this Word of Life; the Life was made *manifest*, and we *saw*
it . . . that which we have *seen* and *heard* we proclaim to you also,
so that you may have fellowship with us: and our fellowship is with
the Father and with his son Jesus Christ. . . . And this is the
message we have heard from him and proclaim to you, that God is
Light, and in him there is no darkness at all."[16]
These words from the beginning of the first Epistle of John

[16] I John 1, 1–5.

might almost have been written—perhaps they were written—to underline the opposition of primitive Catholic and Evangelical Christianity to gnosticism. It is the opposition of those committed to the Whole to the view which would restrict the Whole to a Part. It is instructive to note in passing, that according to the Catholic Irenaeus himself, while the Catholics were antagonistic to gnosticism, the gnosticists were not antagonistic to Catholicism. They were something that Irenaeus found much more trying: they were patronisingly superior. Catholicism, they held, was all very well for *hoi polloi*, for the average Tom, Dick or Harry. The esoteric gnostic revelations were not anyhow for such as these; and they, the gnosticists, alone really *knew*—as the Catholics did not—what the Catholic beliefs and practices themselves really meant. Again we have a sidelight on gnosticism which is by no means out of date.

But the opposition cuts deeper than that; and here we touch upon Dr. Jung's antinomy of gnosis and faith. Without committing Dr. Jung, I think we may express this antinomy best in the words of Bacon: "*Animus ad amplitudinem Mysteriorum pro modulo suo dilatetur; non Mysteria ad angustias animi constringantur*," "Let the conscious mind, so far as it can, be open to the fullness of the mysteries; let not the mysteries be constrained to fit the narrow confines of the mind." In the first we have the attitude of *faith* in the Unknown; in the second the attitude, not necessarily of gnosis, but certainly of gnosticism. The first is the attitude of religion, humbly accepting a Divine revelation it knows it cannot fully comprehend; the second is essentially the attitude of magic, seeking to subject the mystery to the comprehension of Ego, and utilising transcendent power and knowledge for its own ends and aggrandisement. The message of the Gospels and the apostolic writings was a message of salvation by *faith;* and by faith operative in *works* of *love*. Gnosticism says in effect: to know is all. The enlargement of consciousness, inward-turned to the Realm of the Mothers, the "*mysterium tremendum et fascinans*" of the archetypes, away from the chaos of the hard, cruel world of fact and human history and society: there lies salvation. Know the names and origin of the archetypes and projections of the unconscious; know their conflicts and triumphs and falls and recoveries; and you will be their master and will be saved. Not so, says Faith; that is the very *hubris* of your own Sophia-Acamoth: her lust for the impossible comprehension of the fathomless Abyss, which imprisons her in the very matter which she despises and subjects her to the cruel tyranny of the very archetypes she would excel. Let her rather recognize the insolubility of her conflict and the impossibility of her yearning, let her be thankful for the restraint of the *Horos* who saves her from annihilation in infinite unconsciousness, let her open her mind to the mysteries and not seek to enclose the mysteries in her mind. But then she will be no longer a gnosticist *Sophia;* but perhaps she will be *Pistis Sophia—Faith-Wisdom.*

For while gnosticism has no room for faith, faith has room, indeed need, for gnosis. Gnosis cannot be a substitute for faith, but the possession of gnosis is part and parcel of the gifts to the faithful *Ecclesia.* In the Body of Christ are many members, each with their several functions: and those of the gnostic are among the most honourable. Without the intuitive understanding of what in faith she believes, the Church herself would be incomplete—uncatholic. But it is gnosis *in* faith, not in despite of faith; and it is for the benefit of the whole body and not only for the individual member. Gnosis is not supreme: it must be ruled by Faith and Hope and Charity, and the greatest of these is Charity. "If I have prophetic powers," writes St. Paul in a famous passage, "and understand all mysteries and all *gnosis,* and even if I have all faith, so as to move mountains, but have not love, I am nothing. . . . Love is patient and kind, love is not jealous or inflated, is not arrogant. . . . Love never ends; but as for *gnosis,* it will pass away. For our *gnosis* is imperfect, but when the perfect comes, the imperfect will pass away. . . ." (I Cor. 13). The Church also will have her introverted intuitives, her contemplatives and mystics, nay, her alchemists and cabbalists. She will have her esoterics: those with a deeper gnosis of the Divine mysteries. But never with the idea that theirs is a superior perfection denied to mankind at large. Union with God, if we may adopt the useful Sanscrit terminology, is not *only* to be attained by *Jnana* (or *Gnosis*) nor by *Jnana* without Faith and Love; but also and no less, given Faith and Love, by *Bhakti* and *Karma.* And indeed, selfless works of love and service enjoy a certain priority, for it is in the visible image of God in man that the invisible God revealed in Jesus Christ is to be worshipped and served.

I have a suspicion that in the perplexing first two documents of the *Pistis Sophia* we have a record, radically gnosticist indeed, of

the titanic psychological visions and struggles of a gnosticist, probably a Valentinian, who has felt and faced the tension of his gnostic
vision with the counterclaims of Catholic and Evangelical Christianity. This theory would require a paper in itself to develop; but it
is a hypothesis which would solve many of the difficulties which the
text has presented to scholars, and, read in this light, it may be
found to be a work which many of us in our day may study with
personal profit. Here the whole setting is typically gnosticist. After
the introduction to the complex heavenly hierarchy, of which we
have already spoken, we are shown Jesus on the Mount of Olives,
eleven years after the Resurrection, talking to his disciples. They
are well content with the revelation he has already made, but that
had had to do only with the God of this world of change and decay,
and he has more to tell them; this he does from a blinding light
which terrifies them. Jesus, here, it progressively dawns upon
them, is no inferior Aeon, he is one with the First Mystery which is
also the twenty-fourth encompassing all others. His humanity is
still, perhaps, a little misty and ethereal, but we are left in no doubt
that it is also with the historical Jesus of flesh and blood that we
have to do, and there is no attempt, as in regular gnosticism, to
divorce the man Jesus from the celestial Saviour-Christ. He relates
how he has discovered Sophia, cast out from the Pleroma by her
proud lust for the Father; but she has fallen into another error, and
a still greater corresponding misfortune. She has mistaken the light
of the Aeons for the One True Light in which she had previously
believed. It is her constant *faith* in the True Light, the Light which
she rediscovers in Jesus, that saves her. She is not just Sophia—she
is Pistis Sophia—Faith-Wisdom. Here we have gnosis indeed, but
paradoxically it is a gnosis of salvation not *by* gnosis but by faith;
one in which the perils attached to the gnosis of the Aeons are
exposed, and Jesus is Saviour precisely in transcending, in con-
quering, and even upsetting the whole Pleroma of the gnosticists.
The story is told as a dialogue between Jesus and his disciples. It is
of extraordinary psychological interest, for it is a lesson not only in
psychological insight into the interior world, but still more in psychological courage and patience, and perhaps most of all in its
insistence that, at each stage of the successive vision, its content is
to be linked up with conscious material: in this case the Psalms and
the other Scriptures with which the Disciples are already consciously familiar.

I am not contending that in the *Pistis Sophia* we shall find the pure milk of the Gospels, or an unimpeachably correct statement of Catholic belief. We certainly have nothing of the sort. But if it is not, so to speak, the case history of a gnosticist whose response to his very gnosis is freeing him from gnosticism, and who is discovering the "rescuing power" in the "danger itself," I must join my elders and betters in agreeing that we do not know what it is all about. Towards the end of the story, even the very sectarianism and exclusiveness of gnosticism is repudiated. "Maria the Magdalen, said she to Jesus, 'My Lord. . . . Not only are we now compassionate of ourselves, but we are compassionate of all the races of mankind, that they should be delivered from all the Judgments that are cruel . . . that they should not come into the hands of the Rulers [*i.e.*, the planetary, archetypal Forces] that are cruel, and that they should be delivered from the hands of the Receivers [presumably their passive counterparts] which are cruel in the Darkness.'"

It is perhaps to be regretted that the contemporary Christian critics of gnosticism were not always better psychologists. Irenaeus obviously is striving hard to be just and not to misrepresent the gnosticists;[17] but he is no psychologist. He is a busy, conscientious diocesan bishop and pastor, mainly anxious that the flock entrusted to him be not led astray by hirelings, and, inevitably, much more concerned with *what* the gnosticists said, with what it threatened to the faith and practice of which he believed himself the guardian, than with trying to understand sympathetically *why* they said it. Even he, and still less Tertullian, commonsense men that they were, cannot restrain themselves from making fun of the gnosticist's phantasies. They are easy game. Origen and Clement of Alexandria are no less firm, but perhaps more understanding—and indeed perhaps more experienced in the labyrinthine ways of the mind and the functions of its phantasies and mysteries; we may say perhaps, in the very crooked lines whereby God sometimes writes straight. I, too, have dared to be critical, but I trust I have not mocked. There is a still greater figure in Catholic history, whose scalding, ironic words forbid me. He himself, in the course of the long and intrepid spiritual struggle which he relates in his *Confessions*, had had his gnosticist phase, and had been an adherent of the

---

[17] See the monumental work of F. M. Sagnard, O. P., *La Gnose valentinienne et le témoinage de Saint Irénée* (Paris, 1947).

great Manichaean movement which stands in direct line of succession to the gnostic sects of earlier centuries, and which possessed many of their distinctive features. I cannot do better than conclude my notes on gnosticism with the words whereby, in later years, St. Augustine prefaced some of his:

"Let those be angry with you," he says to the gnosticists of his time, "who do not know with how great toil truth is attained, or how difficult it is to avoid mistakes. Let those be angry with you who do not know how rare a thing it is, and how hard a thing, to be free from the phantasies which arise within us. Let those be angry with you who know not how painful is the healing of the inner eye of man if it is to behold its true Sun—not that image of the Sun in the sky which you know, but that Sun of which it is written, 'The Sun of Righteousness is risen upon me,' and of which the Gospel says, 'This was the true Light that Enlighteneth every man that comes into this world.' Let those be angry with you who do not know what sighs and tears are needed if the real God is to be known—even in the tiniest degree. Lastly, let those be angry with you who have never been led astray, as you, and I, have been led astray. But for me to be angry with you, is utterly impossible. . . .

"But in order that neither may you be angry with me . . . I must beg this one favour of you. Let us, on both sides, lay aside all arrogance. Let us not, on either side, claim that we have already discovered the truth. Let us seek it together as something which is known to neither of us. For then only may we seek it, lovingly and tranquilly, if there be no bold presumption that it is already discovered and possessed. But if I may not ask so much as this of you [Knowing Ones], grant this at least that I may listen to you, and talk with you, as with people whom I, at least, do not claim to know."[18]

---

[18] *Contra Epistolam Manichaei*, cap. 3.

Chapter 12. Gilles Quispel, "Jung and Gnosis"

In this bold, if discursive, essay Gilles Quispel tackles multiple topics: (1) the influence of Jung's Seven Sermons on Hermann Hesse's Demian; (2) Martin Buber's attack on Jung as a Gnostic; (3) Jung's reliance on Basilides for a positive view of the Demiurge and so for the necessity of a devil to account for evil; (4) Jung's departure from Basilides, for whom the god Abraxas is the Demiurge rather than, as for Jung, the highest god and for whom Abraxas is wholly good rather than, as for Jung, evil as well as good; (5) the likely Jewish origin of both the Demiurge and Abraxas; (6) the likely Jewish origin of the name "Abraxas"; (7) Jung's psychologizing of Gnosticism and consequent characterization of the final state as reunion with oneself rather than with God; and (8) Jung's Gnostic-like concern with religion as experience rather than as mere belief. On Quispel and Jung see, in my introduction, the section on "Gilles Quispel."

This essay was originally published as "C. G. Jung und die Gnosis" in Eranos-Jahrbüch, *37 (1968), 277–98 (reprint. as "Hesse, Jung und die Gnosis" in Quispel,* Gnostic Studies, *vol. 2 [Istanbul: Nederlands Historisch-Archaeologisch Instituut, 1975], chap. 29). It has not previously been translated into English.*

"C. G. Jung and Gnosis: The *Septem Sermones ad Mortuous* and Basilides" (1968)

I was about eleven years old when I met Max Demian. At the time I pretty much lived in two worlds. There was the pious home with the righteous father, who read aloud from the Bible at the dinner table and sang chorals at evening devotions. This was a world of mild luster, clarity, and cleanliness; friendly conversations, washed hands, tidy clothes, and good manners were the norm. The liberal arts prep school that I attended was simply an extension of the parental home: Homer's sun smiled so cheerfully, and the True, Good, and Beautiful were venerated. It was a serene and cozy world, but indeed only half the world.

On the other hand there was a kind of underworld in our little city. Here there were servant girls and workmen, ghost stories and scandalous rumors, a multicolored flood of atrocious, enticing, terrible, and puzzling things like slaughterhouses and prisons, drunks and quarrelsome women, calving cows, collapsed horses, stories of thefts, murders, suicides.

I had already come into contact with this world in that I had inwardly subjected myself to a certain schoolmate who blackmailed me and made me his slave. It was Max Demian who freed me from that dependency. But as the years progressed and slowly awakening sexual feelings seized me, I discovered that this dark world was now deep within me.

In this underworld Demian was my spiritual guide. He gave me religious instruction with negative prognosis and with the help of the Bible, which he found to be true in a most literal sense. Consequently, he found Cain to be an honorable person, Abel a coward, and the mark of Cain most distinguished. The conversion of that wretch on the cross he considered a sentimental fairy tale of a treatise. "First he was criminal and did abhorrent deeds, God knows what all, and now he melts away and partakes in such whiny celebrations of repentance and regret. What kind of sense does such repentance make when one foot is already in the grave, tell me that!"

And then he revealed to me his understanding of God and his criticism of the Biblical God:

The matter is that this God, of old and new alliance, is indeed an exemplary figure, but is not what he should actually represent. He is the good, the noble, the patriarchal, the beautiful, and even the elevated, the sentimental—indeed! But the world is also made of something else. And that something is merely ascribed to the devil, and this whole part of the world, the entire half, is undermined and passed over in silence. Just as when they praise God as the Father of all life, but simply ignore sexual activity, upon which life itself is based, and even declare it to be the devil's work and sinful! I have nothing against honoring this God Jehovah, not in the least. But I think we should worship and hold sacred all of the world, and not just this artificially separated official half! Thus it follows that we should have not only divine services, but demonic services as well.

Actually it was not that we wanted to have two cults. We searched instead for a new god, since the old one had failed. I eventually found him.

Above our main entrance there was a coat of arms with a bird in it, which I once drew. It was a scavenger bird with a sharp and audacious sparrow hawk's head. Half of its body stuck in a dark earth-sphere, out of which it worked its way out as out of an enormous egg, with a blue sky in the background.

I sent Max Demian the picture of the sparrow hawk and received the answer: "The bird is fighting its way out of the egg. The egg is the world. Whoever wishes to be born must destroy a world. The bird is flying to God. The God is named Abraxas."

By pure chance I soon after heard from a teacher at the school that Abraxas was a deity of the ancient world. He was mentioned in conjunction with Greek magic formulas and had the symbolic duty to reconcile the divine with the demonic. But it became obvious to me that I myself was this deity.

Such is the way one can summarize Hermann Hesse's *Demian* (1917 [publ. 1919]) for the purposes which we are pursuing. It is clear that Demian is a roman à clef; it is said that Hesse wrote it just after he had undergone analysis in Lucerne in 1917 with J[oseph]. B. Lang, a friend and student of Jung.[1]

Miguel Serrano has written a book with the title *Jung and Hesse*.[2] In it he writes about his visits with Hesse in Montagnola and with Jung in Locarno and Küsnacht. He also presents some interesting observations about *Demian* and *Septem Sermones ad Mortuous*. But of their earlier relationship, at the time that Hesse wrote *Demian*,

---

[1] J. C. A. Fetter, *Menschbeschouwing en Zielzorg* (Zeist, 1933), p. 153. [On Lang see C. G. Jung, *Letters*, ed. Gerhard Adler and Aniela Jaffé, trans. R. F. C. Hull (Princeton, N.J.: Princeton University Press, 1973), vol. 1, p. 552.—ED.]

[2] M. Serrano, *C. G. Jung and Hermann Hesse: A Record of Two Friendships* (London, 1966).

Serrano says nothing. He does not even mention that Hesse had read Jung's *Septem Sermones ad Mortuous* and used it as a source for *Demian*, though this must be obvious to everyone who has read both works.[3]

This would provide a nice theme for a dissertation by a student of German literature. We will let it suffice to determine that Hesse assimilated these "Seven Sermons to the Dead," which Jung composed in 1916 under the name of the Gnostic Basilides, into his novel, which is so characteristic of the moods and hopes of the period immediately following the First World War.[4]

This paper—a modern apocrypha, or rather pseudepigrapha—was first published in Aniela Jaffé's 1962 biography of Jung [i.e., Jung's *Memories, Dreams, Reflections*, ed. Jaffé].[5] Therein it is impartially reported that Jung had these "Seven Sermons to the Dead" privately published as a booklet. He occasionally gave copies to friends. It was never obtainable at bookstores. He later called this venture a "youthful sin" (Jung was already forty-one years old in 1916, but remained youthful until his death) and regretted it.

According to Miguel Serrano, the book was written under the most unusual and even unbelievable circumstances: "The most extraordinary things happened just before that book came to be written. Jung's house was filled with noise, the atmosphere was tense, and the rooms seemed to be filled with invisible presences. Both he and his sons (!) had strange dreams, and they all felt that something like a personified Destiny had entered their daily lives to spy on them. All these experiences ceased the moment the book was finished."

More important, it seems to me, is the question of what the Latin title *Septem Sermones' ad Mortuous* actually means. According to an oral tradition which reached me, it is said that at the time Jung's father was a priest in Basel, one occasionally delivered sermons to the dead. If this is true, Jung was probably thinking of this strange

---

[3] On Hesse's possible knowledge of the Seven Sermons at the time of *Demian* see Stephan A. Hoeller, *The Gnostic Jung and the Seven Sermons to the Dead* (Wheaton, Ill.: Theosophical Publishing House, 1982), 9–10, 93–95.—ED.

[4] A psychological interpretation is given by Judith Hubback, *Journal of Analytical Psychology*, 11/2 (1966), pp. 95–111.

[5] Aniela Jaffé, *Erinnerungen, Träume, Gedanken von C. G. Jung*, pp. 389–398.

custom when he gave the book this title. There must, then, have been seven sermons to the dead.

Even before its publication Martin Buber used this composition as the basis of his attack on Jung in the book *Eclipse of God* (1953 [*sic:* 1952]), about which I will make a few observations. The book *Eclipse of God* shows Buber at his best. In coming to terms with important contemporary philosophers, he demonstrates the affliction of our times, rooted in the *absentia realis Dei*. It is impressive that even a man like Hermann Cohen has suffered because of it! Buber demonstrates that he has completely understood the philosophers that he discusses and recapitulates their ideas with great clarity and a sovereign command of the language. He does, however, become a bit biased when he connects Heidegger's inability to create a synthesis of Time and Being to his political attitudes.

Buber reproaches Jung with being a Gnostic who remained true to his Gnostic convictions, kept secret, to the very end. Buber concedes that Jung accomplished remarkable things in the sciences, but that does not soften the attack: for Buber, he remained a Gnostic who wanted to put the devil on the throne of God.

When, as an outside observer, one reads this sharp and thoroughly annihilating critique, one is reminded of Unamuno's novel *Abel Sanchez*, in which an old man murders his lifelong friend with good reason. As the "philosopher of the encounter," Buber must have increasingly taken offense at Jung's philosophy of individuation precisely because such an established, old liberal, and good-Nietzschean philosophy could say little about the "Other," the most proximate God. Two structures [i.e., Jung's and Buber's viewpoints] are juxtaposed against each other here and are not easy to reconcile.

To be sure, it is a bit alienating that Gnosis now becomes the scapegoat. Why should Gnosis be contemptible? Ferdinand Christian Bauer wrote his marvelous book *Christian Gnosis* (1835) in order to demonstrate that the German Idealism of Schelling and Hegel was the Gnosis of the nineteenth century. Even Goethe allowed himself to be influenced by ancient Gnosticism, as he relates in his autobiography, *Poetry and Truth*. In his biography *Sigmund Freud and the Jewish Mystical Tradition* (1958) David Bakan has attempted to show how Freud is entirely based on the Gnostic tradition of Judaism and is most understandable from that point of view. And our friend [Gershom] Scholem has punctiliously shown that Buber was himself a Gnostic in his youth, before he had hidden his thoughts under the terminology of existentialism.[6] This should show us that every Gnostic is in good company: Gnosis is a splendid cause, not an insult with which to slander and slay an accomplished researcher.

And even the ethical Buber does not emerge from the battle unscathed, for it is not becoming to publicize the contents of a personal manuscript which is not intended for publication and which one happens to come across purely by chance.[7] However, what remains is the objective statement which claims that Jung was essentially a Gnostic: "The psychological doctrine which deals with mysteries without the attitude of faith towards mystery is the modern manifestation of Gnosis. It . . .—and not atheism . . .— is the real antagonist of the reality of faith." This is the accusation we want to examine by comparing the *Septem Sermones* with the conception of the Gnostic Basilides.

Jung begins his manuscript with the following words:

The dead came back from Jerusalem, where they found not what they sought. They prayed me let them in and besought my word, and thus I began my teaching.

Harken: I begin with nothingness. Nothingness is the same as fullness. In infinity full is no better than empty. Nothingness is both empty and full. As well might might ye say anything else of nothingness, as for instance, white is it, or black, or again, it is not, or it is. A thing that is infinite and eternal hath no qualities, since it hath all qualities. (Sermon I)

It is quite clear that he here let himself be inspired by Basilides, and in particular by the interpretation given by Hippolytus (*Refutatio* VII.20.2ff.). Jung seems not to have considered the other interpretation of the instruction, which was transmitted by Irenaeus (*Adv. haer.* 1.24.3–7) and cannot, in my opinion, be authentic:

[6] G. Scholem, "Martin Bubers Auffassung des Judentums," *Eranos-Jahrbüch* 35 (1966) (Zürich, 1967), pp. 1–52.

[7] Prior to its publication as an appendix to Jung's *Memories, Dreams, Reflections* Buber was given a copy of the Seven Sermons, which he cites as the most irrefutable evidence that Jung is a Gnostic. See Buber, *Eclipse of God*, trans. Maurice Friedman et al. (New York: Harper & Row, 1952), p. 137. See also Hoeller, p. 9.—ED.

Basilides says: "It was, he says, when there was nothing and even the Nothingness was not something existent, but was simply nothing, without ulterior motives and without any sophistry. And when I, so he says, ' was.' I don't mean to say, I say that nothing was. It cannot even be said to be 'unsayable,' that which is so-called. We call it unsayable, but it is not that; because the 'not-even-unsayable' is not called unsayable, but is rather elevated beyond any name which one can give it."[8]

This presentation of the unknown God is very impressive, but it is not unique. It is, for example, also found in the *Tractatus Tripartitus* of the Jung Codex or in the *Apocryphon of John*. It is how a Gnostic manuscript usually begins. But not only Gnosticism designates God as Nothingness; the Christian mystics do so, too. Johannes Scotus Erigena taught that the world was created out of the void, and that means out of God, for God is the void. And in the later history of mysticism more and more voices were heard that bore the same witness such as Nicholas of Cusa, Jacob Boehme, and Angelus Silesius. But certainly the Gnostic Basilides was the actual source for Jung. And that should now help us to understand his terminology. He mentions that created being is the opposite of the pleroma, or the void. We humans, as created beings, are fundamentally different and infinitely far from the pleroma because we are limited in time and space:

Creatura is not in the pleroma, but in itself. The pleroma is both beginning and end of created beings. It pervadeth them, as the light of the sun everywhere pervadeth the air. Although the pleroma pervadeth altogether, yet hath created being no share thereof, just as a wholly transparent body becometh neither light nor dark through the light which pervadeth it. We are, however, the pleroma itself, for we are a part of the eternal and infinite. But we have no share thereof, as we are from the pleroma infinitely removed; not spiritually or temporally, but essentially, since we are distinguished from the pleroma in our essence as creatura, which is confined within time and space. (Sermon I)

[8] Translated Robert Haardt, *Die Gnosis, Wesen und Zeugnisse* (Salzburg, 1967).

Created being presupposes a creation out of Nothingness. Basil-ides does indeed teach this as well. Though he claims with unsur-passed boldness that the nonexistent God has brought forth the nonexistent world out of the Nonexistent, this probably means that the God who himself is above all thought and all categories creates a "world-germ" in which the still to be evolved and yet nonexistent world is potentially contained. But Basilides is a consistent thinker: he has considered whether the world originated through an emana-tion from God or rather from pre-existent material (22.2–3). But he repudiates these solutions, which had been applied already by other Gnostics of his time, as for instance by Valentinus, or in the *Apocryphon of John:* he means quite seriously that the creation is from nothingness.[9]

This is where Jung fundamentally changed Basilides. According to him [Jung], the essence of created being is the *principium indi-viduationis:* dissimilarity. The word reminds one of Schopenhauer's philosophy. Created being is, moreover, termed a characteristic of the pleroma. One supposes he means that the pleroma as uncon-scious will brings forth dissimilarity, which is no doubt a secretion or an emanation of the unconscious will. In interpreting Basilides in a Schopenhauerian manner, Jung has made him even more Gnostic than he already was.

And so I arrive at a third point of agreement between Basilides and Jung: that offensive opinion, that though God and devil are most real, they belong to creatura. I must explain this more fully. In his old age Jung gained worldwide fame by announcing the good tidings of the "evil man." He was able to bring an American play-boy to his knees by making his corruption clear to him. The entire English nation wept when Jung appeared on television with that impressive head of his and explained to his listeners how horribly evil they all were. Jung continually emphasized the reality of the devil. The Church, however, did not value Jung's theories. The Barthians above all constantly reproached him with being an athe-ist, which Jung persistently denied.

The "Seven Sermons to the Dead" give the unequivocal answer:

In the night the dead stood along the wall and cried:
    We would have knowledge of god. Where is god? Is god dead?

---

[9] W. Foerster, "Das System des Basilides," *New Testament Studies* 9 (1963), p. 237.

God is not dead. Now, as ever, he liveth. God is creatura, for he is something definite, and therefore distinct from the pleroma. God is quality of the pleroma, and everything which I said of creatura also is true concerning him.

He is distinguished, however, from created beings through this, that he is more indefinite and indeterminable than they. He is less distinct than created beings, since the ground of his being is effective fullness. Only in so far as he is definite and distinct is he creatura, and in like measure is he the manifestation of the effective fullness of the pleroma.

Everything which we do not distinguish falleth into the pleroma and is made void by its opposite. If, therefore, we do not distinguish god, effective fullness is for us extinguished.

Moreover god is the pleroma itself, as likewise each smallest point in the created and uncreated is the pleroma itself.

Effective void is the nature of the devil. God and devil are the first manifestations of nothingness, which we call the pleroma. It is indifferent whether the pleroma is or is not, since in everything it is balanced and void. Not so creatura. In so far as god and devil are creatura they do not extinguish each other, but stand one against the other as effective opposites. We need no proof of their existence. It is enough that we must always be speaking of them. Even if both were not, creatura, of its own essential distinctiveness, would forever distinguish them anew out of the pleroma.

Everything that discrimination taketh out of the pleroma is a pair of opposites. To god, therefore, always belongeth the devil.

This inseparability is as close and, as your own life hath made you see, as indissoluble as the pleroma itself. Thus it is that both stand very close to the pleroma, in which all opposites are extinguished and joined. (Sermon II)

Thus God and the devil are determinations of a higher being but have polarized themselves. They are specified as *summum bonum,* the highest good, and *infimum malum,* the radically evil.

Those who knew Jung well will admit that this theory of his was important to him. In his later works he always returned to it, sometimes by insinuation, sometimes expanding on it. At the same time it was this theory that alienated many well-wishers from him and led them to accuse Jung of teaching the devil's work.

That which is most repulsive and incomprehensible to his contemporaries is on the other hand almost banal to the student of Gnosticism. For here one finds anew the Gnostic juxtaposition of the Demiurge and the highest god.

In the last few years more has become known of this unusual dogma. Paradoxically, its origin appears to be found in Judaism.[10] For there existed in Judaism a pre-Christian sect of Magharians, who taught that God had in the beginning created one single angel. It was this angel which created the world and empowered the prophets. When in their writings they spoke of God in an anthropomorphic manner, it was actually the angel to which they were referring. Almost all Gnostics described the Demiurge as an angel or archon. And since Gnosis is in such proximity to Judaism, one cannot suppress the intuition—and it is later confirmed by Harry Wolfson—that the Gnostics took over the idea of the Demiurge from Jewish heterodoxy and applied it in their own way. They did this because they wanted to free their highest god from any and all guilt concerning evil and the world. It would be an exciting problem to try to present just how the Gnostics tried out these thoughts. In the newly found *Apocryphon of John* the Demiurge is identified with the Old Testament God, held in lowest esteem, and called by such names as Jaldabaoth, Son of Cahos, and even Saklas, or "fool."[11] Valentinus, who was probably influenced by the mythology of the *Apocryphon*, continually emphasized that the Demiurge was guilty of causing the death of man.

In the Western, Italian schools of Valentinianism a change occurred: the Demiurge was no longer considered evil, rather just and symbolic of the highest god. That led one to the view, in the fourth manuscript of the Jung Codex, the *Tractatus Tripartitus* (which was in my opinion written by Heracleon, a student of Valentinus), that the Demiurge was a thoroughly positive character and

---

[10] H. Wolfson, "The preexistent angel of the Magharians and Al-Nahawandi," *Jewish Quarterly Review*, 51 (1960), pp. 89–106.

[11] The etymology Jaldabaoth = "Son of Chaos" seems confirmed by the circumstance that the recently discovered "Hypostasis of the Archons" has Jaldabaoth appearing "in the depths of the water" (Labib 148.11). Cf. R. Haardt in *Wiener Zeitschrift für die Kunde des Morgenlandes* 57 (1961), p. 101. A. Böhling, *Die koptisch-gnostische Schrift ohne Titel aus Codex II von Nag Hammadi* (Berlin, 1962), p. 149, is correct in asserting that the manuscript he published confirms this etymology. One reads there: "Without being seen, she spoke: You are wrong, Samael—that is, 'the blind God.' An immortal, luminous man exists before you, who will reveal himself in your patterns. He will crush you like potter's clay, and you and yours will descend to your mother, the abyss (or: Chaos)" (151.17–24 [Böhling, p. 49]).

was an instrument, a "hand and eye" of wisdom itself, who determines good and evil for the benefit of man and his education in history. It is interesting to see how Gnosis transcends itself in this treatise, by attributing evil to God's influence.

But back to Basilides! This exemplary and preeminent Gnostic from second-century Alexandria was one of not a few systematic thinkers in the history of theology and philosophy who were fascinated by the concept of chaos. According to him, there existed a primordial chaos, a primordial confusion and entanglement, which contained the seed for the entire development to come. There is no mention whatsoever that this chaos is the result of a Fall or that it represents a nullity not willed by God. Instead, God created chaos as the source of all order. This conception reminds one of the dogma of the *rationes seminales*, which is to be found in the works of St. Augustine and Scotus Erigena, among others, and in which God is said to have created everything as potentiality that gradually unfolds itself into actuality. In the background is the Stoic dogma of the *rationes seminales*, which is applied to the history of the universe.

In order to clarify this, Basilides employs various images: the chaos is the seed of the world in which everything is contained, as the mustard seed contains the entire plant to be, or the egg of a peacock contains the entire bird to be in all its motley splendor, or as children only gradually grow teeth which have been there all the time.

It is in such a manner that chaos contains everything in itself: the spiritual, which Basilides designates rather than strangely as "the threefold sonship," also the two archons of the world—this formless sublunar world in which we live. The purpose of the world process is the freeing of the human spirit [i.e., spark], the "third sonship." Added to that is the bestowing of the otherworldly Gnosis upon Jesus, who represents the prototype of the spiritual human and is the beginning of the return of the spirit to God. In this cosmic evolution the two archons are also a moment of the unfolding. Both are innerworldly figures and belong entirely to creatura—i.e., they are products of chaos:

Since henceforth the firmament was present, which lies above heaven, the great archon issued from the cosmic seed and from the seed-fullness of the multitude and was created, the head of the world and of inexplicable beauty, greatness, and power. It is more inexplicable than the inexplicable, stronger than the strong, wiser than the wise, superior to any excellence one can name. When he was created, he swung his entire being upwards and climbed into the firmament, where he remained, thinking that it was the end of the upward climb and elevation and that nothing existed beyond it. He was indeed wiser, more powerful, more towering, and brighter than any other worldly thing, and surpassing the worldly in every conceivable quality of excellence, with the exception of the sonship, which remained in the seed's fullness. He did not know that it was wiser, stronger, and superior to himself. Since he assumed he was Lord, master, and wise architect, he began to create the world. . . . This is the Ogdoad [eightness], so-called by the Basilideans, in which the great archon reigns. The entire heavenly, that is the ethereal, creation has set the great and wise Demiurge to work. (23.3–7)

Naturally, one is speaking of the traditional Gnostic Demiurge. It seems clear to me that Basilides presupposes and reworks the vulgar Gnostic view of the ignorance of the Demiurge. In the *Apocryphon of John* the Demiurge is thus called Saklas, "fool," because he does not know that there is a spiritual world above him. One must assume that Basilides already knew of a Gnostic myth such as the one contained in the *Apocryphon of John* and perhaps even knew the original version of this treatise, for he has hellenized and christianized the vulgar Egyptian Gnosis. The interpretation that the Demiurge is actually an archon, an angel, is taken from the already existent Gnostic tradition.

But the transformation of the Demiurge has already begun with Basilides. In the *Apocryphon of John* the Demiurge is a disgusting and gruesome being. But Basilides cannot praise his beauty and wisdom highly enough. That might have influenced Jung to call his creaturely God *summum bonum*.

After the Demiurge a lower archon comes into being:

After the entire ethereal world was ordered, another archon rose from the seed's fullness, greater than everything that was to be found below him, with the exception of the remaining sonship, although fundamentally inferior to the first archon. Even this one is considered ineffable. This place is called Hebdomas [sevenness]. This archon is regulator and Demiurge of all that is below him. (24.3)

It is not made explicit that this archon is the devil. Even such an excellent commentator as Werner Foerster has denied that Basilides conceived of an evil principle.[12] That is going too far, for even Valentinian Gnosis distinguished the devil from the Demiurge. Thus we think we have established the source of Jung's theory of the *summum bonum* and *infimum malum*. And we are of the opinion that such an examination of sources helps [us] to understand Jung's thinking at this very difficult point.

We do not mean to imply that Jung slavishly adhered to his source. Quite the contrary, for in comparing the Basilidean system with the *Septem Sermones* it becomes obvious what Jung did not take from Basilides.

For Basilides, the Christ episode is of central importance. Christ mediates Gnosis to the unconscious spirit [spark] so that man can extricate himself from his entanglement with the world, become conscious of himself and of his spiritual seed, and return to the spiritual world. According to him, Christ is the prototype and exemplar for spiritual man—at once the redeemer and the first one redeemed. For Jung, on the other hand, Christ was of no importance at this time. It was still many years before he arrived at his psychological interpretation of Christianity.

The greatest difference, however, lies in the interpretation of Abraxas. Influenced by Hesse and Jung, the interpretation has spread among scholars that the Gnostic [highest] god—namely, Abraxas—is the source of [both] good and evil.[13] That is not at all the case. One could rather say, Gnosticism arose out of protest against such an interpretation.

Certainly the Gnostics pose the question, *Unde malum?* But it was thereby presupposed that the godhead had nothing at all to do with evil. When the Biblical God was discussed as being the source of evil, it then followed that he was a lesser god, some lowly De-

---

[12] *Op. cit.*, p. 246.
[13] M. Buber, *Gottesfinsternis*, p. 111: "This god who unites good and evil within himself, whose contradictory nature expresses itself in his man-womanhood, is a Gnostic figure."

miurge and not the highest godhead. Tertullian expresses it in this way:

> Marcion, you see, interesting himself idly (as many persons do even now, and especially the heretics) in the Problem of Evil ("Where does evil come from?"), and finding (as a result of his thick wits, dulled by the very enormity of his curiosity) that the Creator proclaims, "I am He who am the source of evils," . . . presumed that there had to be another god. (*Adv. Marc.* 1.2)

Translates Kellner:

> Plagued, like many people, especially heretics, even now by the question of evil and its source, and stupified by the power of his groveling spirit itself, he [Marcion] finds that the creator once said, "It is I who created evil." He has imagined it was that god who was the founder of evil.

That is how it is with Basilides. For him, Abraxas is identical with the lowly Demiurge. Irenaeus says for instance: "Moreover, he who is thought to be the God of the Jews is their leader" (*Adv. haer.* 1.24.4). "Moreover, their leader is Abrasax [*sic*] and because of this he has the number 365 in him" (*Adv. haer.* 1.24.7). But this is also found in Hippolytus' reports (VII.26.6). This is something very new and unheard of in the history of ideas.

We have found excellent new investigations of Abraxas which have determined his importance even further. One finds the name and figure of Abraxas recorded on numerous magical cameos. These were probably made primarily in Alexandria and reflect religious sentiments which pervaded the metropolis. But then one must also assume that the stereotypical illustration of Abraxas originated in Alexandria and can be traced back to Alexandrian representations.

Abraxas is portrayed as a monster: half man, half animal, and representative of a warlike god. He has the head of a cock, the body of a man, and two snakes as legs: "The torso seemed to be covered with a constricting armor with epaulieres and mantling which went down right to the knees." This is the uniform of the Caesars and high officials of the third and fourth centuries. The monster carries a shield on his right arm and swings a whip with his left. There is some variance to this type: Abraxas is also portrayed with a lion's head.[14]

The source of this godhead is unknown. The heathen cults do not know of it. Certainly Abraxas is the highest god of magic. The pictures are often accompanied by the legends of Iao Sabaoth or Adonaios. That shows that Abraxas was identified with [only] the Jewish God [i.e., Demiurge]. It seems to me that Abraxas is actually the Jewish God who was once also a god of the holy war and was prescribed by magicians for their purposes.[15]

To be sure, the magicians omitted or added certain characteristics. The cock is the animal of the sun. Abraxas has also taken on other solar characteristics.[16] On the other hand the snake is the animal of the earth. Thus Abraxas unified opposites within himself: uranian and tellurian, the light and the dark.

But what does "Abraxas"—or, rather, "Abrasax"—mean? A. A. Barb presented a fascinating but also controversial hypothesis on this matter.[17] He brings to our attention that Abrasax begins with "Abras." He connects that with the Hebrew *arba*, "four." The Hebrew name of God contains four letters: J H W H. *Arba* would thus imply the Tetragrammaton—the sigma being added by the Greeks, as in "Judas," "Thomas," and "Saklas," The metathesis *arba* → *abra* would be comparable with the metathesis *Arbathiao* ("Fourness" is "Lord") → *Abra iaoth* (Preisendanz, *Gr. Zauberpapyri* I, 106). Abrasax would thus be the signification of the god whose name is the Tetragrammaton: J H W H, the "Lord."

The addition of *ax* is believed by Barb to come from numerology. By adding two further letters, the magician would have created a complete sounding magical world made of seven letters and thus corresponding to the seven planets. That the warlike god Abrasax

---

[14] A. Delatte/Ph. Derchain, *Les intailles magiques gréco-égyptiennes* (Paris, 1964), p. 23.
[15] Delatte-Derchain, *op. cit.*, p. 25: "That the shield might be generally called Iao on the one hand invites us to look for an explanation of the figure in Jewish tradition where God is often called the shield of men." A. A. Barb, *Abraxasstudien, Hommages à Waldemar Deonna*, Collection Latomus, 28 (Brussels, 1957), p. 85: "I believe that Perdrizet, Bonner, and others err in constructing a contrast between the God of the Jews and the "grand Dieu du syncrétisme solaire," who is given names such as Iao, Iabaoth, etc. in Hellenistic magic. The Jewish folk religion of this period recognized no such contrast, as the material compiled by Goodenough in his extensive work should now demonstrate."
[16] Campbell Bonner, *Studies in Magical Amulets* (Ann Arbor, 1950), pp. 123–139.
[17] Barb, *op. cit.*, pp. 67–86.

has a cock's head Barb attempts to explain with a Hebrew word game: *gibor*, the "experienced warrior," has in Hebrew, when vocalized *geber*, not only the meaning "man" but also the meaning "cock." Such games are certainly possible in the magic arts but remain uncertain. To understand the meaning of "Abrasax," one must hold to that which is certain.

According to the Church Fathers Irenaeus and Hippolytus, "Abraxas" has the numerical value 365. Thus the Leiden *Kosmopoiia*, 1.23–24: "You are the number of the years Abrasax."[18] This is understood from the numerical worth of the Greek letters: $\alpha = 1, \beta = 2, \varrho = 100, \alpha = 1, \sigma = 200, \alpha = 1, \xi = 60; 1 + 2 + 100 + 1 + 200 + 1 + 60 = 365$.

So we see that Abraxas represents the sun. But that he was also identified with the God of the Jews is shown by the inscription "Iao," which often accompanied pictures of him.

Basilides also thought of Abraxas as identical with the Jewish God. That he made Abraxas the lowest Demiurge was his new Gnostic addition. That this was accomplished presumes that the connection of the solar god with the Jewish creator god was already made prior to his existence—i.e., before the first half of the second century in Alexandria, the native city of the Abraxas concept.

I do not consider it impossible that the name Abrasax was created with reference to *arba*, "four," and is not only magical senseless babble. Besides, there is one Abraxas cameo on which is inscribed not Abrasax but the form "Abra-el,"[19] which probably means "Four (i.e., J H W H) is God."

I would now like to add my own individual contribution to the Abraxas game. It has to do with a Coptic magical papyrus that I bought in 1956 from the Carl Schmidt estate in Berlin, together with Coptic papyri, including a fragment of the Apocryphal Acts of Andrew. On the left side one finds the names: Io, Jaltaboth (?), El, Gabriel (?), Souriel (?), Ainchoooch, Abrbeloth, Abrasax; on the right side: Adonai, Istrael, Michael, Ouriel.

Ialdabaoth and Barbelo are often cited in Gnostic sources as designations for the lowly Demiurge and as the wife of the highest

---

[18] A. Dieterich, *Abraxas* (Leipzig, 1891), p. 17.
[19] Delatte-Derchain, p. 28: "An eel-footed spirit with a cock head capable of divination, its head placed to the left, armed with a shield and a whip. The bust of a bearded man, framed by seven rays, to the left. Inscribed on the bevel: Abrael Adoneu Bane."

God. Thus we may perhaps consider this papyrus to be a Gnostic one. It is noteworthy that Israel (as angel, as is often the case in the magical papyri) is invoked in connection with Michael and Uriel.[20] This shows how strongly magical, Gnostic, and Jewish trends were bound together in this Egyptian text.

For us it is important that Barbelo is called "Arbeloth." Does that really have nothing to do with *arba*, "four"? One also finds in the magical papyri names like Barbarioth, Barbar Adonai, Brabel, Abraiaoth, Abraal, Abriel.

It seems to me that this form could somehow be related to the Hebrew *arba*, "four." Perhaps *abrbeloth ← arba-el:* "J H W H is God." One could surmise the same for Abrasax. The name would then be a cryptic designation for the cosmic God of the All [i.e., Demiurge].

Now it is thoroughly characteristic for Basilides that he has not made Abraxas the highest god. We may suppose that he had already found the presentation of the monstrous Demiurge in his source—namely, in the myth of the *Apocryphon of John*. In it the Old Testament God is already identified with the Aeon of the Mithras mysteries: he has the head of a lion and ends as a snake.[21] It is probably because Abraxas is also portrayed with a lion's head that Basilides identified the lowly Demiurge with Abraxas. He is, as far as I know, the only one who has done that.[22]

It is just as noteworthy and characteristic of his religious experience that Jung did not imitate Basilides in this respect and restored Abraxas to honor again, because for him Abraxas is without a doubt the highest god, who unifies opposites and is the source of good and evil.

[Sermon III of the "Seven Sermons" is given in full here.]

There is no doubt in my mind that Jung intentionally made this modification. He was well read in the ancient history of religion and

---

[20] Jonathan Z. Smith, "The Prayer of Joseph," *Religions in Antiquity* (Leiden, 1968). All passages from Jewish and magical literature are indicated here, where Israel appears as an angel.

[21] G. Quispel, "Gnosticism and the New Testament," *Vig. Chr.* 19 (1965), p. 75.

[22] Basilides is thus also the misunderstood source for the title of Hesse's book *Demian* (from "Demiurge")—as if the Demiurge was the highest god from the Gnostic perspective!

must have been aware of the Abraxas cameos. Moreover, he must certainly have read *Abraxas* by Albrecht Dieterich (Leipzig, 1891). But that means that the objectionable and fundamentally Jungian interpretation, according to which the representation of God, and thus the godhead, encompasses both good and evil, has no analogy in the Gnostic sources. It is not Gnostic at all. One can call it magical, but only a magic with a Jewish foundation. The Lord says in Isaiah, "I am the one who establishes the foundations of evil" (45.7).[23] And Amos says (3.6), "Does evil befall a city, unless the Lord has done it?"

In the *Manual of Discipline,* which was found at the Dead Sea, it says that God made both the Spirit of the Light and the Spirit of the Dark: "And he created the Spirits of the Light and Dark, and on them he based his entire work" (1 Q S III.25 [translated E. Lohse]).

To the Jewish Christians the devil was the left hand of God. Ps.-Clem., *Hom.* XX.3.6: "He kills with his left hand—namely, through evil—which is created in such a manner that it takes pleasure in hurting the godless. But He saves and does well with the right hand—that is, through the good—which is created in order to do justice to the just and to save them."

This certainly bears witness to the authenticity of Jung's religious experience. But it also shows that discovering a new god is not very easy. For when one looks closer, one finds that the new god is actually very old or that even the old god is still surprisingly lively.

Jung's concluding remark about the one god of the human individual is without analogy in Basilides:

> At immeasurable distance standeth one single Star in the zenith.
>
> This is the one god of this one man. This is his world, his pleroma, his divinity.
>
> In this world is man Abraxas, the creator and the destroyer of his own world.
>
> This Star is the god and the goal of man.

[23] The Vulgate itself has a different reading for Isaiah 45.6b–7: "I [am] the Lord, and there is no other: shaping the light and creating the darkness, making peace and creating ill; I [am] the Lord, the one who does all these things."—ED.

This is his one guiding god. In him goeth man to his rest. Toward him goeth the long journal of the soul after death. In him shineth forth as light all that man bringeth back from the greater world. To this one god man shall pray. (Sermon VII)

Stated like this, Jung is not in conformity with Gnosis. He has obviously formulated and experienced this in a completely independent manner. These words express that a relationship and an experience with God is possible only in the individual's soul. It is a denial of the possibility of having a direct encounter with God, long before existentialist philosophy and Martin Buber. Jung encountered only his self. It is thus not at all surprising that a conflict arose between these two men because Jung's religious experience simply does not comply with the existential category of encounter [i.e., with something outside oneself].

Recently, the accomplished American historian of religion [Wilfred] Cantwell Smith wrote a book on *The Meaning and End of Religion* [1963]. Therein he asserts that the essence of all religion is the relationship between man and God. His thesis breaks down with the fact that there is no such relation in the Gnostic and Manichaean religions. It may sound uncouth to say that Gnostics were not interested in God, but that is exactly what their writings tell us. The Gnostic is interested only in the Self. Valentinus describes how the guardian angel, which is the Self, gives the person Gnosis, and is thus fatefully connected with him because only when the I and the Self are interconnected and in Dualitudo can they achieve perfection and eternity. Mani encounters the "twin," who endows him with his teaching and accompanies him until his death.[24] Henry Corbin has created the designation "kathénothéisme" for this.[25] And it is becoming ever clearer that this is the characteristic and basic assumption of Gnosis.

Jung's experiences must also be considered "kathénothéisme." That does not mean that Jung was not a scientist. He devoted his entire life to ascertaining those motifs [i.e., archetypes] he experienced in the dreams of others and in unfamiliar religions. Thereby he tried to prove these motifs to be universal—a priori in the soul and capable of being structured in scientifically plausible forms.

[24] *Eranos-Jahrbüch* 36 (1967) (Zürich, 1968), pp. 1ff.
[25] *Eranos-Jahrbüch* 17 (1949) (Zürich, 1950), pp. 121–187.

Whether he has accomplished this is the decision of the specialist. It is a thoroughly scientific attempt.

Nevertheless, C. G. Jung's experience is interesting for the student of Gnosticism as well. For it demonstrates that the Gnostic conceptions which are found in the sources are traceable to authentic experiences occurring even in our times. Gnosis is not artificial myth or dressed-up philosophy bound to a particular period but is rather authentic myth, imagistic thought—a breakthrough of images that is thus possible for every theistic religion and perhaps every person. If the *experience* of the images did not take place first, contemporary man would not be so gripped by and subjected to these ancient, frightening myths. Jung shows that even today there are experiences which lead man to make use of Gnostic symbols in order to make himself understood. That is why there exists a world history of Gnosis from antiquity to the Middle Ages to the present.

Chapter 13. Gilles Quispel, "Gnosis and Psychology"

In the following essay, originally published in the proceedings of the 1978 Yale Conference on Gnosticism (The Rediscovery of Gnosticism, ed. Bentley Layton, vol. 1 [Leiden: Brill, 1980)], 17–31), Quispel discusses the purchase of the Jung Codex, Jung's interest in Gnosticism, and most of all Quispel's own synchronistic rather than projective interpretation of Gnosticism. Again, see, in my introduction, the section on "Gilles Quispel."

"Gnosis and Psychology" (1978)

During the war we had plenty of time: you could not go out, or eat, or resist, or participate in public life. It so happened that I was a teacher of Greek and Latin in a small provincial town of the Netherlands and was working on my dissertation. For this I had to read Christian Fathers of the second century, heresy hunters like Irenaeus and Tertullian. And then, in the particular constellation of that time and that moment in my life, I found that the heretics were right. Especially the poetic imagery of a certain Valentinus, a second-century Gnostic, the greatest Gnostic that ever lived, made a deep and lasting impression upon me. Only a few fragments of his writings remained, but the reports about the views of his pupils were so numerous that it was tantalizing to try and reconstruct the original doctrine of the Master himself. This I did from 1941 till 1945—I told you I had nothing to do—and after the war I published an article about it. You know what happens in such circumstances. You are young; when you have laid an egg, you think it is the world egg, in short I sent an offprint of this article to Aldous

Huxley in California, Karl Barth in Basel and Carl Gustav Jung in Zürich. At that time I was disappointed that the first two mentioned did not answer; now I am rather astonished that Jung, at that time already a world celebrity of seventy-one, replied with a personal and encouraging letter. This led to an invitation for a conference in Ascona, Switzerland, one of the so-called Eranos Conferences, which Jung and his followers used to visit every year. Of course I lectured about my Valentinus, Jung said a few words of appreciation and then everybody liked me. This was in 1947.

Soon afterwards the news spread that Gnostic manuscripts in Coptic had been discovered in Egypt. It was said that among them there was the so-called *Gospel of Truth* which according to a Father of the Church was in use among the Valentinians. And there was more.

One day the French professor Henri-Charles Puech, when sitting in the underground railway of Paris, was turning over the leaves of transcriptions from Nag Hammadi which a young Frenchman, Jean Doresse, had given to him. His attention was drawn to the beginning of one writing, which runs as follows: "These are the secret words which the Living Jesus spoke and Didymus Judas Thomas wrote."

In a flash it occurred to him that he had read that before. When the train stopped, he ran home and took a book from the shelf of his bookcase. It was so: the famous fragments of the sayings of Jesus in Greek, found at Oxyrhynchus in 1897 and 1903, began with the same words and turned out to belong to one specific writing, the *Gospel of Thomas*. For the first time in history a collection of sayings of our Lord, independent of the New Testament and in some cases completely new, had come to light. Puech had discovered this. And he had no possibility to get access to the manuscript. He wrote to me, I wrote to Jung, and in 1951 we had the opportunity to discuss certain matters in Ascona with Jung and his associate C. A. Meier. Why was this?

At that time the whole collection of Coptic writings known as the Nag Hammadi Library and discovered in 1945 could have been published completely. The Director of Egyptian Antiquities, the French priest Etienne Drioton, would have surveyed the whole enterprise and distributed the writings to French scholars exclusively. A start had already been made: Jean Doresse and Pahor

Labib made an edition and translation of the very important *Apocryphon of John*, printed at the Imprimerie Nationale of Paris, which I have seen with my own eyes, but which was never published. But there occurred a revolution in Egypt, Drioton had to leave the country, Doresse could no longer get a passport, not even from his own government, and this precious treasure of mankind fell into the hands of a people not really interested in it. The legal owner of most of these manuscripts was persuaded to bring them to a place and later to the Coptic Museum for expertise, where they were seized (the reason for which remains unknown) and left in Tano's suitcase, where I found them in 1955. No contacts with other scholars were made; at a later date it was even stipulated that the greatest experts, Puech and Walter Till, were not to participate in the edition, for reasons unknown. How little some people cared is obvious from the fact that the whole file with correspondence on Nag Hammadi had gotten lost in the Coptic Museum. And yet experts urged the authorities to proceed. Prominent scholars of Harvard, among them Arthur Darby Nock, wrote in this sense to Mustafa Amr, the successor to Drioton, unselfishly adding that they themselves did not know Coptic. In these circumstances Jung and Meier have rendered an invaluable service to impatient students of Gnosticism. The old man had considered what he could do and had come to the conclusion that he would help these manuscripts to be put at the disposal of the qualified scholars who had already waited so long (in his own words: "den zuständigen Gelehrten zur Verfügung gestellt werden sollten"). Therefore one codex which had left Egypt was to be acquired and after publication given back to the Egyptian government on the condition that the other manuscripts would be released for serious study. So I acquired the Jung Codex on May 10, 1952. Now imagine what it is for a scholar to study Valentinus during a whole war and afterwards to acquire a whole manuscript with five authentic and completely new writings of Valentinus and his school. Is not that an act of God?

So in 1955 the lacking pages of the Jung Codex were found in the Coptic Museum and an arrangement was made which was accepted at a meeting of an international committee in Cairo in 1956: (1) The Jung Codex was to return to Egypt and an international committee of experts was to publish all the writings of Nag Hammadi; (2) the firm Brill at Leiden (and not the French Institute at Cairo) was to publish them; (3) the Rask Oersted Foundation at Copenhagen was to finance the photographic edition of the manuscripts; (4) the Bollingen Foundation at New York was to pay all the expenses of the committee, including the travel of some Egyptian members to Paris. Of course, everybody concerned signed the convention that only members of the committee would have access to the manuscripts. This solemn pledge was broken and pirated editions were published in Germany.

And then the decline of classical studies became only too obvious. All these writings have been translated into Coptic from the Greek. Knowledge of Greek is a must for everybody who wants to study these documents, if only because so many Greek words still occur in the text. The mistakes made against the Greek in these pirated editions are appalling. In these texts the spouse of God, a female symbol of wholeness, is sometimes called Metro-pator, Motherfather, because she has synthetized the male and the female principle. This extremely profound imagery is completely obscured by the unspeakable translation: "Grandfather" ("Grannie is now in heaven"). Moreover, these editors proved too prudish for Gnosis; they translated *métra* as "mother," and *physis* as "nature," whereas it means in this context "uterus."

And even those who translated the Coptic correctly did not establish and fix a text, but printed manuscripts, sometimes even three. There has been, however, since antiquity, a technique of edition. The first rule of it is that you have to establish a text of your own choice, based upon the manuscripts available, but with the necessary conjectures and emendations, of which account is given in the critical apparatus under the text. I'm sorry to say that quite a few editions are completely deficient in these respects. Therefore it was right that Antoine Guillaumont, of the Collège de France in Paris, urged UNESCO to publish photographic editions. This desire has been implemented at last. Moreover, we may trust that our American friends, under the inspiring leadership of James Robinson, will see to it that the Coptic, the Greek, and the art of editing will be adequately dealt with in their future editions. It will be only then that Jung's wish that these texts might be put at the disposal of the qualified scholars available will be realized.

What was the reason that Jung, already an old man, had a hunch of the importance of this discovery, whereas so many prominent theologians and philosophers at that time disparaged the perennial religion of Gnosis as "nihilism" and "metaphysical anti-Semitism"? That was because Jung was one of the few outsiders who had really read the fragments of this faith forgotten and was keenly aware of its relevance for scholarship. He had written his doctoral dissertation "On the Psychology of So-called Occult Phenomena" (1902): in this he had interpreted the fancies of a medium, who was none other than his niece Helly Preiswerk, and had rightly called them Gnostic. And yet the youth and mentality of the patient precluded the possibility that she knew the reports of the anti-heretical Church Fathers. Hence the conclusion arises that Gnosis lives unconsciously in the soul even of a modern woman.

Jung was already on the right track at that time, but the rising sun of the "Religionsgeschichtliche Schule" helped him to continue in the right direction. German theology at that period was dominated by the political theology of Ritschl and Harnack, who were very much against Rome, mysticism, and pietism, and all for Luther, justification by faith alone, and the nation. Jung, the doubting son of a clergyman, was as a student already an outspoken opponent of Ritschl.

On the contrary, people like Herman Usener, Albrecht Dieterich, and Wilhelm Bousset loved popular religion, mysteries, syncretism, and Gnosis. They found that God very often had been experienced as a Woman, Mother Earth, that "rebirth" is found also in the Hellenistic cults of the beginning of our era, etc. Dieterich even wrote a book about a cosmic God of good and evil, represented as an officer with the head of a cock and serpentine legs, called Abraxas. They explored what they called "die Grundformen religiösen Denkens," the fundamental patterns (or archetypes) of religious thought. Jung knew this literature. It should be observed that at that time studies had already been made of symbols that were held to be typically Aryan or Indo-Germanic. And others already divided humanity into classes with different patterns of thought. Against these, men like Dieterich found basic forms of religious symbolism that are characteristic for all human beings. The implications of their work are thoroughly liberal and humanistic.

When working in an asylum, Jung one day was told by a patient that the sun had a tail, which caused the wind. Later on he read in a book by Dieterich, *Eine Mithrasliturgie*, that a magical papyrus of antiquity contained the same view. The hallucinations of a mad clerk in Zürich showed affinity with Gnostic lore. This fact led Jung to suppose that our collective unconscious contains basic patterns which he called archetypes.

Jung studied the then available Gnostic literature, especially after his rupture with Freud, when he had terrible experiences and the Gnostics were his only friends. He even made a Gnostic painting reflecting his own state of mind. The stream of Eros starts with dark Abraxas, a world creator of contradictory nature, and leads up to the figure of a youth within a winged egg, called Phanes and symbolising rebirth and the true Self. At the same time he wrote a Gnostic apocryphon called *The Seven Sermons to the Dead by Basilides of Alexandria*, in which he proclaimed a new God beyond good and evil, called Abraxas. The German author Herman Hesse took over these ideas in his book *Demian*. As a matter of fact, the impressive image of individuation, the young bird who picks its way out of the eggshell, comes from Jung. So a whole generation in Europe found the expression of its deepest aspirations in a Gnostic symbol. As Fred Haynes remarked, Jung had renewed and revitalized Gnosticism in Europe after the First World War. And Jung really thought that familiarity with Gnostic imagery and Gnostic experiences helped uprooted modern man to solve his psychological problems. Starting from his own experiences and their parallels in ancient lore Jung tried during a long life to prove that these patterns were to be found in all religions and recur in dreams of modern men (in fact, his theory is also liberal and humanistic). He considered the archetypes as the language of life itself, universal symbols of all men, black, white, yellow, or red, and of all times. He discovered sense in nonsense and thought he could perceive in the soul an inbuilt tendency toward self-realization, the process of individuation.

When man comes to himself, he is, according to Jung, in the first place faced with his shadow of deficiency; then he starts to explore his female side, the *anima*, often accompanied by the wise old man, who incarnates the cumulative wisdom of mankind, until the Self announces itself in dreams and visions, symbolized by the child or the square, heralding the healing of the split between reason and instincts. All these archetypes are and were already then to be found in Gnostic texts: the demiurge as shadow, Sophia as *anima*, Simon Magus as the wise old man, the Logos as child, the *tetraktys* or four fundamental aeons as *quaternio*.

It did not take long for students of Gnosis to realize that this theory and this terminology were useful tools for the interpretation of Gnostic texts. Especially Henri-Charles Puech, once a teacher of Simone Weil, later professor at the Sorbonne and the Collège de France, pointed out that the center of every Gnostic myth is man, not God. These confused and confusing images of monstrous and terrifying beings should be explained according to Puech in terms of the predicament of man in search of himself. The discovery of the *Self* is the core of both Gnosticism and Manicheism. Even before Nag Hammadi this psychological approach was already a necessary supplement to the purely historical or unilaterally existentialistic interpretation of Gnosis which prevailed in other quarters. There is no question that psychology in general is of great help, an auxiliary science, for history in general, which otherwise tends to become arid and pedantic. And more specifically the Jungian approach to Gnosticism, once decried as a soul-shaking spectacle concocted by decadent psychologists and vain students of Judaic mysticism, turned out to be adequate when the *Gospel of Truth* was discovered. For then it became clear to everybody that Gnosis is an experience, inspired by vivid and profound emotions, that in short Gnosis is the mythic expression of Self experience.

This is the state of unconscious man without Gnosis:

Thus men were in ignorance concerning the Father, Him Whom they saw not. When [this ignorance] inspired them fear and confusion, left them uncertain and hesitant, divided and torn into shreds, there were many vain illusions and empty and absurd fictions which tormented them, like sleepers who are a prey to nightmares. One flees one knows not where or one remains at the same spot when endeavoring to go forward, in the pursuit of one knows not whom. One is in a battle, one gives blows, one receives blows. Or one falls from a great height or one flies through the air without having wings. At other times it is as if one met death at the hands of an invisible murderer, without being pursued by anyone. Or it seems as if one were murdering one's neighbors: one's hands are full of blood. Down to the moment when those who have passed through all this wake up. Then they see nothing, those who have passed through all this, for all those dreams were . . . nought. Thus they have cast their ignorance far away from them, like the dream which they account as nought.

And this is how man discovers his unconscious Self:

Therefore he who knows is a being from above. When he is called, he hears; he answers; he directs himself to Him Who calls him and returns to Him; he apprehends how he is called. By possessing Gnosis, he carries out the will of Him Who called him and seeks to do what pleases Him. He receives the repose. . . . He who thus possesses knowledge knows whence he comes and whither he goes. He understands as someone who makes himself free and awakes from the drunkenness wherein he lived and returns to himself.

How gratifying it was to visit the old man in his lonely tower at the border of the lake, where he had cooked the meal himself, and to read these and similar passages from the newly discovered codex which was to be named after him Codex Jung. He is quoted as having said on this occasion: "All my life I have been working and studying to find these things, and these people knew already." And it is true that the best confirmation of a Jungian interpretation of Gnosis is the Codex Jung. On the other hand, Jungian psychology makes us understand that Gnostic imagery is not nonsensical nor a purely historical phenomenon, but is ever recurrent in history—in Manicheism, in Medieval Catharism, in the theosophy of Jacob Boehme and the poetry of William Blake—because it is deeply rooted in the soul of man.

So Jungian psychology has already had a considerable impact on Gnostic research. The term Self is used by practically everyone; the insight that Gnosis in the last analysis expresses the union of the conscious Ego and the unconscious to form one. Self is commonly accepted; nobody, not even the fiercest existentialist, can deny that Jung is helpful in discerning the real meaning of myth.

But students of Gnosis seem not to have observed that among the

Jungians certain new views have been formulated which are relevant for our field. That is, the concept of synchronicity. Because these developments are not generally known, some examples should be given in this context.

Adolf Portmann is a famous biologist and a reputed humanist, who lectured every year at the Eranos Conferences which took place in Ascona in Italian Switzerland. He always extemporized, but, of course, prepared his talks. Once upon a time he had in mind to end his lecture with a story about the praying mantis, not only because it was important for his scholarly aims, but also because it sounded so well in a peroration. Just when he had in mind to broach this subject and felt somehow moved by the insect's beautiful name, *Gottesanbeterin,* through the open window of the lecture hall a praying mantis flew into the room, made a numinous and ominous circle around the head of the professor, then sat down upon the lectern just under the lamp which threw its light upon the lecturer's notes, to the effect that two enormous dark wings, the arms of a praying man, were projected upon the white wall behind Portmann.

Sheer coincidence, of course, and it would be blasphemous and magical to suppose that the state of mind of the lecturer provoked the insect. Such a causal connection is absolutely impossible. But it is true that it would cost the famous biologist several weeks to find a praying mantis in Italian Switzerland. In fact he had never seen one there, though he came there every year. In any case, it is remarkable that the mantis appeared at the moment that the man was emotionally involved in the insect with the telling name. Such happenings Jung calls "synchronicity."

In his old age Jung was fascinated by the symbolism of the fish. He held that mankind was passing in our days from a period of dualism, characterized by the constellation of Pisces, to a long period of unification, indicated by Aquarius. This is what he wrote in his notebook on April 1, 1949:

Today is Friday. We ate fish for lunch. Somebody casually makes a remark about the April-fish. In the morning I noted an inscription: Est homo totus medius piscis ab imo. In the afternoon a former patient shows me some very impressive paintings of fishes which she made herself. In the evening I am shown an embroidery of fish monsters. In the early morning a former patient tells me a dream of her standing on the beach of the sea and a *big fish* landing at her feet.

When some months later he wrote this down again, he found before his house a foot-long fish on the wall of the lake. There certainly is something fishy about this. These coincidences receive a religious dimension when we remember that the fish is the symbol of Christ. *Ichthus* in Greek stands for: Jesus Christ Son of God Savior. But the whole story became uncanny after the publication of the *Gospel of Thomas* found at Nag Hammadi. There we find a very peculiar parable attributed to Jesus:

> And he said: Man is like a wise fisherman, who cast his net into the sea. He drew it up from the sea full of small fish: among them he found a *large* and good fish, that wise fisherman, he threw all the small fish down into the sea. He chose the large fish without regret.

Compare this with a dream of a modern man, written down long before the publication of the *Gospel of Thomas:*

> I came to the bank of a broad streaming river. At first I could not see very much, only water, earth and rock. I threw the page with my notes into the water and felt that I had given back something to the water. Immediately afterwards I had a fishing rod in my hand. I sat down upon the rock and started fishing. Still I do not see anything but water, earth and rock. All of a sudden I get a rise and have a bite: *a large fish* got hooked. He had a silver belly and a golden back. When I drew the fish ashore, the whole landscape was illuminated.

This dream should be interpreted in terms of self-realization. Without knowing it, that man had a bite, a manifestation from the deepest Self, the very center of his personality: he is developing in the right direction, and this is not possible without religious experience. But what really matters about this is that obviously the outside world is in full sympathy with our inner emotions, without any causal connections. Obviously the rationalistic approach towards reality is one-sided: the principles of time, space, and causality should be supplemented by the principle of synchronicity. And this means that both the absurd world of the unconscious within and the absurd nonsense of the world outside is pervaded by a mysterious and awe-inspiring Sense. Old-fashioned people would call it the hand of God.

Jung had collected such stories of meaningful nonsense during a long life. And it seems that synchronistic happenings do occur very often in the life of medical doctors. But he never dared to publish his views, until an American, J. B. Rhine, had proved him to be right by complicated statistics and impressive calculations. And even then Jung found the courage to make his views known only when his friend Pauli, the Nobel prize-winner for theoretical physics, had consented to publish a study about the mechanization of our world picture in the same book. A preview was given by Jung in Ascona in 1951, in the same place and year that it was decided to acquire the Coptic Gnostic codex.

One cannot imagine what impression this lecture made upon his followers. And even Jung himself seemed quite relieved and unusually good humored. All his life he had rummaged in the collective unconscious, but now he had forced a breakthrough from the soul to the cosmos. He beamed when he told me: "Es geht um die Erfahrung der Fülles des Seins"; it is the experience of the fullness, the pleroma, of Being that matters. And he said to me on another occasion that now the concept of projection should be revised completely. Up till that moment Jung had simply taken over from Freud the naive and unphilosophical view of projection, that man is just projecting his own illusions on the patient screen of eternity. Freud in his turn had borrowed it from Feuerbach, and it is already there in the Latin poem of Lucretius. That solution is so simple that it cannot be true.

It is, however, the main associates of Jung who have drawn the consequences from "synchronicity" and who have thoroughly modified the old-time view of projection. Among those present at the conference of 1951 in Ascona, where Jung launched his theory of synchronicity, Erich Neumann, the well-known author of *The Origins of Consciousness* and *The Great Mother,* was most deeply moved. He had returned to the land promised to his fathers, but could not come to terms with the God of his people. Erich Neumann was a sweet soul, but he had a ruthless mind. His logic was as prosaic and rectilinear as a certain Berlin avenue called the "Kurfürstendam": the world is a projection, your wife is a projection, the neighbor is a projection, God is a projection. And now Jung left the limitations of the psyche and found in the cosmos meaningful correspondences, which made sense and seemed to convey a message. This played havoc with Erich's views. And perhaps he had premonitions of his premature death which was to follow soon afterwards. He became more open to reality and disciplined the fancies of his reason. With great emotional relief he told a fascinated audience in 1952 that there was a "Self field" outside the psyche, which created and directed the world and the psyche, and manifests itself to the Ego in the shape of the Self. And this Self in man is the image of the creator. Erich Neumann had found peace with himself, with the world, and with God.

C. A. Meier, Jung's associate and successor, the same who did so much to acquire the Codex, went a different way. He always had had his doubts about the vulgar concept of projection and focused his special attention on Eros, a specifically Jungian theme, ever since the rupture with Freud caused by a different concept of libido. In fact, from the very beginning Jung had conceived this in a sense that was broader than the merely sexual, as a vital energy which can take different forms. And Jung had seen long before the war that his ideas on the subject agreed with the Orphic and Neoplatonic lore on Eros.

Meier has amplified this theory. In his recent book *Personality*, the fourth volume of a systematic textbook on psychology, he conceives Eros as a more than personal force, a stream of love that is principle of wholeness which reconciles creatively all opposites and tensions. In this Meier claims to agree with one of the greatest men of the Italian Renaissance, which was not an anticipation of pragmatism and positivism but in reality the revival and discovery of Jewish Gnosis. Meier quotes extensively the *Dialogues on Love* of Leone Ebreo, a Portuguese doctor living in Italy, who taught his gentile fellows about Cabbalism and androgynous Adam. This man wrote about the circle of Love which originates in God, pervades the universe and descends to matter and Chaos, but returns in human Eros to its source. Meier agrees, and observes: "This renaissance-platonic imagery leads us far from the soul into the cosmos, and yet we would rather not call this a simple projection, but an authentic symbol." And obviously this symbol manifests the truth about reality. Symbolic, imaginative thinking can be true. And Leone Ebreo, who found this key symbol, was right.

I always wonder how it happens that so often Jews are the ones who show us the truth of the image. In our century it was Henri Bergson who warned us that reason is a useful instrument for making tools and machines and cars, but that discursive, intellectual reasoning is neither meant nor authorized to uncover the truth: he thought that truth could only be grasped by intuition and only expressed by poetical images. Ernst Cassirer, so influential in the United States, differed from him insofar as he preferred mathematical, conceptual symbols to imaginitive, mythological symbols; but he brought home the unfamiliar truth that both intellect and intuition produce symbols, and he certainly took myth very seriously. In this general perspective of European Judaism Wolfgang Pauli certainly was no exception to the rule, but it made all the difference that he was a nuclear physicist, and secondly that he was thoroughly familiar with Jungian psychology.

What a man!

Bald, fat, ironic, with bulging eyes. As a student he already frequented nightclubs, then studied, slept the whole morning and arrived towards midday at the seminar. A typical metropolitan, born in Vienna in 1900, known to all as the man of the Pauli embargo, a man who created embarrassment around him wherever he went. He and his friends Niels Bohr and Werner Heisenberg are the founding fathers of our modern world picture and our atomic age. And this man was passionately interested in everything religious and Gnostic. He could listen attentively to a lecture about the *memoria* in St. Augustine. And when on November 15, 1953, the discovery of the Jung Codex was made public, he was among the audience. I will never forget what he then said to me: "This negative theology, that is what we need. As Schopenhauer said, he cannot be personal, for then he could not bear the suffering of mankind. This is it, the Unknown God of Gnosis."

He was interested in this material, because the difference between conceptual, analytic, discursive thinking and magical, symbolic, mythical thinking to him was a vexing problem. In his book on Kepler of 1952 he studied the transition from the earlier magical-symbolic description of nature to the modern, quantitative, mathematical description of nature. A representative of the former organic view is the alchemist Robert Fludd (1547–1637), a representative of the latter is Isaac Newton. Kepler (1571–1630) is just in between. Of course, Pauli does not deny that this development was necessary. But he deplores that in the course of this evolution the sense of the whole got lost. And he underlines that the analytical, quantitative approach is not the only true method, but needs to be supplemented by symbolic, intuitive thinking. Newton was right, but Fludd too.

Pauli says,

Modern quantum physics again stresses the factor of the disturbance of phenomena through measurement, and modern psychology again utilizes symbolical images as raw material (especially those that have originated spontaneously in dreams and fantasies) in order to recognize processes in the collective ("objective") psyche. Thus physics and psychology reflect again for modern man the old contrast between the quantitative and the qualitative. Since the time of Kepler and Fludd, however, the possibility of bridging these antithetical poles has become less remote. On the one hand, the idea of complementarity in modern physics has demonstrated to us, in a new kind of synthesis, that the contradiction in the applications of old contrasting conceptions (such as particle and wave) is only apparent; on the other hand, the employability of old alchemical ideas in the psychology of Jung points to a deeper unity of psychical and physical occurrences. To us, unlike Kepler and Fludd, the only acceptable point of view appears to be the one that recognizes *both* sides of reality—the quantitative and the qualitative, the physical and the psychical—as compatible with each other, and can embrace them simultaneously. . . . Among scientists in particular, the universal desire for a greater unification of our world view is greatly intensified by the fact that, though we now have natural sciences, we no longer have a total scientific picture of the world. Since the discovery of the quantum of action, physics has gradually been forced to relinquish its proud claim to be able to understand, in principle, the *whole* world. This very circumstance, however, as a correction of earlier one-sidedness, could contain the germ of progress toward a unified conception of the entire cosmos of which the natural sciences are only a part.[1]

When I consider these theories of Pauli I think it is permitted to summarize his views in the following parable: An authentic symbol is like a pane of glass, a millinery shop window in one of our big cities. Sometimes it mirrors your own image, sometimes it gives you an insight into the display behind the glass. It all depends upon your own point of view.

In the newly discovered writings of Nag Hammadi, it is said again and again that the world and man are projections. The first Idea, God's Wisdom, looks down on the Chaos below, and the primeval waters mirror her shadowy image: that is the demiurge who orders unorganized matter. So the world originates from the projecting activity of the great Goddess Barbelo. Even today we find the same among the Mandaeans, the only Gnostics in this world who can boast an uninterrupted continuity of the ancient Gnostics; according to them the Holy Spirit (Ruha d'Qodša) produces a dragon, Light (Ur, from Hebrew 'ôr = "light") from the black water of Chaos. According to another version, at the commandment of God ("Life") the heavenly weighmaster, Abatur, looks down from above into that black water; at the same moment his image was formed in the black water, the demiurge, Gabriel or Ptahil, took shape and ascended to the borderland (on high near heaven, near the realm of light).

Or, again, this holy Motherfather reveals herself to the demonic powers of this world through her luminous image in the primordial waters: then these archons, rulers, create a "golem," a robot, the material frame of man, Adam, according to that image. And so, in a way, man too is a projection of Barbelo.

If we could trace the origin of this fascinating and appalling poetry, then the much-debated origins of Gnosticism would be discovered. And I think this possible, if only you allow me to tell a few stories which you may know, but perhaps not precisely:

1. There was a beautiful youth in Greece, called Narcissus, who scorned love and so offended the god Eros. One day he fell in

[1] W. Pauli, "The Influence of Archetypal Ideas on Kepler's Theories," *The Interpretation of Nature and Psyche* (London, 1955) 207–208 and 209.

love with his own image, mirrored in the water when he looked down. He saw his *eidolon*, his reflection, hovering on the water. Therefore he faded away or, according to another tradition, drowned in the water. The story goes to show that the beauty of the body is not real. If you are engrossed in it, you are like this man, who wanted to seize his own reflection upon the water, dived into the deep, and drowned. So your soul dives into the abyss, where you live blind with the phantoms of Hell. Or again in another version: They tell that he, when looking in the water, saw his own shadow, fell in love with it, jumped into the water to embrace his own shadow and so was suffocated. *This is not true* (cf. the *Apocryphon of John:* "not as Moses said"). For he was not suffocated in the water, but he contemplated the transient and passing nature of his material body, namely life in the body, which is the basest *eidolon* of the real soul. Desiring to embrace this, he became enamored with life according to that shadow. Therefore he drowned and was suffocated, as it were perverting his own soul and a really decent life. Therefore the proverb says,"Fear your own shadow." This story teaches you to fear the inclination to prize inferior things as the highest, because that leads man to the loss of his soul and the annihilation of the true Gnosis of reality.

2. The young god Dionysus was set upon a throne as soon as he had been born in a cave on the isle of Crete. But titanic monsters, who wanted to kill the child, gave him a mirror to distract his attention; and while the child gazed in the mirror and was fascinated by his own image, the Titans tore the child into pieces and devoured him. Only the heart of the god was saved. This means that Dionysus, when he saw his *eidolon*, his reflection in the mirror, in a sense was duplicated and vanished into the mirror and so was dispersed in the universe. But Apollo gathers him and brings him back to the spiritual world above, truly the savior of Dionysus. According to the Orphic sages, this means that the worldsoul is divided and dispersed through matter. But the worldspirit remains undivided and pure from every contact with matter.

3. About this distinction between the soul and its image, its *eidolon*, which makes contact with matter, there is still an-

other story. Helen is said to have eloped with Paris and to have
been the cause of the war between Greeks and Trojans. But it
is not true that Helen was ever in Troy: she remained in Egypt
and the Greeks and Trojans fought only about her idol, a
"doll" which resembled her. The Pythagoreans say that this
refers to the soul, which does not become incarnate in the
body proper, but makes contact with it through its *eidolon*, its
lower part, properly speaking its image reflected in a mirror
or in water, but here meant to indicate the subtle or astral
body.

It was after the pattern of these stories that the oldest Gnostics
known to us, Simon Magus of Samaria and his followers, told that
the tragic fate of divine Wisdom, raped by hostile powers and at last
saved from dispersion, was symbolized by the myth of Helen of
Troy and her *eidolon*. And this, I think, throws an unexpected light
upon Gnostic origins.

But more important, these myths enabled the Gnostics to give a
new and original solution to a vexed problem. They knew that such
a thing as projection exists. In fact projection is the literal and
adequate translation of the Gnostic technical term *probolé*. But they
did not agree that God is a projection of man. They rather expressed in their imaginative thinking that the world and man are a
projection of God.

It all depends on whether you agree that a window can have a
double function: from a certain angle you see yourself in it, from a
different angle you can also look through it and see reality and the
truth. For the ancients a mirror is more mysterious than it is for us.
You could see your own reflection in it. But when you used it for
"katoptromancy," i.e., for magic soothsaying, then the gods would
manifest themselves in the mirror and the future could be dis-
cerned in it. The mirror could be a magic mirror, reflecting darkly
the outlines of your face on its bronze surface and yet allowing an
insight into an unknown dimension, which later on will be seen
clearly. "Now we see only through a glass darkly, but then we shall
see face to face, eye to eye," says Paul in 1 Corinthians 13.

I suggest that this is a correct definition of the truth of imaginative thinking as revealed by the Gnostic symbols. The world and
man are a projection of God. And the consummation of the histor-

ical process will consist in this: that man and the universe are taken back and reintegrated into their divine origin. That is eternal life; that is the Kingdom of God. Certainly this is a plausible, spirited, and provocative hypothesis concerning the nature and end of the psyche, the universe, and ultimate reality.

Index

Mythos: The Princeton/Bollingen Series in World Mythology

Otto Rank, Lord Raglan, Alan Dundes, IN QUEST OF THE
  HERO
Gladys Reichard, NAVAHO RELIGION
Géza Róheim (Alan Dundes, ed.), FIRE IN THE DRAGON
Robert A. Segal, ed., THE GNOSTIC JUNG
Philip E. Slater, THE GLORY OF HERA

THE COLLECTED WORKS OF

C. G. Jung

Editors: Sir Herbert Read, Michael Fordham, and Gerhard Adler; *executive editor,* William McGuire. Translated by R.F.C. Hull, except where noted.

In the following list, dates of original publication are given in parentheses (of original composition, in brackets). Multiple dates indicate revisions.

The Soul and Death (1934)
Synchronicity: An Acausal Connecting Principle (1952)
Appendix: On Synchronicity (1951)

9. PART I. THE ARCHETYPES AND THE COLLECTIVE
UNCONSCIOUS (1959; 2nd ed., 1968)
Archetypes of the Collective Unconscious (1934/1954)
The Concept of the Collective Unconscious (1936)
Concerning the Archetypes, with Special Reference to the An-
ima Concept (1936/1954)
Psychological Aspects of the Mother Archetype (1938/1954)
Concerning Rebirth (1940/1950)
The Psychology of the Child Archetype (1940)
The Psychological Aspects of the Kore (1941)
The Phenomenology of the Spirit in Fairytales (1945/1948)
On the Psychology of the Trickster-Figure (1954)
Conscious, Unconscious, and Individuation (1939)
A Study in the Process of Individuation (1934/1950)
Concerning Mandala Symbolism (1950)
Appendix: Mandalas (1955)

9. PART II. AION ([1951] 1959; 2nd ed., 1968)

RESEARCHES INTO THE PHENOMENOLOGY OF THE SELF
The Ego
The Shadow
The Syzygy: Anima and Animus
The Self
Christ, a Symbol of the Self
The Sign of the Fishes
The Prophecies of Nostradamus
The Historical Significance of the Fish
The Ambivalence of the Fish Symbol
The Fish in Alchemy
The Alchemical Interpretation of the Fish
Background to the Psychology of Christian Alchemical Symbolism
Gnostic Symbols of the Self
The Structure and Dynamics of the Self
Conclusion

10. CIVILIZATION IN TRANSITION (1964; 2nd edn., 1970)
The Role of the Unconscious (1918)
Mind and Earth (1927/1931)
Archaic Man (1931)
The Spiritual Problem of Modern Man (1928/1931)
The Love Problem of a Student (1928)
Woman in Europe (1927)
The Meaning of Psychology for Modern Man (1933/1934)
The State of Psychotherapy Today (1934)
Preface and Epilogue to "Essays on Contemporary Events" (1946)
Wotan (1936)
After the Catastrophe (1945)
The Fight with the Shadow (1946)
The Undiscovered Self (Present and Future) (1957)
Flying Saucers: A Modern Myth (1958)
A Psychological View of Conscience (1958)
Good and Evil in Analytical Psychology (1959)
Introduction to Wolff's "Studies in Jungian Psychology" (1959)
The Swiss Line in the European Spectrum (1928)
Reviews of Keyserling's "America Set Free" (1930) and "La Révolution Mondiale" (1934)
The Complications of American Psychology (1930)
The Dreamlike World of India (1939)
What India Can Teach Us (1939)
Appendix: Documents (1933–1938)

11. PSYCHOLOGY AND RELIGION: WEST AND EAST (1958; 2nd edn., 1969)

WESTERN RELIGION
Psychology and Religion (The Terry Lectures) (1938/1940)
A Psychological Approach to the Dogma of the Trinity (1942/1948)
Transformation Symbolism in the Mass (1942/1954)
Forewords to White's "God and the Unconscious" and Werblowsky's "Lucifer and Prometheus" (1952)
Brother Klaus (1933)
Psychotherapists or the Clergy (1932)
Psychoanalysis and the Cure of Souls (1928)
Answer to Job (1952)

The Development of Personality (1934)
Marriage as a Psychological Relationship (1925)

18. THE SYMBOLIC LIFE (1954)

Translated by R.F.C. Hull and others
Miscellaneous writings

19. COMPLETE BIBLIOGRAPHY OF C. G. JUNG'S WRITINGS
(1976; 2nd edn., 1992)

20. GENERAL INDEX TO THE COLLECTED WORKS (1979)

THE ZOFINGIA LECTURES (1983)
Supplementary Volume A to The Collected Works Edited by William
McGuire, translated by Jan van Heurck, introduction by Marie-Louise
von Franz

PSYCHOLOGY OF THE UNCONSCIOUS ([1912] 1992)
A STUDY OF THE TRANSFORMATIONS AND SYMBOLISMS OF THE
LIBIDO.
A CONTRIBUTION TO THE EVOLUTION OF THE HISTORY OF
THOUGHT
Supplementary Volume B to the Collected Works. Translated by
Beatrice M. Hinkle, introduction by William McGuire

Related publications

THE BASIC WRITINGS OF C. G. JUNG
Selected and introduced by Violet S. de Laszlo

C. G. JUNG: LETTERS
Selected and edited by Gerhard Adler, in collaboration with Aniela
Jaffé. Translations from the German by R.F.C. Hull.
VOL. 1: 1906–1950
VOL. 2: 1951–1961

C. G. JUNG SPEAKING: Interviews and Encounters
Edited by William McGuire and R.F.C. Hull

C. G. JUNG: Word and Image
Edited by Aniela Jaffé

THE ESSENTIAL JUNG
Selected and introduced by Anthony Storr

THE GNOSTIC JUNG
Selected and introduced by Robert A. Segal

PSYCHE AND SYMBOL
Selected and introduced by Violet S. de Laszlo

Notes of C. G. Jung's Seminars:

DREAM ANALYSIS ([1928–1930] 1984)
Edited by William McGuire

NIETZSCHE'S ZARATHUSTRA ([1934–1939] 1988)
Edited by James L. Jarrett (2 vols.)

ANALYTICAL PSYCHOLOGY ([1925] 1989)
Edited by William McGuire

DATE DUE

MAR 25 1996			